Versailles and Trianon

Châteaux and Gardens

Guide

Versailles

and Trianon

Guide
to the Museum and National Domain of Versailles and Trianon

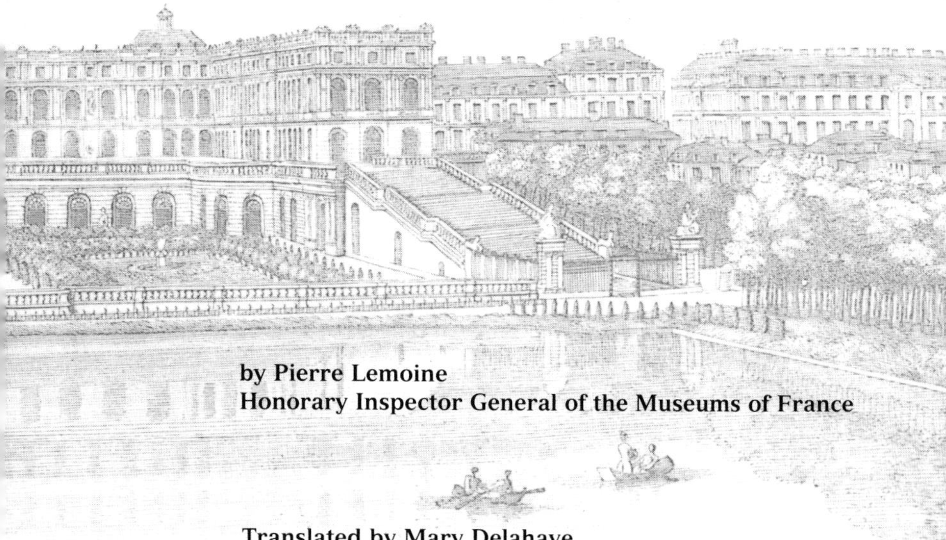

by Pierre Lemoine
Honorary Inspector General of the Museums of France

Translated by Mary Delahaye

Réunion des musées nationaux

ISBN 2-7118-2309-1 (French Edition)
ISBN 2-7118-2310-5 (English Edition)
ISBN 2-7118-2311-3 (Japanese Edition)
ISBN 2-7118-2313-X (German Edition)
ISBN 2-7118-2314-8 (Spanish Edition)

49, rue Etienne Marcel
75001 Paris

Contents

Foreword 8

History 13

The Château 25

The State Apartments 29
The King's State Apartment 35
The Queen's State Apartment 55
The Coronation Room - The Battle Gallery 66
The King's Apartment and the Inner Apartment 71
The King's Apartment 71
The Royal Opera 94
The Private Apartments 98
The Inner Rooms of the Queen and of the Dauphine 99
The Apartments of Madame du Barry, of Madame de Pompadour and of Monsieur de Maurepas 106
The Apartments of the Dauphin, of the Dauphine and of Mesdames 115
The Dauphine's Apartment 117
The Dauphin's Apartment 124
The Lower Gallery 132
Madame Victoire's Apartment 133
Madame Adélaïde's Apartment 139
The Apartment of the Captain of the Guards 145
The History Galleries 150
The Crusades Room 151
The XVIIth-Century Rooms 153
The XVIIIth-Century Rooms 169
The Revolution, the Consulate and the Empire Rooms 170
The Ground Floor Rooms in the South Wing 187
The XIXth-Century Rooms 195

The Gardens 209

The Ornamental Gardens and the Royal Avenue 213
The Wooded Groves 223

Trianon 229

History 231
The Palais de Trianon or Grand Trianon 233
The South Buildings 234
The Peristyle 239
The North Buildings 240
Trianon-sous-Bois 247
The Emperor's Private Apartment 247
The Gardens of Trianon 251
The "New Trianon" or "Petit Trianon" 253
The Château du Petit Trianon 261
The Queen's Hamlet 266
The Great and the Small Stables 268
The Indoor Tennis Court 269

Foreword

As Charles Mauricheau-Beaupré recalled, at the beginning of his guide to Versailles published in 1949, when the collections were being reorganised after the Second World War, the first known descriptions of Versailles were written in 1669, in the reign of Louis XIV, by La Fontaine and by Mademoiselle de Scudéry, and then by Félibien in 1674 when he published the first true guide to the Château and the garden. A reality in constant mutation and a complex assemblage of masterpieces in the field of architecture, landscape design, interior decoration and furniture, collections of paintings and sculpture, Versailles is periodically in need of new cicerones, for the visitor must be sure of finding an up-to-date account to help him discover the apartments recently restored and furniture lately acquired inside the Château, as well as new arbours in the gardens, to enable him to gain a better appreciation and understanding of the reorganisations which have been carried out in one of the most perfect ensembles conceived by the genius of man.

This present work is due to our friend Pierre Lemoine who spent practically all his career at the Château de Versailles, where he was chief curator for seven years, from 1980 to 1986. Following in the line of his eminent predecessors, - Pierre de Nolhac, Charles Mauricheau-Beaupré, Gérald Van der Kemp, - he did much to pursue the work of restituting the historical decors and presenting them to public view, particularly the ground-floor apartments occupied, in the course of succeeding generations, by the Dauphin, the Dauphine and the daughters of Louis XV. He was therefore the very person to write this new guide. Here we find descriptions of the apartments and collections in an order which corresponds to the logical organisation of the historical settings and to the direction followed by the visitor. This was a most challenging task. Indeed the Princes' apartments are situated traditionally in two opposite suites of rooms facing each other, one for the husband and one for his wife. Thus, if we start a visit to one of the apartments from the antechamber, which is quite logical, this means that the other one is necessarily approached through the washroom or the bedroom, which is far less so.

Any description of Versailles must come to terms with this dual disposition and explain its contradictions. It must also take account of changes in the routes followed by the conducted tours. The spectacular rise in the number of visitors, increasing each year, (about four million in 1989), means new measures have to be taken to regulate the flow of people and avoid overcrowding in this inestimable and fragile historical place. Great care is taken to improve the welcome given to the public and facilitate access to the private apartments and the historical galleries. This aim will be another reason for further modifications in the years to come of certain circuits, certain conditions for visiting.

That is why the Great and the Small Stables are not mentioned in this book. Built on the Place d'Armes by Jules Hardouin-Mansart between 1679 and 1685, they are (like the *Grand Commun* outbuilding now housing the Dominique Larrey Military Hospital), essential annexes to the Château. These two architectural blocks, built in the days when the horse was the indispensable friend of all those who frequented Versailles, also providing a theme for a true art, are used today as various administrative offices. The collections taken from the Château to be preserved in the galleries, the coaches and the sculptures brought inside from the park are not in a condition to be exhibited at the present time. We can only hope that this will become possible in the near future.

I am convinced that visitors coming to Versailles from all over the world will find this book the finest of companions.

5 September 1990

Jean-Pierre Babelon

Director of the Museum and the national domain of Versailles and Trianon

The numbers beneath the titles indicate the dimensions of each room : length x width x height

The numbers in brackets in the text (fig. 00) refer to the illustrations

The numbers in superscript (°°) refer to the plans

History

The etymology of the name Versailles is uncertain. In former times *"versail"* designated land which had been cleared of weeds, so that the name of the most famous castle in the world could have derived its origin from this word. Anyway, for a long while it was a country covered with woods, ponds and marshes, and the last of these were not drained until the XVIIIth century.

The first mention of Versailles appeared in 1038, in the deeds of St. Père Abbey at Chartres, which bore among others the signature of a certain Hugo de Versailliis. The foundation of the seigneury and of the parish dedicated to Saint Julian most probably dates back to this period.

The lords of Versailles were not particularly powerful, but they were subject to the direct authority of the King. Their modest castle, no more than a manor house dominating the church and the village, stood on the southern slope of the mount where later the present castle would be built.

After the tumult of the Hundred Years War, the castle was raised from its ruins thanks to a new titular of the fief, the Sire de Soisy. It consisted in those days of a main building with a wing at one end, preceded by a gateway with a turret on either side. The estate comprised two courtyards, a garden, a cultivated enclosure, pigeon-cotes, some windmills and stables and 80 *arpents* (1 arpent = approx. 1 acre) of woods, fields and arable land.

In 1561, the seigneury belonged to Martial de Loménie, Charles IX's Finance Minister who increased the domain to 450 arpents, or 150 hectares. He was assassinated on 24 August 1572, on the night of St. Bartholomew, and the estate was bought from his heirs, who had not yet attained their majority, by Albert de Gondi for the sum of 35 000 *livres*. He was the most illustrious member of a family of Florentine origin which came to France in the suite of Catherine de Médicis. Gondi was soon made Duc de Retz and Maréchal of France and at Versailles he received the visit of Henri III and his brother-in-law, the King of Navarre, the future Henri IV of France. The latter knew the castle well for he had already been invited in 1570, at the time of Loménie, and he spent three days there from 7 to 9 July 1589, less than a month before ascending the throne of France.

Henri IV enjoyed hunting on his friend's land abounding in game, and his passion for hunting, which would be shared by all his descendants, was to determine the destiny of Versailles. Indeed, the King was sometimes accompanied by his eldest son, the young Dauphin and future Louis XIII, who thus acquired a liking for this rather wild place. On becoming king he returned there frequently to hunt in the company of close friends, among whom was the young Duc de Saint-Simon, later to become the father of the famous memorialist.

In 1623, to avoid having to put up at the inn, he had a pavilion built on the top of the mount, where formerly a windmill had stood, a pavilion in brick and stone, capped by a tiled roof with a main building twelve *toises* by three (1 toise = approx. 2 metres) and two narrow wings.

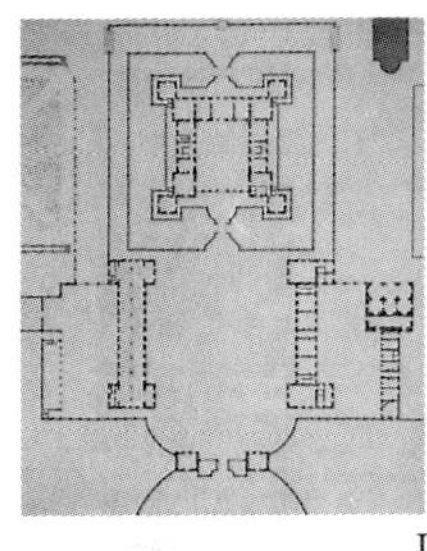
1

This was the building to which Maréchal de Bassompierre would allude at the Assembly of Notables in 1627, when he evoked "the meagre little castle of Versailles which even the simplest gentleman would have no vanity in owning".

However, a few years later, from 1631 to 1634, Louis XIII transformed and enlarged this hunting lodge. He ordered Philibert Le Roy to extend the main building by one *toise* (two metres), reconstruct the wings and flank the angles with four jutting pavilions. This is how the "small house of cards" was conceived, of which Saint-Simon was to speak later, and which still exists today, encapsulated in Louis XIV's vast constructions.

While work was in progress, Louis XIII acquired more land and, on 8 April 1632, he bought back the seigneury of Versailles from Jean-François Gondi, Archbishop of Paris and Albert's heir. From then onwards he decided that he would

2

3

retire there as soon as the Dauphin reached his majority "to have no thought other than a concern for his salvation". His premature death prevented him from realizing his wish.

During the early years of his reign, Louis XIV rarely visited Versailles, but, once married, he brought the Queen and the court there. From 1661, work commenced to rapidly transform the retreat of a man in search of solitude into a pleasant residence suitable for the royal family. On the first floor in particular, two symmetrical apartments were created for the King and Queen, linked by a central reception room (fig. 1). The two *communs* (outbuildings) were erected to house the kitchens and stables, around a forecourt enclosed by railings and preceded by a square whence three avenues radiated in a web-foot pattern (see fig. 2). Meanwhile Le Nôtre landscaped new gardens and Le Vau built the Orangery (fig. 3) and a "Menagerie" (fig. 4).

Once these renovations were completed, the castle became a place for entertainment. A pantomime called *"Les Plaisirs de l'île enchantée"* (Pleasures of the Enchanted Island) was performed there in May 1664 and on 18 July 1668 the *"Grand Divertissement Royal"* (Grand Royal Entertainment) (fig. 5) took place, dazzling the spectators and bringing renown to the name of Versailles throughout Europe.

1
Plan of the Château
c. 1662

2
Pierre Patel
Bird's-eye View of the Château, 1668

3
Adam-Frans van der Meulen
View of the Château from the Satory Hills,
c. 1665

Veüe et Perspectiue de la Menagerie du costé de l'entrée

4

La Salle du Bal donné dans le petit Parc de Versailles
IV.

5

However the King wished to further enlarge the castle which had become too small and he asked Louis Le Vau to draw up plans. Le Vau submitted several different projects: some required the former castle to be pulled down and replaced by a palace in the Italianate style; others were in favour of keeping it, while merely adding a new wing in stone at each end.

Louis XIV appears to have hesitated between these two possibilities, but finally, no doubt counselled by Colbert, he adopted a combination of both: the "house of cards" was to be preserved and enveloped on three sides by a taller stone building with a flat roof, and no attempt would be made to

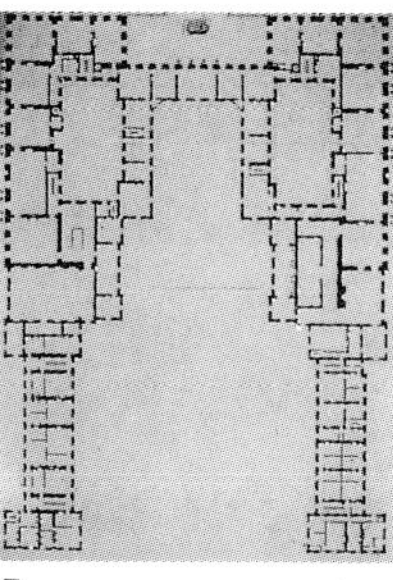
7

6

harmonize this with Louis XIII's construction. From now onwards the old Château (Château-Vieux) will be distinct from the new one (Château-Neuf), though the differences in material, scale and style between the two imply that this was to be a temporary solution. Obviously the King had every intention of demolishing the brick building later and replacing it with a main building in stone, in keeping with the façades of the "envelope". Le Vau first of all, followed by Mansart, put forward many projects, but the wars which cast a gloom over the second part of his reign prevented Louis XIV from carrying out his "great plan" (grand dessein). He left it to Louis XV who delayed its execution for a long while. It was not until the close of his reign that he resolved to carry it out. The financial difficulties which marked the reign of Louis XVI were to thwart the ambitious plans for reconstructing the palace presented by Gabriel and his successors: the "Gabriel wing", and the pavilion erected by Dufour in the reign of Louis XVIII to match it, are the only tangible signs of a dream which never came true.

Versailles is then an unfinished castle or rather, it is formed of two castles, one embedded within the other, partly justifying Saint-Simon's pithy remark: "One part is beautiful and the other ugly, one is a vast expanse and the other a throttled space, all patched up together".

Thus, the façade overlooking the gardens is the only true expression of the wishes of Louis XIV and his architects: a vast palace in the Italianate manner, with flat roofs concealed by a balustrade bristling with trophies and flame ornaments, and façades punctuated by salient *avant-corps* with columns surmounted by statues. The Baroque character of this archi-

4
Adam Pérelle
The Menagery, 1663

5
Jean Le Paultre
The Grand Divertissement Royal, 18 July 1668:
the Ball

6
The Garden Front
of the Château,
c. 1675

7
Plan of the first Floor
of the Château in
1675

8

8
Pierre-Denis Martin
View of the Château from the Courtyards

9
The Garden Front of the Château

10
Pierre-Denis Martin
The Courtyards of the Château and the Stables, 1722

tecture is further accentuated by the creation of a huge terrace, set back on the first floor and framed by two massive pavilions (see fig. 6). On either side of this terrace the two symmetrical state apartments are situated, the King's State Apartment at the north and the Queen's State Apartment at the south, corresponding to the royal private apartments (fig.7) in the Old Château.

The brick and stone castle, momentarily preserved, was further embellished: the façades were adorned with Rance marble columns, gilt wrought-iron balconies, busts placed on

9

10

brackets and allegorical statues on the balustrades; the roofs were decorated with gilded lead ornaments; the courtyard was paved in marble. The outbuildings were heightened and linked to the original castle to form the Royal Court enclosed by gilt railings. A forecourt was created beyond, flanked by two wings to accommodate the Secretaries of State, separated by gilt railings from the Parade Ground (Place d'Armes) where three avenues converged (fig. 8).

Meanwhile, from 1678 onwards, the garden front was renovated: the central terrace disappeared and a new façade was erected between the two pavilions, behind which the Hall of Mirrors was built (fig. 9).

Indeed, the Peace of Nijmegen, ensuring the supremacy of the King in Europe and marking the zenith of Louis XIV's reign, provided the impetus for further enlargements. It is now that Jules Hardouin-Mansart erects two long wings at the south and north ends to accommodate the princes and courtiers, the Great and Small Stables for the saddle- and draught-horses and the carriages (fig. 10) and the *Grand Commun*

11
The Château on the Side of the Orangery

11

(Great Outbuilding) for the *Bouche* (kitchens) and lodgings for the numerous servants.

As for the gardens, the considerable extension of the buildings had tripled the surface of the castle and huge embankments had to be made, with the result that the original small mount was increased to the size of a vast platform in order to support the new buildings. André Le Nôtre now produced a definitive design for the gardens: the flowerbeds and lawns were enlarged to match the scale of the immense palace; a new Orangery of cyclopean dimensions replaced that of Le Vau which had become too small (fig. 11); the perspectives were increased; the Grand Canal and the ornamental Swiss Pool at the end were dug; innumerable groves were planted, fountains were installed, all at great cost and requiring extensive canalizations.

Thus the masterpiece known as the "jardin à la française" came into being, and the greatest sculptors of the time contributed to its decoration: marble and bronze statues evoke the celebrated "villas" of Roman Antiquity and make these gardens the most extraordinary open-air museum of sculpture imaginable.

Yet, anxious perhaps to preserve a trace of the intimate character of the original Versailles, Louis XIV had a small palace built at the far end of the park. Saint-Simon aptly sums up the way it evolved: "The Trianon, in this same park, at the gateway to Versailles, first a porcelain house where one could take refreshments, later furnished for spending the night, and finally a palace of marble, jasper and porphyry, with delightful gardens" .

Meanwhile, an entire town was being constructed, conceived around the great axis of the Château and gardens; thus arose the most magnificent achievement in town planning, a contemporary and rival of the Champs-Elysées. The town was the indispensable complement to the palace with its numerous adjoining buildings, already housing some five thousand people. However there was not enough room there for the courtiers, attached by their functions to the Court, to lodge their servants, so they had to build mansions in the town to accommodate their domestic staff, horses and carriages. Taverns and inns contributed to the animation of the town, the population of which never ceased to grow until, on the eve of the Revolution, it numbered seventy thousand inhabitants.

This prosperity was due to Louis XIV's decision to transfer the seat of the court and the government to Versailles. They settled in on 6 May 1682. From then onwards and for over one hundred years, apart from a brief interruption at the time of the Regency, Versailles was to be the political and administrative capital of the kingdom.

This astonishing decision, which deprived Paris of its ancient privilege and foreshadowed the creation of the great modern capital cities such as Washington or Brasilia, was an answer to a certain number of the King's preoccupations. Louis XIV, still rankling from the dangers and humiliations of the Fronde uprising, was anxious to protect his royal person and the government from any outbursts on the part of the Paris mob. Moreover, he had not forgotten the revolt of the princes and great lords who, in his youth, had almost succeeded in shaking the very foundations of the monarchy. By enticing them to the court in Versailles and maintaining them there in a state of dependence and idle luxury, he deprived them of their freedom and any temptation to rebellion.

Moreover, he dreamed of erecting a palace which would bear the stamp of his own time, for, at the Louvre and the Tuileries, he was hampered by the work of his predecessors. Besides, in Paris he suffered from lack of space. An accomplished rider and an impenitent hunter, he loved the open air and vast expanses.

Finally and above all, the creation of Versailles corresponded to his great political and economic plan. By taking personal command of the affairs of the realm and reorganizing the administration, increasing its centralized character, the King wished to assemble around him the ministers and their offices. Reinforcing economic protectionism, which was to rob Italy of its monopoly of luxury industries (marble, mirrors, velvet, brocade), he reopened the marble quarries which had been left unexploited since the fall of the Roman Empire, reorganized the former royal manufactures and created new

12

12
Gabriel's "Great Plan"

ones such as the Gobelins tapestry works and the St. Gobain crystal factory. With its gates wide open to all and sundry, even to the most humble, the palace became a sort of permanent exhibition of French art and crafts. Within less than twenty years, France developed into the principal producer and exporter in the whole of Europe. The economic prosperity which she enjoyed during the XVIIIth century and the renown of French art throughout the world originated then with the creation of Versailles.

The end of the reign will be marked essentially by the construction of the Chapel, not completed until 1710. Its ample proportions and rich decoration make it the magnificent crowning work of Louis XIV's reign.

During the Regency, young Louis XV lived at the Tuileries Palace in Paris, but on 15 June 1722, six months before attaining his majority, he decided to go back to reside in Versailles and to make it once more the seat of government.

His long reign is, for the Château, a period of intense artistic activity, marked it is true by some deplorable demolitions, such as that of the Bathing Apartment and the Ambassadors' Staircase, but also by many remarkable creations, such as the Hercules Room, the Opera and the Small Trianon. Meanwhile, the apartments of the King, the Queen and the Princes of the royal family were gradually transformed to comply with contemporary taste and to make them more comfortable. Ange-Jacques Gabriel surveyed these new arrangements and produced drawings for the admirable wood panelling which was enhanced by splendid, elaborate furniture, made by the best cabinet makers of the day.

In the reign of Louis XVI, the evolution in taste is evident in the appearance of new decorations and furniture, in which the return to the antique is expressed with discreet elegance. At the same time, magnificent plans are concocted for the partial reconstruction of the Château, which the Revolution was to prevent from being carried out (fig. 12).

At the end of the *Ancien Régime* (of Absolute Monarchy), the palace was without doubt the most sumptuous royal residence in the whole of Europe, and the works of art that the kings had accumulated there for over a century had turned it into an incomparable museum.

At the Revolution, the pictures, antiques and jewels were sent to the "Museum" in Paris, now the Musée du Louvre, books and medals went to the Bibliothèque nationale, while clocks and scientific instruments were transferred to the School of Arts and Crafts (Conservatoire des Arts et Métiers). With few exceptions, the furniture was sold at public auction.

It was decided however that the Château would be "preserved and maintained at the expense of the Republic to serve for the entertainment of the people and to set up useful establishments for agriculture and the arts". These included a Natural History Collection, a Library, a School of Music and finally a Museum especially devoted to the French School of Art (Musée spécial de l'Ecole française) containing about three hundred and fifty paintings, as well as two hundred and fifty statues from the gardens. These arangements were of short duration though and the paintings in particular were soon dispatched to the Louvre.

With the proclamation of the Empire, once again the palace became an official residence of the Crown. Napoléon had it restored and decided he would spend the summer months there; but he abdicated before being able to carry out his project. Likewise, the Restoration was too short-lived to allow Louis XVIII or Charles X to settle down again in the Château where they were born.

In 1830 the palace was practically intact, but in danger. In order to save it from possible destruction or an unworthy use, Louis-Philippe, with a care for national reconciliation, decided to transform it at his own expense into a museum dedicated "to all the glories of France". He assembled there a collection of portraits and historical scenes which, with regard to their number (over six thousand pictures and two thousand sculptures), documentary interest and, quite often, artistic value, made Versailles the most important museum of History in the world.

Nevertheless, though he kept the Chapel, the Opera, the the Hall of Mirrors, as well as the major part of the decoration of the royal apartments, in order to create his vast exhibition halls, Louis-Philippe had no hesitation in demolishing most of the apartments of the princes and courtiers, thus annihilating masterpieces of the decorative art of the XVIIth and XVIIIth centuries.

Today the Château presents a dual aspect: on the one hand there is all that survives of the former royal residence - about one hundred and twenty rooms - where a systematic policy of scrupulous restoration has been carried out in an effort to give it back its former aspect and furniture; and on the other, the Museum of History which Louis-Philippe called "les Galeries Historiques" comprising one hundred and twenty rooms.

The Château

The visitor enters through the forecourt with the Ministers' wings on either side, and by an iron gateway flanked by two groups of sculpture symbolizing, on the left, the *Victories of Louis XIV over Spain* by François Girardon and, on the right, his *Victories over the Empire* by Gaspard Marsy. The statues of *Peace* by Jean-Baptiste Tuby on the left and *Abundance*, on the right, by Antoine Coysevox are in recess. Originally these statues framed the gateway of a second railing separating the forecourt from the Royal Court. The theme of War and Peace is found again in the decoration of the Hall of Mirrors and the rooms on either side of it and also in the gardens. The second railing, pulled down during the Revolution, was transferred to the place where the equestrian statue of *Louis XIV* by Cartellier and Petitot was to stand; this was not erected until 1836.

The Marble Court is the oldest part of the Château; the buildings bordering it date from Louis XIII and were considerably altered and embellished by Louis XIV (fig. 13).

The clock above the central avant-corps is framed by the statues of *Mars* by Marsy and *Hercules* by Girardon. The statues placed on the balustrades of the wings projecting at each end symbolize: on the right, *Renown* by Le Conte, *Asia* by Massou, *Europe* by Le Gros, *Peace* by Regnaudin, *Diligence* by Raon, *Prudence* by Massou, *Wisdom* by Girardon, *Justice* by Coysevox and *Munificence* by Marsy; on the left are *Victory* by Lespingola, *Africa* by Le Hongre, *America* and *Glory* by Regnaudin, *Wealth* and *Authority* by Le Hongre, *Generosity* by Le Gros, *Force* by Coysevox and *Abundance* by Marsy.

13
The Marble Courtyard

13

In order to appreciate the general structure of the buildings and, in particular, the implantation of the Old Château in relation to the New Château, it is advisable to walk round the central building, taking the north passage into the gardens (on the right in the Royal Court) and returning by the south passage.

A detailed visit of Versailles and Trianon requires at least two full days, and more still in order to see the "History Galleries".

Those with only one day to spare should restrict their visit to the main parts:

– the Château itself (the King's Private Apartment, the Opera, the Chapel, the State Apartments of the King and the Queen, the Hall of Mirrors),

– the gardens and Trianon.

To avoid the crowds, it is best to start by visiting the gardens and Trianon.

A brief visit should be limited to the Chapel, the State Apartments and the Hall of Mirrors (entrance A, at the end of the Chapel courtyard, for individual visitors; entrance B, on the right in the Royal Court for groups having booked).

All conducted tours led by National Museum guides begin at Entrance C in the passage on the left side.

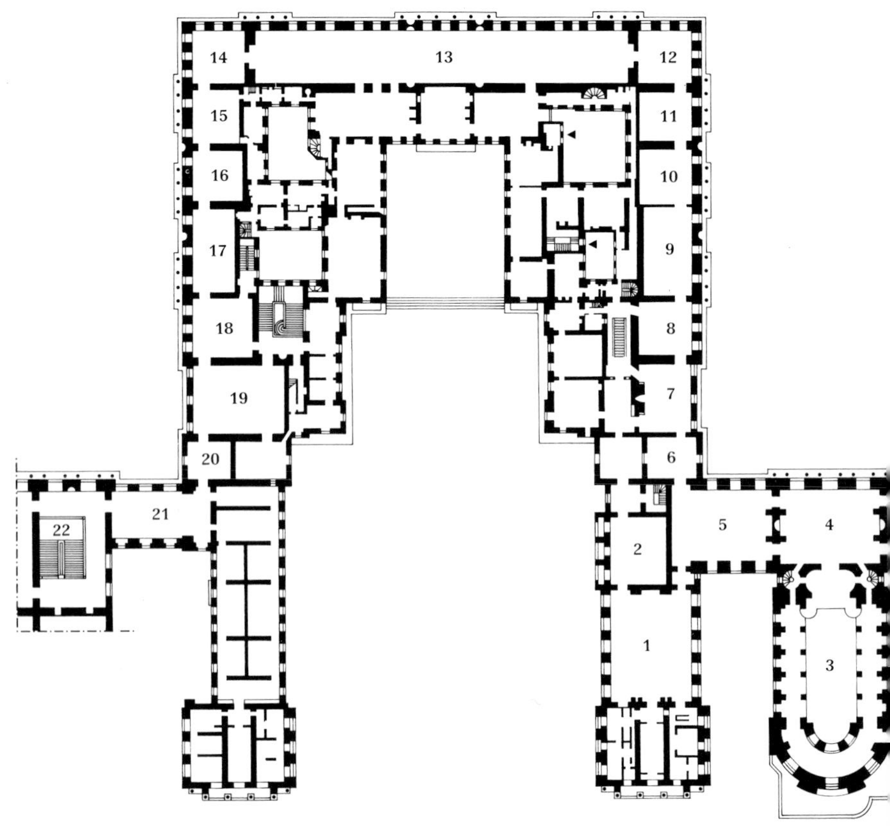
14
13
12
15
11
16
10
17
9
18
8
19
7
20
6
21
22
5
4
2
1
3

The State Apartments

Unaccompanied visit

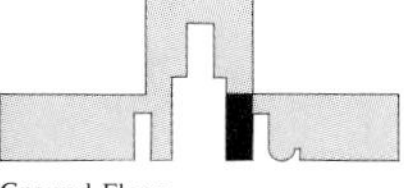
Ground-Floor

Individual visitors can reach the State Apartments by Entrance A, situated at the back of the Chapel Court. Originally the first room opened on to the courtyard and the garden and served as a public passageway. Today the Information Bureau, the ticket offices, the counter for the hire of cassette-guides and the cloakroom are all found here.

Groups having booked go in by Entrance B on the right of the Royal Court. They enter the "Gabriel Vestibule" leading to the Great Staircase[1] (fig. 14) beyond which is the States General Hall[2] and the Hercules Room at the entrance to the King's State Apartments. This staircase was intended to replace the Ambassadors' Staircase, pulled down in 1752 to comply with Gabriel's plans. Operations on the original project were soon interrupted though and it was only in recent times that they have been resumed and were completed in 1985.

14

14
The Great Staircase

The Chapel Vestibule
(15.50 m × 13.92 m × 6 m)

This great colonnaded room, paved with marble, occupies the site of the Thetis Grotto, erected in 1665 and destroyed in 1685. The large haut-relief in marble represents *Louis XIV crossing the Rhine*. This work by Nicolas and Guillaume Coustou was meant to adorn the fireplace in the War Room; it was placed there by Louis-Philippe.

The Royal Chapel[3]

This magnificent edifice (44 m × 17.82 m × 25.59 m) is the fourth chapel to be built for the Château, the three preceding ones having been merely temporary. Work began in 1699 according to the plans of Jules Hardouin-Mansart and was completed in 1710 under the direction of his brother-in-law Robert de Cotte. In accordance with the tradition of Palatine chapels, it consists of two floors. The main tribune above the entrance was reserved for the royal family, the side tribunes for the royal princes and the principal court dignitaries, while the rest of the congregation remained on the lower floor (fig.15).

15

15
The Royal Chapel

16
Antoine Coypel
The Paintings on the vaulted Ceiling, 1709

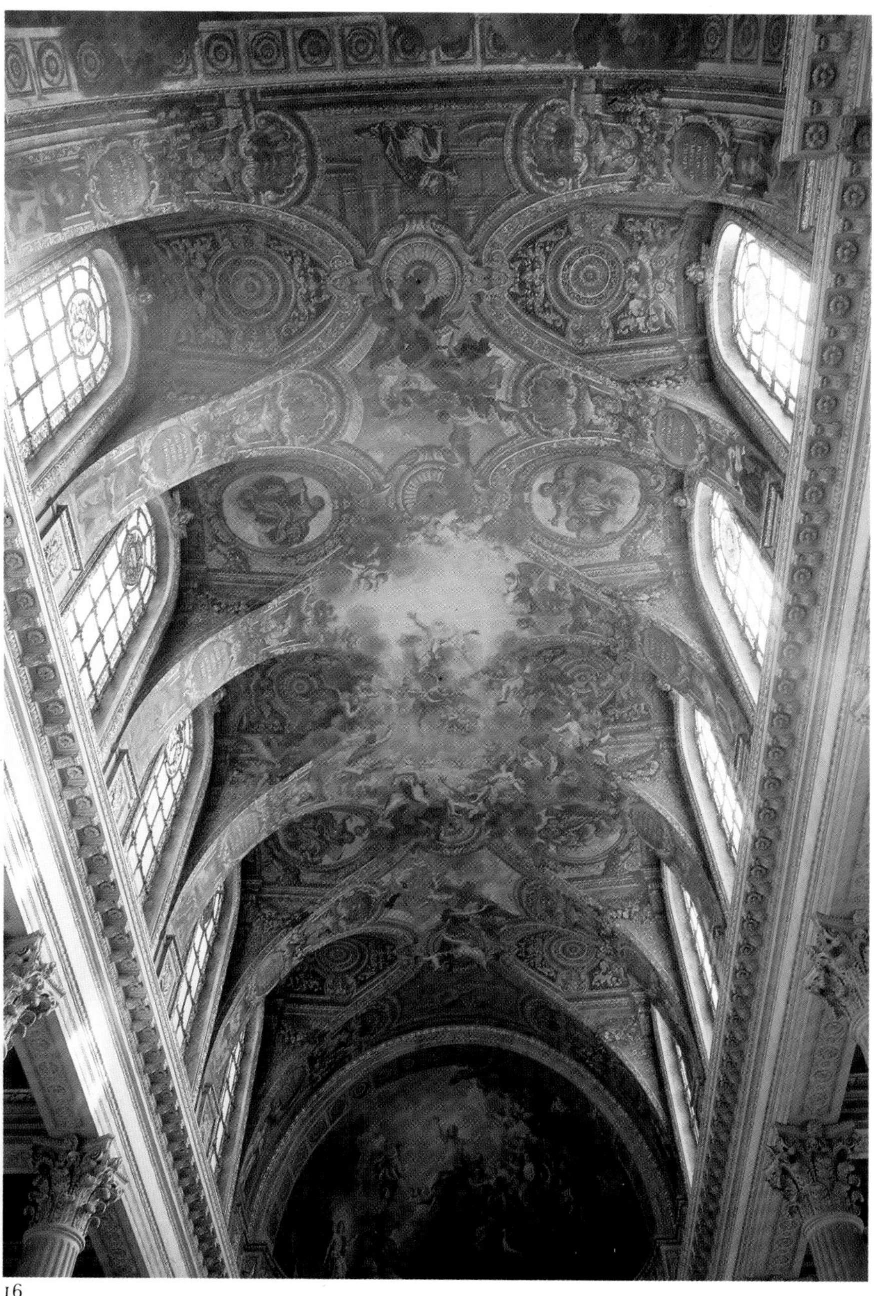

16

The luminosity of this majestic nave, the nobility of the architecture and the exceptional quality of its decoration make this chapel one of the great masterpieces of religious art.

The pallor of the stone is discreetly heightened by the golds of the high altar and the organ, as well as by the polychrome marble paving and the painting on the arched ceiling.

The entire decoration clearly illustrates the parallelism existing between the Old and the New Testaments. The ceiling paintings (fig. 16) represent the three figures of the Trinity: in the centre, *God the Father in his Glory offering to Mankind the Promise of Redemption* by Antoine Coypel; in the half-dome of the apse, *Christ's Resurrection* by Charles de La Fosse; above the royal tribune, *The Holy Ghost descending on the Virgin and the Apostles* by Jean Jouvenet. At each extremity of the vault, two medallions in imitation gilt bronze represent Saint Louis, to whom the chapel is dedicated, and Charlemagne. Between the tall windows, the twelve Prophets prefigure the twelve Apostles, portrayed on the ceilings of the side tribunes.

This parallelism is also found in the bas-reliefs of the the choir ambulatory where Nicolas Coustou displays the symbols of Judaism (the seven-branched Candlestick, the Tables of the Law and the Ark of the Covenant) beside the instruments of Christ's Passion. The rest of the carved decoration consists of figures of the Virtues crowning the windows of the tribunes: angels are holding the instruments of the Passion in the archivolts of the arcades on the ground floor, and in the bas-reliefs on the pillars, scenes recall the different stations of the Cross, alternating with admirable trophies on religious themes. All these sculptures, executed with exceptional delicacy, are the work of a whole team of sculptors, including Guillaume and Nicolas Coustou, Le Lorrain, Thierry, Frémin, Magnier, Le Moyne, Le Pautre, Van Clève, among others.

The high altar in gilt bronze is entirely due to Van Clève. He carved the *Glory* with the name of *Jahveh* shining forth, the angels in adoration and the bas-relief representing *The Dead Christ on his Mother's Knees* (fig. 17).

The fine organ is situated in the tribune above the high altar, with a mechanism due to Cliquot and the magnificently carved chest of drawers gilded by Le Goupil. Around this organ, the most famous titulary of which was François Couperin called "the Great", stood the musicians and choristers responsible for interpreting the great motets of Lully, Charpentier and Delalande.

The side altars are dedicated to the patron saints of members of the royal family, the two main ones being placed in a small construction of two superimposed chapels projecting northwards: on the ground floor, the Saint Louis Chapel, adorned with a painting by Jouvenet, *Saint Louis succouring the Wounded at the Battle of Mansourah* and on the floor

17
The High Altar
and the Organ

17

above the Virgin Chapel with an *Annonciation* by Louis de Boulogne above the altar. In the next tribune the altar of Saint Theresa is decorated with *The Saint in Extasy* by Jean-Baptiste Santerre.

The remaining altars, placed in the aisles and the ambulatory on the ground floor, were not completed until Louis XV's time. They are adorned with admirables bronze bas-reliefs: *Saint Adelaide taking leave of Saint Odilon* by Lambert Sigisbert Adam; *Saint Anne instructing the Virgin* by Jacques Verberckt; *Saint Charles Borromeo during the Plague in Milan* by

Edme Bouchardon; *The Martyrdom of Saint Victoire* by Nicolas Sébastien Adam.

Until the end of the *Ancien Régime*, the chapel served as framework for the religious celebrations of the French Court; masses were given for the Ordre du Saint-Esprit (the Order of the Holy Ghost), the *Te Deum* for military victories and the baptisms and weddings of the princes, the most famous of all no doubt being the one which took place on 16 May 1770 when the Dauphin, the future Louis XVI, married the Archduchess Marie-Antoinette. During these ceremonies the King took up his position on a prayer stool at the centre of the nave, contrary to his usual habit of attending mass from the royal tribune above, situated just over the entrance door.

This door is flanked by two spiral staircases going straight to the Chapel Room. The Stone Gallery leads to the Opera and to the History Galleries, which include the Crusades Room and those of the XVIIth and XIXth centuries. A visit to the XVIIth-century galleries provides an excellent introduction to the State Apartments, the last of which opens on to the Chapel Room

The Chapel Room[4]
(14.17 m × 12.85 m × 11.57 m)

Situated above the Chapel Vestibule and opening directly on to the royal tribune, it shares the same architecture as that of the Chapel: a floor paved with marble, Corinthian columns, and figures of the Virtues above the doors and windows. The stucco work in the angles of the ceiling represent the four

18

18
The Chapel Room

parts of the world (fig. 18). The statues were placed in their niches in 1730: on the right, *Magnanimity* by Jacques Bousseau; on the left, *Fame holding the Portrait of Louis XV* by François Antoine Vassé.

The main door opening on to the royal tribune bears an admirably engraved lock by Desjardins. The Savonnerie carpet emblazoned with the royal coat of arms was woven especially for this tribune where, every morning, the King and the royal family knelt down to follow mass. At each end of the tribune there are two circular balconies, formerly protected by mirrored niches framed in gilt bronze baguettes, where the King sometimes sat on the left and the Queen on the right. The side doors are surmounted by bas-reliefs depicting the *Presentation at the Temple* by Poirier and *Jesus instructing the Doctors of Law* by Guillaume Coustou. The painting on the arched ceiling represents *The Descent of the Holy Ghost on the Virgin and the Apostles on the Day of Pentecost*; it is a reminder that the King, on the day of his coronation, received the same unctions as a Bishop would, and for this reason he was also considered a successor of the Apostles.

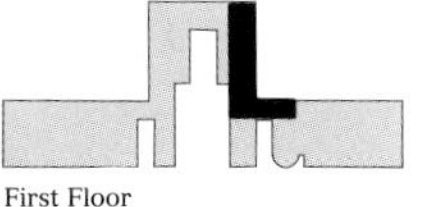

First Floor

The King's State Apartment

Originally the King's State Apartment comprised seven rooms: the Drawing Room reached by the King's Grand Staircase, the Guardroom, the Antechamber, the Bedchamber and three private rooms, the last of which opened on to the terrace occupying the centre of the main front overlooking the gardens, at the other end of which began the suite of rooms of the Queen's State Apartment.

The decoration, in particular the ceilings adorned with paintings in gilt stucco coffers, draws inspiration entirely from contemporaneous Italian palaces. The general theme was borrowed from the famous Planets Apartments in the Pitti Palace in Florence, where Pierre de Cortone had been in charge of the work that Le Brun had the occasion to admire. This theme was particularly appropriate for Versailles, where the decoration was based on the solar myth. Félibien has described it in these terms: "As the Sun is the emblem of the King, the seven planets have been chosen as the subject of the paintings in the seven rooms of this apartment, so that in each of them those actions of the Heroes of Antiquity must be represented which relate to each of the planets and also to each of His Majesty's actions. The symbolical motifs are seen in the carved ornaments of the cornices and on the ceilings". Indeed, ever since Antiquity, the planets bear the names of the principal gods of Olympus and, just as the planets revolve round this star, so do the Olympian gods accompany Apollo, the Sun King.

This ambitious, well-conceived programme was never completed however. From 1678 onwards, in fact, the construction of the Hall of Mirrors had entailed alterations to the decoration of the Council Room and the disappearance of two others. This loss was partly compensated by the creation at the other extremity of two new rooms, the Venus Room and the Room of Abundance.

In 1684 Louis XIV had a new apartment decorated and furnished in the Old Château, where he was to reside until the end of his life, and his successors after him. Consequently the State Apartment was put to another use and henceforth served only for entertainment and fêtes. On reception days (*jours d'appartement*), on Mondays, Wednesdays and Thursdays, the King, the royal family and the entire court assembled there for four hours, from six o'clock till ten o'clock in the evening. Each room was then allotted a different purpose, etiquette was relaxed and the King became merely a host presiding over the entertainment offered to his guests. This is what Madame de Maintenon called "the delights of Versailles" (*les délices de Versailles*).

The walls of the State Apartment are cased in marble, either from top to bottom or as far as the window-rest and Félibien drew attention to the fact that "care has been taken to use only the most rare and precious marbles in all places closest to the King, so that as one proceeds from one room to the next, there is more and more wealth, not only in the marble, but also in the sculptures and in the paintings embellishing the ceilings".

At first Louis XIV wanted the doors in gilt bronze, but he soon gave up this idea. They were subsequently made in carved and gilded wood and can still be seen there. Their decoration is closely related to the symbolism of each corresponding room.

In the rooms entirely cased in marble, statues and busts in the Antique style belonging to the royal collection were exhibited. In the others, above the dado work, the walls were lined with fabrics on which the paintings were hung. These are now almost all kept in the Louvre. The fabrics varied according to the season: in winter, it was crimson velvet, trimmed with braiding and gold fringes and in summer, a brocade or a damask. The screens placed in front of the doors were made of the same material, which was also used to cover the stools and benches. The curtains at the windows were of damask or white taffeta edged with gold fringes, with the King's monogram embroidered in gold thread.

The furniture made of engraved silver was the work of the greatest silversmiths of the day, such as Claude Ballin: it consisted of chandeliers, candelabras, sconces, fire-dogs, tables, stools, pedestal tables bearing girandoles, etc. This sumptuous furniture was even more valuable for its work than for its material. It was in fact melted down twice, in 1689 and 1709, to pay for the costs of war and was then replaced by furniture in carved and gilded wood, which was dispersed at the Revolution.

In 1710 the State Apartment was extended eastwards by the creation of a new room, the Hercules Room, which communicated with the Chapel Room.

The Hercules Room[5]

(18.32 m × 13.85 m × 11.57 m)

This room replaces the third chapel, built for the castle in 1682, which, once the present Chapel we have just seen had been completed, was demolished in 1710. A floor was laid down at the level of the former tribunes, making it easier to communicate between the central building and the north wing. The decoration of this new room was undertaken in 1712 under the direction of Robert de Cotte, but was interrupted first by the death of Louis XIV in 1715 and then by the Regency, and only resumed in 1729 and completed in 1736.

The marble casing and twin pilasters foreshadow the decoration of the Hall of Mirrors, situated at the far end of the State Apartment; the exceptional quality of the marbles and the splendour of the bronzes on the chimneypiece, chiselled by Antoine Vassé, contribute to making this room one of the

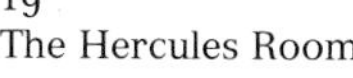

19
The Hercules Room

19

most beautiful in the palace ((fig. 19). Without doubt though it is the paintings above all which hold our attention.

We are entitled to say that the entire decoration has been conceived around the great painting by Paolo Veronese, occupying one whole wall. *The Repast at Simon's House,* executed by the great Venetian artist for the refectory of the Servi Convent, was offered to Louis XIV in 1664 by the Republic of Venice (fig. 20). Placed as it is here in a superb frame moulded by Jacques Verberckt, who was likewise responsible for framing the picture above the chimneypiece, *Eliezer and Rebecca,* also by Veronese, it has inspired the fake architectures and harmonious colours of the ceiling.

This ceiling, one of the largest in the world, is also, thanks to its skilled composition, elegant figures and fresh colours, one of the great masterpieces of French decorative painting. François Le Moyne, who painted it between 1733 and 1736, depicts *The Apotheosis of Hercules* (fig. 21). The hero, having vanquished all the vices and monsters, is ascending Mount Olympus on a chariot drawn by the spirits of Virtue. *Jupiter and Juno,* surrounded by the gods and goddesses, present Hebe the goddess of Youth to him, who will become his wife. Farther along we see the graceful group of *Zephyr and Flora* who are playing with a garland wreathed by Cupids; *Aurora,* surrounded by stars, and *Iris,* recognizable by her rainbow, attract attention to the group of *Muses* dominated by *Apollo and the Spirit of the Fine Arts.* This beautiful ensemble aroused the admiration of all contemporaries, and Louis XV appointed

20

21

Le Moyne to be his Principal Painter *(Premier Peintre)*. Alas, a few months later, exhausted by this gigantic task and suffering from depression, the unfortunate artist committed suicide.

The Hercules Room was inaugurated on 26 January 1739 by a full dress ball, on the occasion of the marriage of Louis XV's eldest daughter to an Infante of Spain. That night the room was lit by seven rock crystal chandeliers, one hundred and nine other chandeliers and four sprays of twenty-five golden lilies bearing candles and crystal festoons. Fifty musicians wearing blue dominoes were placed before the chimneypiece; tiered seating covered with crimson rugs had been erected in front of the Veronese painting for the ladies of the court who were not dancing, and in the window recesses for those who had come from Paris. The royal procession arrived at seven o'clock to the sound of music. Louis XV was wearing a costume of blue cut velvet and a jacket of gold brocade, with diamond buttons matching those on his plaque of the Saint-Esprit. Queen Maria Leszczynska had donned the ceremonial court dress with a white background, embroidered with wreathed gold columns scattered with silk flowers. Her bodice was entirely covered with precious stones and she wore a necklace of large diamonds with the "Sancy" pendant, while the "Regent" glittered in her hair. After the formal ball, a meal was served in vermeil bowls, and then a masked ball

20
Paolo Veronese
The Repast at Simon's House, 1576

21
François Le Moyne
The Apotheosis of Hercules, 1733-1736

took place until dawn in the State Apartment, where three hundred musicians wore dominoes in variegated colours.

The door on the left of Veronese's great picture opens on to the King's new Grand Staircase; we have already passed by the foot of it.

The Room of Abundance[6]
(8.65 m × 7.56 m × 7.55 m)

This small reception room (fig. 22), arranged in 1680, for long served as a vestibule to the Collection Room or Room of Rare Objects (Cabinet des Curiosités or des Raretés) reached by the door at the end after mounting five steps. In this study, which under Louis XVI will become the King's Gamesroom, Louis XIV kept some of his rarest pictures, objets d'art which are now exhibited in the Louvre, and above all his famous collection of gold medals kept in twelve medal cabinets inlaid with copper and tortoiseshell. This is now at the Cabinet des Médailles in the Bibliothèque nationale.

The ceiling was painted by René-Antoine Houasse, who depicts on the surround the most valuable pieces in the Room of Rare Objects, in particular the King's "ship", an ornament symbolizing sovereign power, and in the centre, *Royal Munificence and the Progress of the Fine Arts.*

22

23

22
The Abundance Room

23
Hyacinthe Rigaud
Philip V, 1700

The four bronze busts were brought here from former royal collections. The portraits are those of Louis XIV's descendants: on either side of the door, *The Dauphin*, his son and the *Duc de Bourgogne*, his eldest grandson, by Hyacinthe Rigaud; on the left, his second grandson, *King Philip V of Spain*, also by Rigaud (fig. 23) and on the right, his great-grandson, *Louis XV*, by Jean-Baptiste Van Loo.

When a reception was held in the Apartment, a buffet was laid out in the Room of Abundance on three tables laden with gold and silver vessels containing hot chocolate, tea, coffee, lemonade, iced water, sorbets and diverse liqueurs.

The Venus Room[7]
(13.27 m × 8.90 m × 7.38 m)

This reception room, in Louis XIV's day, was the main entrance to the State Apartment: the door at the end, on the left, opened on to the Ambassadors' Staircase, destroyed in 1752 (fig. 24) then leading to the next room. The floor was paved with variegated marbles

The walls are cased in marble with Ionic columns in Rance marble on either side of the doors at the end (fig. 25). The same columns, painted in trompe-l'oeil, are repeated in the fake perspectives with which Jacques Rousseau decorated the narrow sides of the room and which appear to increase its dimensions (fig. 26). The same artist was responsible for the trompe-l'oeil statues placed between the windows, representing *Meleager* and *Atalanta*. In the recess at the end stands a statue of Louis XIV in antique attire by Jean Warin. Six antique busts complete the decoration (fig. 27).

24

The ceiling was painted by Houasse. In the centre he represents *Venus subjugating Divinities and Powers to her Empire*; on either side there are two imitation medallions in gilt bronze depicting *The Rape of Europa and of Amphitrite*; in the corners are couples of famous lovers: *Theseus and Ariadne, Jason and Medea, Antony and Cleopatra, Titus and Berenice*.

25

26

27

The pictures in the covings deal with themes from ancient history all containing an allusion to contemporary events: *Augustus presiding over the Circus Games* (Carrousel of 1662); *Nabonassor and Semiramis building the Hanging Gardens of Babylon* (work carried out on the royal households); *Alexander weds Roxana* (marriage of the King); *Cyrus takes up Arms to save a Princess* (War of Devolution or of the Rights of the Queen). These paintings appear to hang above false bas-reliefs: on the narrow walls, *Apollo and Daphne* and *Pan and Syrinx*; on the longer sides, four ravishments symbolizing *The Four Elements*. On evenings when receptions were held, refreshments were placed on tables laden with silver bowls containing sweetmeats, fresh fruit and candied fruits.

24
The Ambassadors' Staircase (model)

25
The Venus Room

26
Jacques Rousseau
Fake Perspective, 1677

27
Jean Warin
Louis XIV in antique Costume

The Diana Room[8]
(10.34 m × 8.70 m × 7.55 m)

Like the preceding one, this room provided access to the State Apartment, and the door on the far right opened on to the second flight of the Ambassadors' Staircase. Originally the floor was paved with variegated marbles.

The walls are cased in Campan and Rance marble on a background of white marble (fig. 30).

28

29

30

In the centre of the ceiling, *Diana, accompanied by the Night Hours and the fresh Morning Hours, presides over Hunting and Navigation*, by Gabriel Blanchard; in the covings: *Jason and the Argonauts* and *Alexander hunting the Lion* by Charles de La Fosse; *Cyrus hunting wild Boar* and *Julius Caesar sending a Roman Colony to Carthage* by Claude Audran. On the mantlepiece, decorated with a small bas-relief representing *The Flight into Egypt*, attributed to Jacques Sarrazin, *The Sacrifice of Iphigenia* (fig. 28) by La Fosse; facing, *Diana and Endymion* by Blanchard. Above the doors, imitation gold bas-reliefs of *Diana and Acteo*, *Diana protecting Arethuses*, *Sacrifice to Diana* and *Offering of Flowers*.

At the end of the room, on a pedestal adorned with bronze cast by the Keller brothers, stands the bust of Louis XIV made by Lorenzo Bernini in 1665. The brilliant execution of this sculpture makes it one of the masterpieces of this great Roman artist and without doubt the finest portrait of the King in his youth (he was twenty-seven at the time) (fig.29). The two antique busts on either side and the four busts in porphyry of Roman emperors stood in the same place before the Revolution.

The Diana Room served as a billiard room; it is well known that Louis XIV was a master at this game.

The Mars Room[9]

(17.53 m × 9.20 m × 7.58 m)

This was really the first room (fig. 31) of the State Apartment, during the odd ten years that the King lived there. It was the Guardroom and this destination explains its warlike character and the subjects of the decoration.

In the centre of the ceiling, *Mars on his Chariot drawn by Wolves, accompanied by the Spirit of War and of History writing to the Dictation of Fame* by Audran,; on the left, *Victory supported by Hercules and followed by Abundance and Felicity* by Jouvenet; on the right, *Terror, Fury and Wrath pursuing Fear and Pallor* by Houasse.

Each of the imitation gilt bronze bas-reliefs in the covings is an allusion to the re-establishment of discipline and to the King's military justice: *Caesar reviewing his Troops* by Audran; *Cyrus haranguing his Troops* by Jouvenet; *Demetrius storming a Town* by Audran; *The Triumph of Constantine* and *Alexander Severus demoting an Officer* by Houasse; *Mark Antony appointing Albinus as Consul* by Jouvenet.

In the corners there are some magnificent gilt stucco works: two trophies evoke the alliance between the Holy Roman Empire, Spain and Holland against France; a naval trophy recalls the trade with the East Indies; a trophy of Turkish weapons commemorates the victory of St.Gothard.

28
Charles de La Fosse
The Sacrifice of Iphigenia, 1712

29
Lorenzo Bernini
Louis XIV, 1665

30
The Diana Room

31

33

32

Above the doors, four pictures by Simon Vouet: *Justice, Temperance, Force* and *Prudence*, painted before 1638 for the Château de St. Germain, replace Titian's pictures there beforehand.

Above the fireplace, *David playing the Harp* by Domenichino. During the *Ancien Régime*, in wintertime, this picture hung in the alcove of the King's Bedchamber.

When, in 1684, the King no longer lived in this apartment, two marble tribunes were set up on either side of the fireplace for musicians as, on reception evenings, the Mars Room was reserved for concerts. These tribunes were dismantled in 1750 and the room acquired its present aspect: two false doors were made to match the real ones and the walls were hung with crimson damask trimmed with gold braid.

Two large pictures were put back on either side of the fireplace: *The Family of Darius at the Feet of Alexander* by Charles Le Brun (fig. 32) and *The Pilgrims of Emmaus*, an early copy of the original painting by Veronese, now in the Louvre. On the narrow sides of the room are portraits of *Louis XV* and *Queen Marie Leszczynska* with the royal arms on the borders (fig. 33), both by Carle Van Loo.

The beautiful Savonnerie carpet, like those in the next rooms, were all woven in the reign of Louis XVI for the Great Gallery in the Louvre.

The Mercury Room[10]

(10.25 m × 9.93 m × 7.58 m)

Originally an antechamber, this room later became the State Bedchamber (*Chambre du Lit*) in which stood the parade bed embroidered entirely with gold. The rest of the furniture was in silver: the balustrade in front of the bed and the eight candelabras, the chandelier, the fire-dogs, the table placed between the windows and the frame of the mirror above it. The walls were lined with two alternate brocades, one on a gold and the other on a silver background, where hung, among others, *The Pilgrims of Emmaus* and *The Entombment* by Titian, now in the Louvre.

Jean-Baptiste de Champaigne was given the task of painting the ceiling: in the centre, *Mercury on his Chariot with the Morning Star, Arts and Sciences*; in the ceiling coves, *Alexander receiving a Mission of Indians, Ptolemy conversing with some learned Men, Augustus receiving a Mission of Indians* and *Alexander receiving various Animals sent from all over the World for Aristotle to describe* (an allusion to the construction of the Menagerie in the Park at Versailles); in the corners, figures of women and children hanging up garlands of flowers, on camaieu medallions, symbolize *Physical Dexterity, Knowledge of the Fine Arts, Royal Justice* and *Royal Authority* .

Above the doors are *Acis and Galathea* by Michel Corneille

31
The Mars Room

32
Charles Le Brun
The Family of Darius at the Feet of Alexander, 1660

33
Carle Van Loo
Queen Marie Leszczynska, 1747

34

35

and *Apollo and Daphne* by Antoine Coypel, both paintings brought from the Château de Meudon, the Dauphin's residence.

On the crimson damask, restoring to the room the aspect it bore in the XVIIIth century, hang the portraits of Louis XV painted by Hyacinthe Rigaud in 1730 (fig. 34) and of Marie Leszczynska by Louis Tocqué in 1740. The tapestry at the end is part of a set on the *History of the King*, woven at the Gobelins workshops: it represents *Louis XIV granting an Audience to the Papal Legate at Fontainebleau, on 29 July 1664*.

The clock with automata, due to the clockmaker Antoine Morand and offered to Louis XIV in 1706, stood in this room in the XVIIIth century. The two fine chests of drawers were made in 1709 by André-Charles Boulle for the King's bedroom at Trianon (fig. 35).

On evenings when informal receptions were held in the apartments, this room was set aside as a gamesroom for the royal family. The Duc d'Anjou, Louis XIV's grandson, who was proclaimed King of Spain on 16 November 1700, occupied this room for three weeks before departing for his new land.

34
Hyacinthe Rigaud
Louis XV, 1730

35
André-Charles Boulle
Chest of Drawers, 1709

36
The Apollo Room

The Apollo Room[11]

(10.25 m × 9.90 m × 7.50 m)

This used to be the most sumptuous room of the whole State Apartment, which is hardly surprising for it started by being the King's Bedchamber before it became the Throne Room when the royal bed was moved into the preceding room. It still retains important vestiges of its former splendour, particularly the marbles (sérancolin, sea-green and Genoese), as well as the ceiling (fig. 36).

This ceiling is without doubt Charles de La Fosse's masterpiece and it illustrates the colourist's talent. In the centre we see *Apollo on his Chariot, accompanied by the Figure of France and the Procession of the Seasons*; in the corners are allegories of the *Four Continents*. The paintings on the coved panels represent *Coriolan relieving the Siege of Rome*, *Vespasian constructing the Coliseum*, *Augustus building the Port of Mycenae* (an allusion to the construction of the port of Rochefort) and *Porus led before Alexander*. The beautiful stucco moulding, and above all the graceful Muses holding the frame of the central painting, give added richness to this ceiling.

On the overdoors are an *Allegory of the Birth of the Dauphin* by Blanchard and a picture by Bonnemère *of Renown spreading the Fame of the King to the four Parts of the Earth*.

36

37

37
Hyacinthe Rigaud
Louis XIV, 1701

38
Toussaint Foliot
Pedestal Table, 1769

39
The War Room

The Louis-XV damask cannot efface though the memory of the extraordinary wall fabrics which, in the reign of Louis XIV, covered the walls of the Throne Room: in winter, crimson velvet dotted with motifs embroidered in gold and silver, and the pictures, particularly Rubens' *Thomyris* and *The Labours of Hercules* by Guido Reni, today in the Louvre; in summertime, the famous wall hanging, consisting of a set of embroideries on the theme of Peace, in gold and silver thread and coloured silks, placed between gold and silver pilasters.

The throne itself was in silver. Almost three metres high, it stood at the far end of the room on a platform, beneath a canopy; the bolts are still visible. Here the King gave ordinary audiences, but when he received a foreign envoy, the throne was transported to the Hall of Mirrors. On reception evenings, the Apollo Room was set aside for dancing. The King, himself an excellent dancer, was fond of attending, sitting informally on the steps of the throne.

The chimneypiece was surmounted at all seasons by the portrait of Louis XIV in royal regalia, painted by Rigaud in 1701 and today in the Louvre. The copy replacing it is also the work of Rigaud; the King had intended it for his grandson, the King of Spain (fig. 37). Facing it is the portrait of Louis XVI by Callet.

The six pedestal tables in gilded wood are part of a set of twenty-four made in 1769 for the Hall of Mirrors by Toussaint Foliot (groups of children) (fig. 38) and Augustin Pajou (women holding cornucopias).

38

The War Room[12]
(10.26 m × 10.26 m × 11.50 m)

At first this was the Council Room (Grand Cabinet du Roi) or the Jupiter Room (Cabinet de Jupiter) where Louis XIV held council. Then it was decorated with pictures related to the story of Jupiter and to the restraint of princes (*la Justice du Prince*). All these paintings were removed to the Queen's new Guardroom when work started on the Hall of Mirrors, after which the room acquired its present aspect (fig. 39).

Its decoration, and that of the Peace Room symmetrical to it, closely resemble that of the Hall of Mirrors separating them. These three rooms occupy the entire west front of the main building of the Château, forming a homogeneous ensemble, so that the whole enfilade of the State Apartment ends in a veritable apotheosis. The walls are entirely cased in precious marbles, adorned with gilt bronze trophies and mirrors. At a time when mirrors were relatively small and very costly, it was a manifestation of unheard-of lavishness to decorate three rooms, measuring nearly one hundred metres in length, almost entirely with mirrors. It was also proof that henceforth France, with the Manufacture Royale de St.Gobain, had robbed Venice of a longstanding monopoly.

39

Charles Le Brun took charge of the decoration of the arched ceiling in the Hall of Mirrors and the two reception rooms. These painted panels, retracing the great events of the reign, since the time the King first ruled in his own right (1661) until the Peace of Nijmegen (1678), are the Principal Painter's masterpiece and the accomplished model for a grand royal setting.

In the centre of the cupola, the figure of *France, bearing on her Shield the Portrait of Louis XIV* is surrounded by Victories one of whom presents the coat-of-arms of the City of Strasbourg, reunited to France in 1681. In the covings are *Bellona*, goddess of war, and the three powers which united in 1672 to combat France: the Empire, Spain and Holland.

The masks and garlands on the overdoors symbolize the Four Seasons; but the most striking ornaments are the gilt bronze trophies adorning the panels, admirably chased by the goldsmith Ladoireau.

Above the fireplace, its chimney closed by a bas-relief representing *Clio writing the History of the King*, is a superb stucco moulding where Antoine Coysevox has portrayed *Louis XIV, victorious and crowned by Glory*; this oval medallion rests on some captives enchained with garlands of flowers and is surmounted by figures of *Fame* holding the royal crown. In 1725, it was decided to replace Coysevox's great medallion with a haut-relief commissioned from the Coustou brothers; but no doubt their work was judged inferior to that of Coysevox, for it was never installed. A century later, Louis-Philippe gave it a permanent place by integrating it into the decoration of the Chapel Vestibule. In front of the pier mirrors are three of the six busts of Roman emperors in porphyry, marble and gilt bronze which formerly stood there.

The Great Gallery or Hall of Mirrors[13]

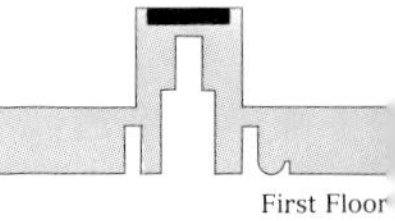

This vast room (73 m × 10.50 m × 12.30 m) occupies the site on which stood the two end cabinets of the King's State Apartment, a terrace and the two end cabinets of the the Queen's State Apartment (see plan). The Saturn Room or Small Bedroom corresponded to the first two windows of the Gallery, the Venus Room to the next two, the latter with three french windows opening on to the terrace which, in turn, corresponded to the nine centre windows. Paved with black, white and red marble, this terrace had an ornamental basin in the middle, decorated with a group of children in gilt lead.

The Gallery (fig. 40), built in 1678 by Jules Hardouin-Mansart, was cased in marble in 1679. The sculptors completed their work in 1680 and Le Brun painted the arched ceiling between 1681 and 1684. Opposite the seventeen arched windows are seventeen corresponding arcades adorned with mirrors, separated by engraved gilt copper baguettes. The arches

40

41

40
The Hall of Mirrors

41
Pierre Ladoireau
Bronze Trophy, 1702

are surmounted alternately with a head of Apollo and the skin of the Nemean lion. The pilasters are in Rance marble on a background of white marble, with capitals adorned with fleurs-de-lys and Gallic cocks, a souvenir of the "French Order" imagined by Le Brun. Trophies of gilt bronze decorate the green Campan marble piers, engraved like those of the War and Peace Rooms by the goldsmith Ladoireau (fig. 41).

The Gallery is decorated with eight busts of Roman emperors in porphyry and Rance marble and eight statues, seven of them antique: *Bacchus, Venus, Modesty, Hermes; the Venus of Troas, Uranus* and *Nemesis*; the eighth one, *Diana* sculpted by Frémin for the gardens at Marly, occupies the place of the famous *Diana*, now in the Louvre.

The vaulted ceiling (fig. 42, see foldout) is Charles Le Brun's masterpiece. He gave free course to his inventive genius, multiplying the allegories, the trompe-l'oeil, the fake perspectives, the real or imitation stucco work. The great paintings evoke the most glorious episodes from the Dutch War (1672-1678), while the painted or fake bronze medallions on a gold background recall the victories of the War of Devolution (1667-1668), as well as the main administrative and economic reforms carried out during the early years of the reign. Thus the paintings on the vault illustrate all the civil and military achievements accomplished by the King in less than twenty years.

The general composition evolves round the great central painting which is the main focus point and should be examined first of all. It shows, confronting the great powers, *The young King turning away from Pleasure and Sports to contemplate the Crown of Immortality proffered to him by Glory, to which Mars, the God of War, is pointing*. From there one should return to the entrance to the War Room and follow the events depicted in chronological order as far as the arcade of the Peace Room.

The Gallery has had three successive sets of furniture: the one in silver sent by Louis XIV to be melted down in 1689 was replaced by a new set in gilded wood. This in turn was followed by another in 1769 and dispersed at the Revolution, some elements of which can be seen in the Apollo Room.

One should try and imagine how this great gallery looked at the height of its splendour. The windows were curtained in white damask with the King's monogram embroidered in gold and the furniture was made of silver: there were chandeliers, pedestal tables bearing crystal girandoles, tables laden with precious vases, stools, tubs with orange trees placed on barrows. Whenever a foreign ambassador was received at court, the silver throne was set up in front of the arcade of the Peace Room, under a dais and on a platform covered by a Persian rug with a gold background. Then the Gallery truly became a "sort of royal beauty unique in this world" as the Marquise de Sévigné declared.

Today the furniture consists of some large porphyry and onyx vases, four tables with porphyry vases and twenty-four pedestal tables, faithful copies of the original ones of 1769.

Normally the Gallery served as a passage room. It was also the direct way for the sovereigns to reach the Chapel each morning and crowds gathered there to admire the brilliant procession going by. This also provided the opportunity to give a *"placet"* or petition to the King in person. It was moreover an incomparable setting for the great Court ceremonies: extraordinary audiences to receive the Doge of Genoa (15 May 1685), the Envoys of the King of Siam (1 September 1686), the Ambassador of the Shah of Persia (19 February 1715), the Ambassador of the Sultan (11 January 1742), among others. Formal or masked balls for the princes' weddings were also held there, such as those of the Duc de Bourgogne (11 and 14 December 1697) and of the Dauphin, Louis XV's son (25 February 1745).

The overthrow of the monarchy did not however deprive the Hall of Mirrors of its historic role. Here, on 3 January 1805, Pope Pius VII, a tiara on his head, appeared on the centre balcony to bless the crowds gathered on the terrace; on 18 January 1871, King William I of Prussia received the imperial crown; on 28 June 1919, the treaty was signed, putting an end to the First World War. Today, it is in the brilliantly illuminated Hall of Mirrors that the foreign heads of state are entertained on official visits.

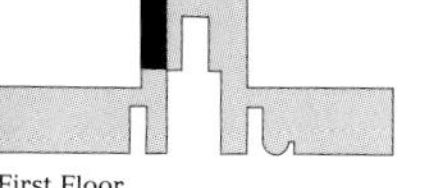
First Floor

The Queen's State Apartment

The Queen's State Apartment, exactly symmetrical to that of the King, was originally composed of the same number of rooms as his. The ceilings were decorated with the same divinities and planets as those of the corresponding rooms in the King's apartment. Only the paintings in the coves represented heroines instead of heroes of Antiquity.

Just as with the King's apartment, the construction of the Hall of Mirrors eliminated the last two small rooms of this apartment, the windows of which corresponded to the last four windows of the Hall of Mirrors. Moreover, Marie Leszczynska and Marie-Antoinette made considerable alterations to certain rooms in their State Apartment, so that it no longer had the fine homogeneity characterizing that of the King.

The Peace Room[14]

(10.26 m × 10.26 m × 11.55 m)

First of all this was the Queen's Large Drawing Room, and it was completely transformed at the same time as the

War Room. Its redecoration was finished in 1686. We find the same marbles and gilt bronze trophies as in the two preceding rooms, but here the musical instruments of the attic are in keeping with the peaceful theme of the general decoration (fig. 43).

It was in fact the benefits of Peace that Le Brun was determined to evoke in the paintings of the cupola: *France victorious offering the Olive Branch to the Powers which had united against Her*; France is seated on a chariot drawn by doves symbolizing the marriages of the princes which have just united her to Bavaria and to Spain. In the corners, Germany, Spain and Holland are seen returning joyfully to their traditional occupations, while Christian Europe lords over piles of Ottoman weapons symbolizing the recent victories over the Turks.

It is also Peace that Louis XV offers to Europe in the charming picture above the chimneypiece, painted by François Le Moyne in 1729. The young sovereign, in all the splendour of his nineteenth year, proffers an olive branch and receives his two elder daughters from the hands of Fecundity and Piety; in the distance Discord tries in vain to open the doors of the Temple of Janus (fig. 44).

43

Fig. 42

The paintings on the vaulted ceiling of the Hall of Mirrors

*1. Alliance of Germany and Spain with Holland, 1672.
2. Holland receives Support against the Bishop of Munster, 1665.
3. Relief for the People during the Famine, 1662.
4. Reparation for the Attack of the Corsican Guards, 1664.
*5. Crossing the Rhine in the Presence of the Enemies, 1672.
*6. The King seizes Maestricht in thirteen Days, 1673.
7. Defeat of the Turks in Hungary by the King's Troops, 1664.
8. Putting a Stop to the Passion for Duels, 1662.
9. The Pre-eminence of France recognized by Spain, 1662.
*10. The King orders simultaneous Attacks on four of the greatest Strongholds in Holland, 1672.
*11. The King arms on Land and on Sea, 1672.
12. Navigation is resumed, 1663.
13. War against Spain for the Queen's Rights, 1667.
14. The Reform of Justice, 1667.
*15. The King rules in his own Right, 1661.
*16. The Splendour of France's neighbouring Powers.
17. The State Finances are restored to Order, 1662.
18. The Peace concluded at Aix-la-Chapelle, 1668.
19. Protection accorded to the Fine Arts, 1663.
*20. Franche-Comté conquered for the second Time, 1674.
*21. Resolution taken to wage War against the Dutch, 1671.
22. Founding of the Royal Army Pensioners Hospital at the Invalides, 1674.
23. The Acquisition of Dunkirk, 1662.
24. Embassies are dispatched from the far Corners of the Earth.
*25. Capture of the Town and Citadel of Ghent in six Days, 1678.
*26. The Measures taken by the Spanish are annulled by the Capture of Ghent.
27. Renewal of the Alliance with the Swiss, 1663.
28. Police and Security are established in Paris, 1665.
29. Joining the Two Seas, 1667.
*30. Holland agrees to Peace and breaks with Germany and Spain, 1678.

* See illustration

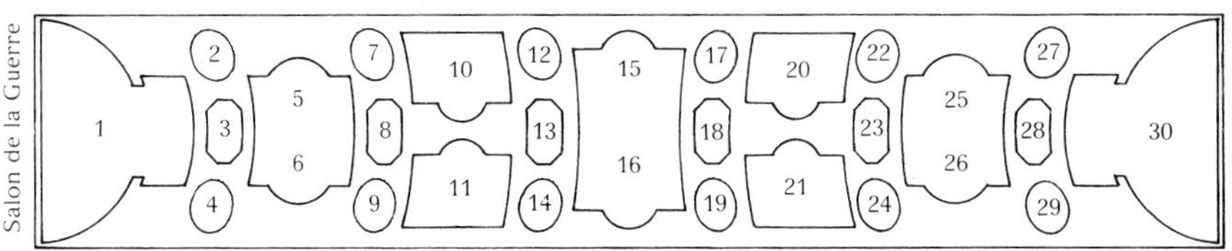

2

5

I

3

4

6

15

16

17

18

19

7 10 12

8 13

9 11 14

25

26

27

28

29

30

20

22

23

21

24

The Peace Room was always considered an integral part of the Queen's State Apartment. Moreover, as early as 1712, in the arcade separating it from the Hall of Mirrors, a mobile panel and door were installed, easily removed to restore the perspective.

It served as the Queen's Gamesroom. There too, every Sunday, Marie Leszczynska gave concerts of sacred or profane music which played an important role in the musical life of Versailles. Marie-Antoinette held her games parties there and had the beautiful "fire" in engraved gilt bronze, from a model of Boizot, placed in the fireplace.

The Queen's Bedchamber[15]
(10 m × 9.45 m × 7.50 m)

This was the largest room in the Queen's State Apartment where she spent the greater part of her time. Each morning, on awakening, she received the ladies of the court; she gave private audiences there and above all, this was where she gave birth to the heir to the throne. Two Queens, Marie-Thérèse and Marie Leszczynska, and two successive Dauphines, Marie-Anne de Bavière and Marie-Adélaïde de Savoie, died there and nineteen Children of France were born there, among them the future Louis XV and Louis XVII (fig. 45).

44

43
The Peace Room

44
François Le Moyne
Louis XV offering Peace to Europe,
1729

No trace remains of the decoration created for Marie-Thérèse. The present admirable decoration was carried out for Marie Leszczynska, between 1730 and 1735, under the direction of Robert de Cotte and Jacques Gabriel. The wood panelling is the work of Degoullons, Le Goupil and Verberckt and the mirror frames and overdoor panels are particularly remarkable.

Marie Leszczynska had expressed the desire to have the portraits of her children constantly before her. At that time she had five, so that we can see above the door *The Dauphin and his two elder sisters, Mesdames Élisabeth* and *Henriette* by Jean-François de Troy and opposite, *Mesdames Adelaïde* and *Victoire* by Natoire.

The ceiling, with coffers dating from the time of Marie-Thérèse, is adorned with gilded grisailles embellished with the intertwined monograms of the King and Queen and four camaieu medallions in which François Boucher presents figures of the Virtues: *Charity, Abundance, Fidelity* and *Prudence*. The stuccoed corners were redone for Marie-Antoinette in 1770 and show the arms of France and Navarre alternating with the two-headed eagle of the Holy Empire. Above the mirrors, Marie-Antoinette also installed portraits, in Gobelins tapestry, of her mother the Empress Maria Theresa, her

45

46

47

brother Joseph II and her husband Louis XVI (today the latter has been replaced by a painting).

The mantlepiece in griotte marble adorned with engraved bronzes by Forestier dates from 1786 (fig. 46). On it stands a bust of Marie-Antoinette executed in 1783 by Félix Lecomte. The Queen's splendid jewel-case in mahogany with mother of pearl and gilt bronze was made in 1787 by Schwerdfeger (fig. 47).

The bedroom has been restored to the state it was in when Marie-Antoinette left it on 6 October 1789, never to return. The alcove curtain, in figured silk with bouquets of lilac and peacock feathers on a white background, has been rewoven at the Lyons silkworks which had produced the original material in 1787. The bed, *"à la Duchesse"* (surmounted by a curtained canopy), has been scrupulously copied from documents in the archives, with the exception of the quilt which is original. The embroidered covers of the seats are also reproductions but, as the original wooden frames of the chairs had disappeared, they have been used for two armchairs formerly belonging to Louis XVI, and for eight folding stools, four of which from the bedroom of the Comtesse d'Artois, the Queen's sister-in-law. The balustrade has been reconstituted from ancient documents and the alcove rug has been copied from the original.

The two curtained doors provide access to the Queen's inner rooms, a suite of fifteen small rooms reserved for the

45
The Queen's
Bedroom

46
The Mantlepiece
in the Queen's
Bedroom

47
Ferdinand
Schwerdfeger
Marie-Antoinette's
Jewel Casket, 1787

sovereign's private use and for service purposes. On the morning of 6 October 1789, Marie-Antoinette was to flee from the palace through the door on the left to escape from the mob invading her apartment.

The Nobles' Room[16]

(9.78 m × 9.42 m × 7.53 m)

At first an antechamber for Queen Marie-Thérèse, this room later became the Queen's Audience Room. Here Marie Leszczynska held court and gave solemn audiences, seated on an armchair beneath a canopy on a platform, the bolts of which are still visible. Here too the noblewomen were presented to the Queen (fig. 48).

The ceiling painted by Michel Corneille is all that remains of the original decoration. In the centre is the painting entitled *Mercury, with Eloquence, Poetry, Geometry and the Sciences which He had inspired, extends his Influence over the Arts*; in the corners are the figures of *Vigilance, Immortality, Trade* and *Diligence* with stucco cupids bearing attributes symbolizing *Trade, Eloquence, The Sciences* and *The Arts*. The paintings on the covings represent *Sapho playing on a Lyre, Penelope weaving her Tapestry, Aspasia and the Greek Philosophers* and *Caesisena studying Painting*.

In 1785 Marie-Antoinette renewed the whole of the mural decoration and furniture of this room to suit the fashion of the day. The walls were lined with an applegreen damask trimmed with wide gold braiding. Jean-Baptiste Regnault was commissioned to paint two pictures for the overdoors: *The Origin of Painting* and *Pygmalion begging Venus to bring his Statue to Life*. Riesener made three chests of drawers (fig. 49) and two corner cupboards for which Gouthière engraved bronzes similar to those he had also done for the bluish-grey marble mantlepiece.

The large portrait of *Louis XV* in royal regalia, executed in tapestry by Cozette from a picture by Louis-Michel Van Loo, occupied the same position at the time of Marie-Antoinette. Today, on either side are paintings of François Boucher: *Fishing, Venus and Vulcan, Neptune and Amymone* and *The Fortune-Teller*.

A clock and two candelabras, from the Comte d'Artois' Turkish Boudoir, stand on the mantlepiece, and on the chest of drawers facing it there is a Chinese porcelain stool (Ming) mounted in bronze.

48

49

48
The Nobles' Room

49
Jean-Henri Riesener
Chest of Drawers,
1786

The Antechambre of the Great Dining Hall[17]
(15.53 m × 8.80 m × 7.47 m)

The Antechamber of the Great Dining Hall was originally the Queen's Guardroom, which explains the warlike decoration of the ceiling, resembling that of the corresponding room in the King's State Apartment, the Mars Room. The central painting, the work of Vignon, has disappeared and has been replaced by an old copy of *The Tent of Darius* by Le Brun, the original of which we have seen in the Mars Room. In the coving are two small paintings representing *Fury and War* and *Bellona burning the Face of Cybele*. Above all though we can admire the six bas-reliefs in imitation gold, marvels of the trompe-l'œil manner: *Rodogune at her Toilet* by Vignon, *Artemisia aboard the Vessels of Xerxes, Zenobia combatting the Emperor Aurelianus, Ipsicrate following her Husband to Battle* and *Clelia and her Companions*, all four by Antoine Paillet and *Arpelia rescuing her Husband* by Vignon. The gilt stucco work in the corners represents Cupids perched on trophies of arms.

The panels above the doors depict instruments of military bands and were painted in 1673 by Madeleine de Boulogne.

50
The Queen's Antechamber

51
Élisabeth Vigée-Lebrun
Queen Marie-Antoinette with her Children, 1787

52
Adélaïde Labille-Guiard
Louise-Élisabeth de France, Duchess of Parma, 1787

50

51

52

In 1680 the next room was annexed to the Queen's State Apartment, to compensate for the rooms lost in the construction of the Hall of Mirrors. It was turned into the new guardroom which in turn became an antechamber (fig. 50).

In the XVIIIth century the King and Queen supped here "au grand couvert" (in public). The table was set up in front of the fireplace; the sovereigns sat on armchairs, surrounded by the princes and princesses of the royal family on stools; opposite, against the wall of the guardroom there were tiered steps for the musicians. The courtiers attended the royal supper, standing or remaining seated according to their rank, just like any other person who wished to be there, however humble. The "grand couvert" really was held in public and the sovereigns readily spoke to anyone they knew. Thus, on 1 January 1764, young Mozart, then aged eight, stood throughout the meal beside Queen Marie Leszczynska, who plied him with food while addressing him in German and translating the child's replies for Louis XV.

The two portraits of *Marie-Antoinette* are due to Élisabeth Vigée-Lebrun: in the first one (1779), she is wearing a white dress, and in the second one, painted in 1787 (fig. 51), she is surrounded by her children (Madame Royale, the Dauphin and the Duc de Normandie).

The other three portraits, also painted in 1787, were by Adélaïde Labille-Guiard, Madame Vigée-Lebrun's great rival. They represent Louis XVI's aunts, at the right of the fireplace Madame Élisabeth, the Duchess of Parma in Spanish dress (fig. 52) and, facing the windows, Mesdames Adélaïde and Victoire.

On the chimneypiece is a reduced copy of *Ariadne asleep*, the celebrated antique statue kept in the Vatican.

The Guardroom[18]
(11.75 m × 11.23 m × 7.65 m)

The Guardroom corresponds to the Diana Room in the King's State Apartment, and was sometimes used as a drawing room or as a landing on the Queen's staircase, which could be reached through a door to the right of the bust of the Emperor Vespasian. Then it was paved with marble, but in 1680 it became a new Guardroom for the Queen and the paving was replaced by a wooden floor (fig. 53).

The paintings on the ceiling are the work of Noël Coypel and were brought from the former Jupiter Room, which became the War Room in 1678. In the centre is *Jupiter accompanied by Justice, Piety and Spirits symbolizing the Planet and its four Satellites*. The paintings in the covings evoke royal justice by giving memorable examples from Antiquity: *Ptolemy Philadelphus freeing the Jews, Alexander Severus distributing Corn to the People during a Famine, Trajan dispensing Justice*

53

53
The Queen's
Guardroom

54
Noël Coypel
Sacrifice to Jupiter,
1680

54

and *Solon explaining his Laws*. In the corners, a charming fancy has inspired the artist to represent the lords and ladies of the court leaning over a pretence balustrade to admire the Queen passing by in procession.

Two pictures by Coypel complete the decoration, one above the fireplace is a *Sacrifice to Jupiter* (fig. 54) and opposite, *The Childhood of Jupiter on Mount Ida, with Cybele's priests, the Corybants, dancing*.

On the morning of 6 October 1789, the mob invaded the room: one of the Lifeguards just had time, before being struck down, to open the door of the antechamber a crack and cry out "Save the Queen!".

The door on the right of the fireplace goes to the Fleury Staircase, called after the Duc de Fleury who, under Louis XVI, lodged in the attic above the Queen's State Apartment. This staircase also goes down to the ground-floor apartments of the Dauphin, the Dauphine and Mesdames.

The visit to the State Apartments can be rounded off by a look first at the Coronation Room and from there at the 1792 Room, the Battle Gallery and the 1830 Room, which in fact are part of the "History Galleries".

The Coronation Room - The Battle Gallery

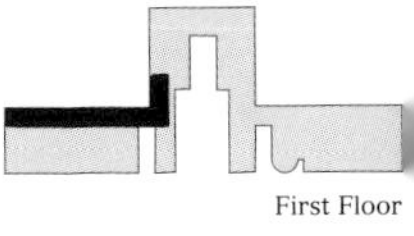

The Coronation Room[19]
(17.32 m × 13.21 m × 10.20 m)

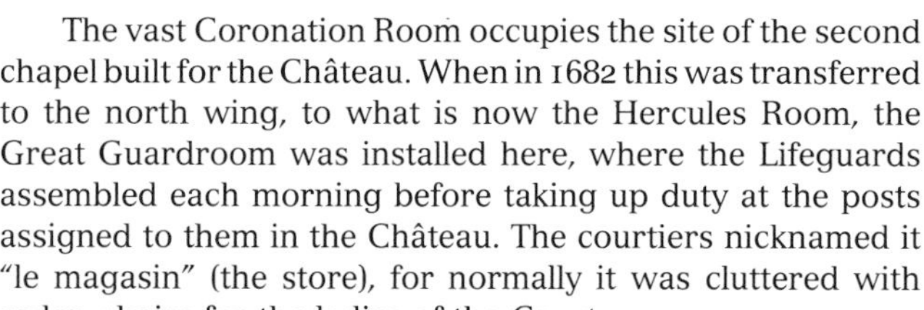

The vast Coronation Room occupies the site of the second chapel built for the Château. When in 1682 this was transferred to the north wing, to what is now the Hercules Room, the Great Guardroom was installed here, where the Lifeguards assembled each morning before taking up duty at the posts assigned to them in the Château. The courtiers nicknamed it "le magasin" (the store), for normally it was cluttered with sedan-chairs for the ladies of the Court.

Here on Maundy Thursday, the Queen washed the feet of thirteen pauper girls and gave them a meal in commemoration of the Last Supper. It was here too on 13 April 1771 that Louis XV held a solemn session of the *"lit de justice"* in the course of which he announced his decision to adjourn the Parlement. Finally it was through this room that the mob, after mounting the Queen's staircase, stormed into Marie-Antoinette's apartment.

Louis-Philippe decided to devote this room to the glorification of Napoléon I and gave it its present decoration. In the centre of the ceiling there is an *Allegory of the Eighteenth Brumaire* (Coup d'Etat) by Callet; above the doors, allegorical figures of *Courage, Genius, Generosity* and *Constancy* by Gérard; between the windows, portraits of Napoléon as First

55
Jacques-Louis David
The Coronation,
1808-1822

55

Consul and then as Emperor, and those of the Empresses Joséphine and Marie-Louise.

The three large pictures covering the walls are particularly famous ones. At the far end there is *The Battle of Aboukir*, commissioned from Gros by Joachim Murat who is depicted in the middle charging the Turks. The other two paintings are the work of Jacques-Louis David: on the left, *The Coronation* (fig. 55), or rather *The Crowning of the Empress Joséphine at Notre-Dame de Paris, on 2 December 1804; The Army swearing Allegiance to the Emperor after the Distribution of the Imperial Eagle Standards on the Champ de Mars, on 5 December 1804*. After first being placed here, the original of *The Coronation* was sent to the Louvre in 1889. It was then replaced by the copy begun by David himself in 1808, but not completed until 1822 when he was living in exile in Brussels.

We now cross a small room where Louis-Philippe placed pictures representing episodes during the wars of the Revolution[20].

The 1792 Room[21]

(18.65 m × 8.25 m × 7.50 m)

The 1792 room, symmetrical to the Hercules Room, served to communicate between the central building of the Château and the south wing. Under Louis XV it was the Merchants' Hall (Salle des Marchands), where they set up their stalls, and under Louis XVI, the Hall of the Hundred Swiss Guards (Salle des Cent Suisses).

Louis-Philippe gave it its present aspect when he grouped together there portraits of heroes of the wars of the Revolution and the Empire, all wearing the uniform and the badges of the rank they held in September 1792, at the proclamation of the Republic.

The Citizen-King, then the *Duc de Chartres*, appears in his uniform of Lieutenant General. The two principal paintings, after Horace Vernet, represent the battles of Valmy (20 September) and of Jemappes (6 November) in which the young prince and his younger brother the Duc de Montpensier, aged respectively nineteen and seventeen, took part. A charming picture by Léon Coignet represents the *Departure to join the Army of the National Guard of Paris, in September 1792*.

The 1792 Room devoted to the war, the Battle Gallery which evokes the main victories of our history, and the 1830 Room concerned with the theme of national reconciliation, were all three conceived by Louis-Philippe as a triptych corresponding to the one formed by the War Room, the Hall of Mirrors and the Peace Room.

The Princes' Staircase[22]

The Princes' Staircase, with its beautiful decoration dating for the most part from the xviith century, links the ground floor and the first floor of the south wing, or the Princes' wing, where the apartments of certain members of the royal family, the royal children of France and some princes of the blood were situated.

The vaulted ceiling which originally capped it was unfortunately replaced in the reign of Louis-Philippe by a heavy coffered ceiling.

The Battle Gallery

(118.88 m × 12.63 m × 13 m)

This gallery (fig. 56), corresponding to two storeys, was installed in 1837 by Louis-Philippe. Thus it occupies the place

56

56
The Battle Gallery

on the first floor of four of the princes' apartments, the walls and the mezzanines which were demolished, and on the second floor, of some ten apartments attributed to courtiers.

Under Louis XIV the King's brother and sister-in-law, the Duc and Duchesse d'Orléans, their son the Duc de Chartres, the future Regent, and the Duchesse de Chartres had lived in the princes' apartments. In the last days of the Monarchy, they were occupied by Madame Élisabeth, Louis XVI's sister, the Comte d'Artois, his brother, and the Comtesse d'Artois.

Louis-Philippe wanted this gallery to display "a grandiose review of our military history" from Tolbiac (496) to Wagram (1809). Among the thirty-five pictures covering the walls, the most remarkable are: *Philippe-Auguste before the Battle of Bouvines* (27 July 1214) by Horace Vernet, *Saint Louis at the Battle of Taillebourg* (21 July 1242) by Eugène Delacroix, *Henri IV entering Paris* (22 March 1594) by François Gérard, *The Battle of Fontenoy* (11 May 1745) by Horace Vernet and *The Battle of Austerlitz* (2 December 1805) by François Gérard.

On the bronze tables are inscribed the names of the princes of the Royal House of France (*Maison de France*), as well as the commanders-in-chief (*connétables*), admirals and marshals killed in battle. Eighty-two busts represent the most renowned among them.

The 1830 Room

(19 m × 10 m × 10.20 m)

This room occupies the place of three previous ones (the first and second antechambers and the large boudoir) belonging to the apartment of the Duchesse d'Orléans, Louis XIV's sister-in-law, where Louis XVI's sister, Madame Élisabeth, later lived.

It has been dedicated by Louis-Philippe to the events which had brought him to the throne. One large painting is especially remarkable in which Eugène Devéria depicts the King on 9 August 1830 pledging to maintain the Charter of 1814.

A stone gallery, punctuated by statues and busts of some of the famous men in French history, leads to the landing of the Princes' staircase and the way out.

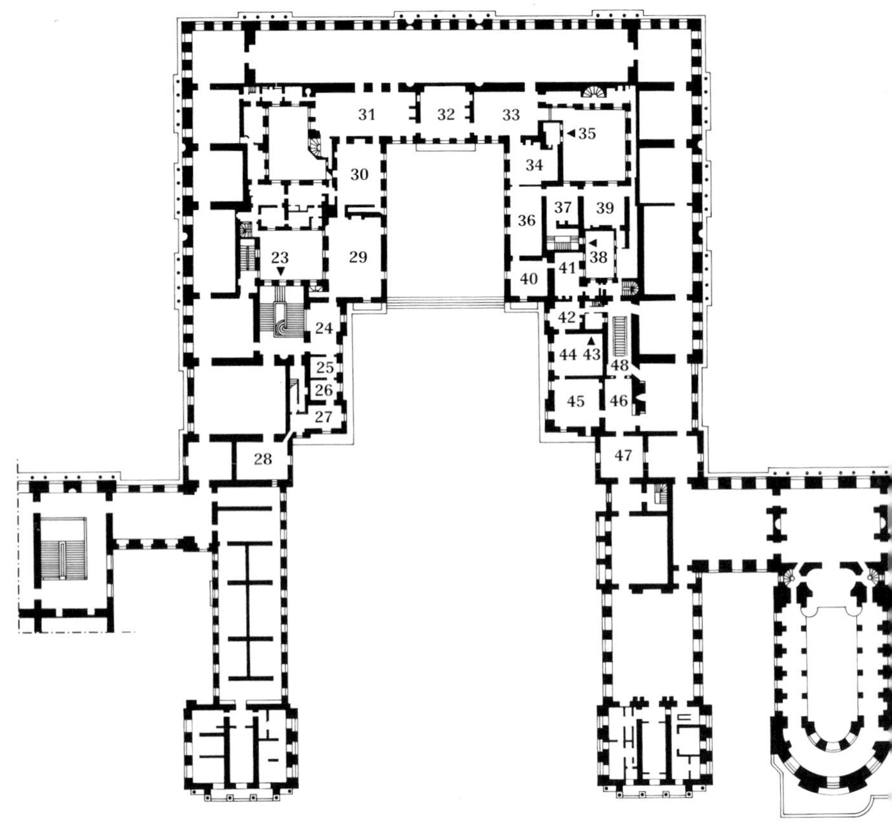

31
32
33
35
30
34
37
39
36
23
29
38
41
40
24
42
44
43
48
25
26
45
46
27
47
28

The King's Apartment and the Inner Apartment

Conducted lecture tours

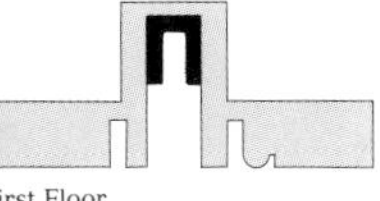

The King's Apartment

Louis XIII's apartment occupied the north part of the main building of the original castle. It was reached by a staircase in the centre and contained three rooms completed by a salient gallery in the right wing.

During his youth Louis XIV lived in his father's former apartment. Soon after his marriage though, he remodelled the first floor of the castle to provide suitable accommodation for the Queen. The central staircase was replaced by a room joining two similar matching rooms, that of the King in the north-west corner of the courtyard and that of the Queen in the south-west corner. Each apartment consisted of four rooms: an antechamber, a bedroom and two small private rooms. Both were reached by a staircase in the middle of each wing. The King's staircase also led to a chapel, while that of the Queen went to the Dauphin's rooms.

The construction of the New Château entailed the destruction of one of the small rooms in both apartments which were then reduced to three rooms each. They became the King's and Queen's Private Apartments, each communicating with their corresponding State Apartment. The sovereigns could retire to these "convenient apartments" to escape the strict formality of court etiquette.

The death of Queen Marie-Thérèse on 30 July 1683, and the completion of the Hall of Mirrors the following year, incited Louis XIV to abandon his State Apartment, which had become a public passage, and settle in the Old Château. He then had his Private Apartment enlarged on the east side and annexed those of the Queen and of the Dauphin, thereby making an apartment of some fifteen main rooms. The King intended this to be a temporary arrangement. In fact though, despite numerous transformations undertaken by Louis XV and Louis XVI, this was to be inhabited by the King until the end of the Monarchy.

The Queen's Staircase[23]

Built in 1680 to match the King's Staircase or Ambassadors' Staircase, the Queen's Staircase rapidly became the most frequented one in the whole palace, for it served both the King's and the Queen's apartments (fig. 57).

The Vestibule[24] leading to it is adorned with a statue of Apollo, commissioned from Guillaume II Coustou by the Marquise de Pompadour for the Château de Bellevue.

The Queen's Staircase is entirely decorated with polychrome marbles, with the exception of the steps which are in stone. It is adorned with a painting representing a *Perspective of Palaces with Figures in oriental Dress*, the work of Philippe Meusnier and Jean-Baptiste Blain de Fontenay; two landscapes had completed this decoration, but they were taken away in the XIXth century.

The first-floor landing is adorned with a gilt lead statue, due to Massou, symbolizing the marriage of Louis XIV and

57
The Queen's Staircase

57

Marie-Thérèse of Austria: two cupids hold up an escutcheon on which the intertwined monograms of the King and Queen are inscribed, surmounted by two doves and torches of Hymen.

The first door on the right opens on to the Queen's Guard-room, and the second one on to the Great Guardroom or Coronation Room. The next one, at the left of the sculpture group, leads to the Stucco Staircase and from there to the Revolution, Consulate and Empire rooms. The last door goes to the vestibule of the King's apartment.

This Vestibule, lined with marble, is in fact a sort of loggia overlooking the Queen's Staircase. From the windows there is a view on to the Marble Court and the Old Château.

The door on the right gives access to the Marquise de Maintenon's apartment, the morganatic wife of Louis XIV, which she occupied from 1684 to 1715. Completely disfigured in the XIXth century, it has retained no trace of its former decoration. The apartment comprised four rooms: two antechambers[25 & 26], a bedroom[27] and a large drawing room[28]. In the bedroom, then lined with crimson damask and a green and gold brocade, the King would work from five till ten o'clock, in the presence of the Marquise, with a different minister each evening. During that time the princes and princesses of the royal family gathered in the large drawing room next door for the King's supper. It was in this large drawing room, its walls lined with gold brocade, that the King enjoyed listening to the "Royal concerts" composed for him by François Couperin. Finally, it was here that Racine's last tragedy, *Athalie*, was performed before a privileged audience.

Today Madame de Maintenon's former apartment is used for temporary exhibitions.

From the Vestibule, the visitor enters on the left the King's apartment.

The Guardroom[29]

(15.07 m × 9.95 m × 8.45 m)

The Guardroom and the room after it were created in 1684 in place of two rooms of the Dauphin's first apartment, the Queen's staircase and the antechamber of the Queen's private apartment. To provide sufficient room, Louis XVI had the south wall of the Old Château pulled down and rebuilt farther away jutting into the inner courtyard.

The King's Lifeguards responsible for his safety were given this room. Over the fireplace a picture by Jacques Parrocel shows *A Battle Scene in which the Guards are present.*

The First Antechamber[30]
(12 m × 8.98 m × 8.50 m)

The first antechamber is decorated with pictures by Jacques Parrocel representing *Battles of Antiquity*.

It is here that, after leaving Madame de Maintenon, Louis XIV supped in public at ten o'clock, to the sound of the "Symphonies for the King's Supper" composed by Michel-Richard Delalande. The King sat with his back to the fireplace, surrounded by members of the royal family.

Here too, every Monday morning, a table was set up covered with a green velvet cloth, behind which a vacant armchair symbolized the King. Any Frenchman who had a petition to make to the King or a favour to seek could deposit it here. All these requests (*placets*) were then brought to the King who made notes in his own hand, indicating the answer to be given. This was a kind of survival of the Capetian tradition of direct justice.

The Second Antechamber[31]
(18.76 m × 7.80 m × 9.70 m)

It occupies the place of two rooms which were first the Bedchamber and one of the two boudoirs in the Queen's Private Apartment, and then, from 1684, the King's Bedchamber and his Second Antechamber, also called the Bassano

58

58
The King's Second Antechamber or the Œil-de-Bœuf Room

59
Jean Nocret
The Royal Family,
1670

Antechamber, because it was adorned with pictures by masters of this illustrious Venetian family of artists.

In 1701 Louis XIV moved his Bedchamber to the next room and joined the two into one to form a large antechamber, the so-called Salon de l'Œil-de-Bœuf (fig. 58), owing to the oval window on the south side in the ceiling frieze.

This large room owes all its charm to this frieze, where Poulletier, Hardy, Hurtrelle, Poirier, Van Clève and Flamen have carved a graceful ring of laughing children on a mosaic background.

The King had works of Venetian artists hung here, particularly those of Veronese, some of which are now in the Louvre. Today we see the portraits in antique costume of *Louis XIV* and of his nephew the *Duc de Chartres* by Pierre Mignard, as well as a curious painting by Jean Nocret representing *The Olympian Gods and Goddesses all with Features of Members of the Royal Family* (fig. 59), brought from the Château de St. Cloud. Particularly worth noting are the portraits on the overdoors of *Queen Marie-Thérèse* and of *Monsieur*, the King's brother, holding a portrait of his eldest daughter. The three busts are of *Louis XIV* by Coysevox, *Louis XV* by Gois and *Louis XVI* by Houdon.

Here the courtiers awaited the moment to be introduced into the royal bedchamber, where there was a Swiss guard at the door. During the day the guard's bed was hidden by a Savonnerie screen. It was also in this room that the marriage contracts of the princes and princesses of the blood were sometimes signed.

Three doors open on to the Hall of Mirrors. Another door on the left, provides access to the Queen's apartment. It was along this passage that Marie-Antoinette fled on the morning of 6 October 1789, to escape from the mob. To the left of the windows, a mirrored door opens on to the staircase leading to the Dauphin's apartment.

The King's Bedchamber[32]
(9.70 m × 9.15 m × 10.15 m)

To begin with, this was the central salon separating the King's Private Apartment from that of the Queen. In those days it had three french windows opening on to the terrace which became doors when the the Hall of Mirrors was built. The decoration of the gilded pilasters dates from this alteration.

In 1684 the room became the King's Dressing Room (Salon où le Roi s'habille), but in 1701 Louis XIV decided to make it his Bedchamber. The three end doors were blocked to make an alcove and Nicolas Coustou was commissioned to carve the beautiful allegory of *France watching over the sleeping King*. This is when the mirror surrounds and the charming figures framing the overdoors were carved. A gilded balustrade, still intact, separates the alcove from the rest of the bedchamber (fig. 61). In Louis XIV's day the furniture here was incredibly splendid. In winter the alcove was lined with a crimson velvet embroidered in gold, on which hung pictures; in summer there was a gold and silver brocade on a background of crimson damask. The same material was used to cover the bed and the seats.

The paintings adorning this bedroom are, with one exception, those chosen by Louis XIV. In the attic: *The Four Evangelists* and *Caesar's Denarius* by Valentin de Boulogne (fig. 60); another picture by Valentin de Boulogne *The Fortune-Teller*, now in the Louvre, was replaced by *Agar in the Desert* by Lanfrance.

60

60
Valentin de Boulogne
Caesar's Denarius,
c. 1630

61
The King's Bedroom

61

Above the door are *Saint John the Baptist* by Carraciole, *Mary Magdalene* by Domenichino and two portraits by Van Dyck, his self portrait and the *Marquis de Moncade.*

It was in this bedroom that Louis XIV sometimes gave audiences and where he dined in private "au petit couvert". The ceremonies of the King's getting up in the morning and going to bed at night *(Lever* and *Coucher)* were also held here, with their succession of "entrances" and strict rites. Here, on 1 September 1715, he died, with a serenity and a nobility which even his enemies admired, after reigning for seventy-two years.

Louis XV had had a new bedchamber arranged in his private apartment, which was more comfortable and not so chilly, but this one continued to be used for his *Lever* and *Coucher.* In 1761 he replaced Louis XIV's single fireplace with the two present ones, on which stand a bust of Louis XIV by Coysevox, a clock-barometer, as well as four candelabras which had belonged to the Comte de Provence, Louis XVI's brother.

Louis XVI used this room as his bedchamber just as Louis XV had done before him. On Friday, 20 March 1778, he received in solemn audience here Benjamin Franklin and other American plenipotentiaries, who had come to sign the "Treaty of Friendship and Trade" between France and the United States. Eleven years later, on 6 October 1789, before leaving

Versailles forever, he was forced to appear with the Queen and their children on the balcony of this room, to confront the crowd massed in the Marble Court. And so it was that this room, where the long reign of Louis XIV had ended and which had served for the public display of Monarchy, was to become the setting for the King's fall from power.

The King's Study or Council Room[33]

(12.53 m × 8.10 m × 7.19 m)

First of all there were two rooms here, the Bedchamber and one of the two small rooms in the King's Private Apartment, each with two french doors opening on to the terrace. In 1684 both rooms became the King's Study or Term Room (Cabinet du Roi or Cabinet des Termes), so-called because of the figures decorating the ceiling. The walls of the two small rooms were then entirely lined with mirrors, against which small gilded pier tables were placed to hold the precious vases and the jewels we admire today in the Apollo Gallery at the Louvre.

It was in the first room that Louis XIV presided over the different Councils, whereas, every evening after his supper, he gathered around him in the Term Room the royal princes and princesses.

62

63

62
The Council Room

63
Clock, 1754

In 1755 Louis XV joined the two rooms together to form the Council Room, as it is today (fig. 62). Ange-Jacques Gabriel designed the admirable wood panelling carved by Antoine Rousseau: on it we see small spirits symbolizing the King's different Councils which took place both in times of war and in times of peace. The overdoors are painted by Houasse and relate *Scenes from the Legend of Minerva*. They come from Trianon.

The fireplace in red and brown speckled marble, enriched with superb gilt bronzes, is adorned with sumptuous objets-d'art commissioned by Louis XV and Louis XVI: a Rocaille clock (1754) and two vases of Mars and Minerva in Sèvres porcelain, with bronzes engraved by Thomire (1787) (fig. 63). The bust of *Alexander the Great* in porphyry, whose breast-plate and draperies are the work of Girardon, and that of *Scipio the African* in bronze, were placed in this room by Louis XV.

The blue and gold brocade on the door-screens, tablecloth and stools was rewoven in Lyons from a pattern designed for Louis XV.

This beautiful room was the hub of court life. It served for the day-to-day business of the King with his ministers, special audiences, the ceremony of swearing allegiance by the Principal Crown Dignitaries, deliberations of the Order of the Holy Ghost, respects paid on the occasion of a royal birth, marriage or death. This too was where the most important decisions were taken during the reigns of Louis XV and Louis XVI, concerning for instance, in 1756, the change of alliances and, in 1775, the participation in the War of Independence which was to lead to the foundation of the United States of America. The mirrored door on the right of the chimneypiece opens on to the Hall of Mirrors. The King passed through it each morning on his way to the chapel. The next door at the left of the large window leads to the King's Bathroom.

The King's Inner Apartment

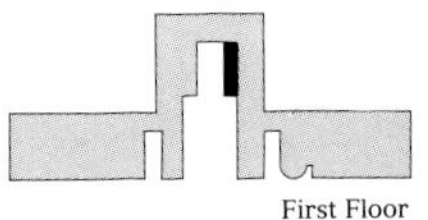

First Floor

The following rooms compose what was known in Louis XIV's day as the Inner Apartment (Appartement intérieur). Except for the members of his family, only very rare privileged people, mostly art-lovers like himself, were invited to enter it. Indeed it was here that he kept the most beautiful pictures in his collection, now in the Louvre.

Louis XV, with a care for his personal comfort and privacy, undertook in 1735 to transform this small museum into a real residence and he gave it very much the same aspect it has today. Jacques Verberckt was responsible for carving the wood panelling from Gabriel's drawings, the most beautiful ensemble of its kind to be found anywhere in France. The greatest cabinet makers of the time produced the furniture, which was completed by silks from Lyons, porcelain from Sèvres, carpets from the Savonnerie, while the bouquets of flowers were constantly renewed. In this elegant apartment Louis XV, and Louis XVI after him, worked with their counsellors and received chosen guests, away from the tumult of the State Apartments.

64

65

64
The new Bedroom

65
The Wardrobe Room

The new Bedroom[34]
(9.95 m × 8.40 m × 5 m)

This room takes the place of Louis XIV's Billiard Room. In 1738 Louis XV turned it into his real bedroom, though he still continued to use the State Bedchamber for official ceremonies. He died here on 10 May 1774 and this is where Louis XVI lived until 6 October 1789 (fig. 64).

The alcove, formerly shut off by a gilded balustrade, is hung with a lampas brocaded in gold, copying the last "summer furnishing" of Louis XVI. Above the doors, portraits of Louis XV's daughters, *Mesdames Élisabeth, Henriette* and *Adélaïde* have replaced pictures by Titian, Antonio Moro, Rubens and Van Dyck, formerly found there.

The magnificent chest of drawers which, under Louis XV, stood facing the fireplace, now belongs to the Wallace Collection in London, whereas the one that replaced it in Louis XVI's reign is now at the Château de Chantilly. The present chest of drawers we see today was made by Levasseur for the bedroom of Louis XVI's brother, the Comte d'Artois, at the Temple Palace in Paris. On it stands a scent-fountain in Chinese porcelain and gilt bronze, made for Louis XV's Wardrobe Room (Cabinet de Garde-Robe) in 1743.

On the fireplace is the bust of the *Duchesse de Bourgogne*, Louis XV's mother, by Antoine Coysevox.

A concealed door in the alcove hangings provides access to Louis XVI's Wardrobe Room[35] (fig. 65). Fine panelling,

66

carved by Rousseau in 1788, represents the attributes of the Sciences, the Arts, War, the Navy, Trade and Agriculture.

The Clock Room[36]
(12.55 m × 6.30 m × 5.03 m)

This occupies the place of the Antechamber and part of the Picture Room (Cabinet des Tableaux) (fig. 66). It owes its name to the extraordinary astronomic clock which is its main ornament (fig. 67), due to the engineer Passemant, the clockmaker Dauthiau and the bronzesmith Caffieri, and was placed in this room in January 1754. It gives the date, the real time, the mean time, the phases of the moon and the movement of the planets, according to Copernicus. The fine barometer, the work of Jean-Joseph Lemaire, was delivered to the King in 1772.

One of the two tables was made by Roumier for Louis XV's apartment at Versailles, and the other by Slodtz for his apartment at Compiègne. Their legs and crossbars are admirable examples of the Rocaille style and their stucco tops display the plans of the estates of Compiègne and Fontainebleau.

The paintings above the doors are early replicas of François Boucher's work. The bronze statuette is a reduced copy by Vassé of the equestrian statue of Louis XV, executed by

67

66
The Clock Room

67
Passemant
Astronomic Clock,
1754

Bouchardon, and intended for the centre of the Place Louis XV – the present-day Place de la Concorde – in Paris. It was already in this room at the time of the monarchy, together with the statuette of Frederick II of Prussia in Sèvres biscuit china.

The Clock Room usually served as a second Antechamber for the private rooms and sometimes, in the evenings, as a Gamesroom.

The Dog Room[37]
(6.05 m × 5.80 m × 5.88 m)

The name of this room and the decoration of its cornice are a reminder that Louis XV let his favourite dogs sleep here. The panelling comes from Louis XIV's former Billiard Room which Louis XV had transformed into a bedroom. The flower paintings above the doors are the work of Jean-Baptiste Monnoyer and Jean-Baptiste Blain de Fontenay. Two of the tables were made by Roumier for the Golden Cabinet next-door, and the third one by the Foliots for the apartment of Madame Adélaïde at Compiègne. Plans of the estates at Versailles, Marly and St.-Germain-en-Laye are displayed on the stucco tops.

This room, usually occupied by the valets serving the Inner apartment, nicknamed the "blue boys" (*garçons bleus*) owing to the colour of their livery, served as a First Antechamber for the inner apartments which in fact opened on to the King's staircase[38]. After having been moved several times, this staircase was rebuilt in 1754 on its present spot, with wrought-iron banisters bearing the monogram of Louis XV. Its access was protected on the ground floor by a small Guardroom. The King could use it to leave or to enter his apartments without having to cross the great antechambers and the Queen's staircase, always crowded with courtiers. Likewise the ministers took the King's staircase when they went to work with the King, just as the guests arriving for the hunt suppers.

The Dining room called "return from the hunt"[39]
(8.60 m × 6.57 m × 5.01 m)

In 1750 this replaced a small Bathing Apartment. Once or twice a week Louis XV gave a supper there for the lords and ladies who had followed him to the hunt, and this invitation was a favour much sought after (fig. 68). The Buffet Room (Pièce des Buffets) next door made it convenient for serving meals. The dishes were prepared in the King's private kitchens situated on the third floor. After supper the King and his guests moved into the Clock Room where the evening ended around the games tables.

The roll-top desk is by David Roentgen and the upright clock by Ferdinand Berthoud.

68

69

The Inner Room or Angle Room[40]

(7.28 m × 6.52 m × 4.93 m)

It occupies part of the former Picture Room of Louis XIV, which Louis XV had made into his study (Cabinet de travail) for work in the daytime, either alone or with one of his ministers.

It is the most sumptuous room in the private apartment (fig. 69). The mirror frames (1738) and the wood panelling (1753) count among Verberckt's masterpieces; the collection of furniture assembled here by Louis XV, and still in place to be admired, with its elegant shapes, delicate inlaid work and magnificent bronzes, is the finest Rocaille ensemble imaginable. It consists of the medal cabinet by Gaudreaux (1738), the corner cupboards by Joubert (1755) and above all the roll-top desk made by Oeben and Riesener between 1760 and 1768, which is probably the most famous piece of furniture in the world.

On the medal cabinet (fig. 70), there are two Sèvres porcelain vases embellished with gilt bronzes and the candelabra made by Thomire in 1783, recalling the determining role played

68
The Dining Room called "Return from the Hunt"

69
The King's Inner Room

70
Antoine Gaudreaux
Medal Cabinet, 1738

70

by Louis XVI in the War of Independence, which ended in the creation of the United States of America. Together with Roque's clock and N.Q. Foliot's chairs, they all combine to give to the Inner Room its air of royal splendour and refined elegance.

The Back Room[41]
(5.96 m × 3.93 m × 4.53 m)

This occupies the place of the Oval Room arranged by Louis XIV in 1692. Decorated with Corinthian pilasters and four alcoves adorned with bronze groups, among which the famous "fire-dogs" by Algarde, this room leads on the right to the Small Gallery (Petite Galerie) and on the left to the Shell Room (Cabinet des Coquilles). In this room, which owes its name to the decorated cornice, Louis XIV kept his most precious manuscripts and books, together with some twenty paintings among which the *Rustic Concert* by Titian.

In 1754, the Shell Room disappeared to make way for the King's staircase and the Oval Room was replaced by a Back Room and a Privy (Cabinet de Chaise). At first the corners of the Back Room were cut off, but Louis XVI had this changed though he kept the carved woodwork and the pictures by Galloche and by Chavanne.

It is here that Louis XV retired in private to go through the reports of his secret agents whom he had posted abroad, and also to write the instructions to send to them. So this was where the "King's secret" (le Secret du Roi) was worked out, a personal diplomacy which Louis XV carried on in the margin of his official foreign policy and which, among other results, was to lead to the "shuffle of the alliances".

The small glass cabinet placed on the right of the window was made by Riesener to hold Louis XVI's collection of watches.

The next rooms were created in 1752 at the place where the Small Gallery and the Ambassadors' Staircase had been.

This Small Gallery had itself replaced in 1685 the apartment of the Marquise de Montespan. It had three windows and was flanked by a small room on each side. These three rooms formed a sort of reduced model of the Hall of Mirrors and the War and Peace Rooms, which Le Brun had just finished decorating.

It was Pierre Mignard, his great rival, who had been given the task of painting the vaulted ceiling of the Small Gallery and the little cupolas in the two side rooms. In the Gallery he represented *Apollo and Minerva protecting the Arts and Sciences*, and in the two other rooms, the legends of *Prometheus* and of *Pandora*. The parquet in all three was inlaid with different types of wood, after a drawing by Oppenordt. On the walls lined with crimson damask hung some fifty paintings, among which Leonardo da Vinci's *Mona Lisa* and the portrait of *Balthazar Castiglione* by Raphael.

The end room opened on to the landing of the Ambassadors' Staircase which led to the Venus Room. Thus, on this side also, the King's Private Apartment communicated with his State Apartment.

In 1736 Louis XV renovated the decoration of the Small Gallery, but in 1752 he had it demolished, as well as the Staircase, to build an apartment in place of them for his favourite daughter, Madame Adélaïde, who had become his eldest daughter since the death of her sister Henriette. One of the main advantages of this apartment was that it was close to the King's. It contained two antechambers, a large drawing room, a bedroom, an inner room, a back room, an oratory and, on the floor above, a library, a bathroom and a lodging for the Princess's lady-in-waiting. In 1769 Madame Adélaïde moved to the ground floor, near her sisters, and her fine apartment was joined on to the King's. Louis XV, and Louis XVI after him, often changed the destination of these "new rooms" and made many alterations to them.

The Gold Plate Room[42]

(5.74 m × 5.67 m × 5.50 m)

This is Madame Adélaïde's former Inner Room (fig. 71). It has preserved some elements of the decoration of the Small Gallery: the cornice, the pilasters and the window frames, completed by new panelling between 1753 and 1767. The

71

panels in the alcove are particularly to be admired; they dated no doubt from 1753 but were not installed in their present place until 1767. Verberckt carved the trophies of musical instruments, reminders of the Princess's tastes, together with fishing tackle and gardening tools.

It was in this beautiful room that Madame Adélaïde took Italian lessons with Goldoni and learned to play the harp with Beaumarchais; it was probably here too, in December 1763, that Mozart as a young boy played the harpsichord before the royal family.

This was where Louis XV, who drank coffee here, later displayed his collection of gold plate. Louis XVI added the extraordinary ebony and mahogany cabinet with porcelain plaques decorated with birds' feathers and butterflies' wings.

On the fireplace stood a fine bust of *Louis XV* as a child, by Coysevox. The two Sèvres porcelain plaques, representing *The Sultana's Toilet* and *The Sultana giving Orders to the Odalisks* after Amédée Van Loo, were commissioned by Louis XVI for his private rooms.

The Bathroom[43]
(3.80 m × 3.30 m × 2.85 m)

This was fitted up by Louis XV in 1773 on the spot where Madame Adélaïde's Back Room (Arrière-Cabinet) had been (fig. 72). The woodwork, carved by the Rousseau brothers and heightened by a play of different golds, evokes all the pleasures of water: bathing, fishing, shooting aquatic birds, swimming lessons, etc.

Louis XVI transformed this charming little room into the King's Privy Purse Room or Very Back Room (Cabinet de la Cassette or Très-Arrière-Cabinet). Its decoration is one of the first signs of the new style which will triumph throughout his reign.

The Library[44]
(9.57 m × 7.54 m × 5.27 m)

This harmoniously proportioned room corresponds to two thirds of the former Small Gallery of which, moreover, the end wall had been pushed back to create Madame Adélaïde's bedroom. In 1769, after the departure of his daughter, Louis XV had it turned into a gamesroom, but, as soon as he came to the throne, Louis XVI immediately had it transformed into a library (fig. 73).

The wood panelling, discreetly elegant, was carved by Antoine Rousseau from drawings by Gabriel and this was to

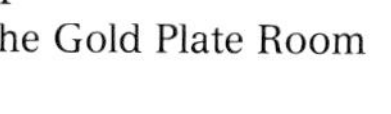

'I
'he Gold Plate Room

72

'2
)etail of the
Voodwork in the
3athroom

73

be these two artists' last work for Versailles. The bas-reliefs represent *France contemplating the Portrait of Louis XVI, Apollo and the Arts*, as well as symbols of the different literary styles. The fireplace adorned by Boizot of children shivering with cold is embellished with bronzes by Gouthière.

The round table, its top made of a single piece of tropical wood measuring 2.10 metres in diameter, was made by Riesener, who was also responsible for the elegant flat desk. The chest of drawers by Benneman and the clock come from the Comte de Provence's bedroom at Versailles. The Valenciennes porcelain group after the *Descent from the Cross* by Rubens, and the two globes, one terrestrial and the other celestial, supported by atlantes, were already in this room at the time of Louis XVI. The seats upholstered with a painted "pekin" fabric had belonged to the King's furniture at the Château de Compiègne.

73
The Library

74
The Dining Room called "in the new Rooms"

The Dining Room "in the new Rooms"[45]
(9.46 m × 9.15 m × 5.27 m)

In 1769 Louis XV created this room by joining the large drawing room to one of Madame Adélaïde's antechambers. From then onwards and until 1789, the King's suppers were served here (fig. 74). Every year at Christmas, in Louis XVI's time, an exhibition was organized here of the most beautiful pieces of porcelain produced by the Sèvres factory in the course of the current year, hence the name sometimes given of "Porcelain Room".

The panelling counts among the finest in the whole apartment. The paintings on the overdoors, done in 1750 by Collin de Vermont for Trianon, represent mythological scenes inspired by Ovid's *Metamorphoses*: *The Rejuvenation of Iolas by Hebe, Jupiter and Mercury visit Philemon and Baucis, The Shepherd Apuleus transformed into an Olive Tree*, and *Bacchus changing the Works of the Maenads into Vine Leaves.*

The Sèvres porcelain plaques were made by order of King Louis XVI, after the tapestries of the *Hunts of Louis XV* by Jean-Baptiste Oudry. The seats, upholstered with sky-blue velvet, were produced by Sené and Boulard in 1786.

74

75

76

75
Riesener
Corner cupboard,
1785

76
The Gamesroom

The Billiard Room[46]
(9.45 m × 5.30 m × 5.20 m)

The Billiard Room occupies the place of one of the flights of stairs and a landing of the Ambassadors' Staircase, the only vestige of which is the magnificent door in carved, gilded wood leading to the Venus Room.

Originally it opened on to a staircase descending to Madame Adélaïde's apartment, which was demolished in the XIXth century. When hunt suppers were being served, it was used as the Buffet Room.

The gouaches representing *The Victories of Louis XV* were commissioned by Louis XVI from Van Blarenberghe. The bench comes from Louis XVI's Billiard Room in the Château de Fontainebleau.

The Gamesroom[47]
(8.75 m × 7.40 m × 4.30 m)

This has taken the place of Louis XIV's Cabinet of Rare Objects, which became an antechamber for Madame Adélaïde in 1753, then in 1769 the lords' dining room, until finally in 1774 Louis XVI turned it into his Gamesroom (fig. 76).

Most of the furniture ordered at that time has been recuperated and put back in place: the four corner cupboards delivered by Riesener in 1774 (fig. 75), nineteen of the thirty chairs made by Boulard in 1785, the bracket sconces and Van Blarenberghe's gouaches placed there by Louis XVI. The card table was made for "the King's use" at Versailles and the crimson and gold brocade was rewoven in Lyons from an old pattern.

The visitor takes the staircase[48], built by Louis-Philippe in place of Madame Adélaïde's staircase, to a small inner courtyard and from there he arrives at the Opera.

The Royal Opera

Conducted lecture tours

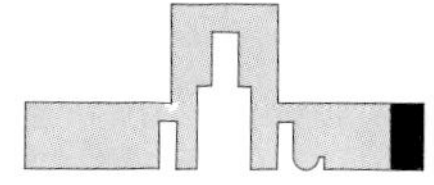

The construction of the Opera at Versailles was the materialization of almost a century of research, studies and projects, for although it was not built until the end of Louis XV's reign, it had been planned as early as 1682, in the year when Louis XIV settled in Versailles. Indeed, the King had put Jules Hardouin-Mansart and Vigarani in charge of drawing plans for a ballet room, and the architect had reserved a place for it at the end of the new wing which was to be built in the course of the following years. The choice of this spot was, moreover, very judicious. The proximity of reservoirs ensured security in case of fire, and the steep slope of the land provided considerable space below stage without having to dig deep underground. This meant that not one of Mansart's successors ever questioned his choice.

The main construction work was put in hand as early as 1685, but was soon interrupted owing to wars and financial difficulties at the end of the reign. Louis XV in turn long shrank from incurring such expenses, so that for nearly a century the French court had to be content with a small theatre arranged beneath the Princes' Passage. Whenever a grand opera was performed, requiring a large cast and complicated stage machinery, a temporary theatre was fitted up in the riding school of the Great Stable and pulled down the following day. A particular occasion occurred when entertainments were organized for the Dauphin's wedding in February 1745. It was however such an inconvenient solution that Louis XV resolved to build a permanent theatre and entrusted his Principal Architect, Ange-Jacques Gabriel, with its construction.

However, this great plan took twenty years to accomplish. Meanwhile, during this long period, Gabriel, who had made studies of the foremost theatres of Italy, particularly those of Vicenza, Bologna, Parma, Modena and Turin, presented different projects to the King, none of which were accepted. It was not until 1768 that the King, anticipating a series of weddings with his various grandchildren, at long last decided that work was to start. This went on apace and the Opera, finished within twenty-three months, was inaugurated on 16 May 1770, the day of the Dauphin's marriage to the Archduchess Marie-Antoinette, with a performance of *Perseus* by Quinault and Lully.

Two stone galleries lead to the Opera; to reach it the King took the first-floor gallery, then either went directly to the

77

royal box or descended the staircase, since demolished, leading to the Guardroom and from there arrived at the foyer and the amphitheatre.

The plan of the theatre, original for the times, took the form of a truncated oval and the traditional boxes were replaced by simple tiered balconies, set back one above the other, with separations elbow high. This lay-out enabled the audience to see and hear better. There are no dead angles in this theatre and the acoustics are really remarkable, all the more so because, being entirely made of wood, the walls resound like a violin.

Its proportions are perfect (fig. 77) and one cannot but admire the elegant colonnade of the third-row boxes. As for the mirrors which line the back of the theatre, in which the half-chandeliers are reflected giving the illusion that they are complete, they emphasize the lightness characteristic of this architecture, the elements of which they seem to repeat endlessly.

The decoration is particularly refined. Jean-Jacques Durameau painted the central ceiling where he shows *Apollo distributing Crowns to the Muses* and the twelve small ceilings of the colonnade where he evokes the loves of the gods. Their delicate colouring harmonizes with the decor in fake marble

77
The Opera

in the theatre itself, dominated by the Campan green and the red speckled with grey sérancolin marbles.

Augustin Pajou carved the bas-reliefs for the first row of boxes where, between the profiles of the Muses and Graces on a lapis-lazuli background, one can see the elongated figures of the Olympian gods and goddesses, and those of the second-row boxes where cupids symbolize the most celebrated operas alternating with the signs of the Zodiac. It was Antoine Rousseau who was responsible for the trophies of musical instruments framing the stage and for the cartouche with the arms of France above (fig. 78).

At the back of the stalls rises the Amphitheatre; on the first row there are armchairs for the royal family and stools for the princes and princesses of the blood and the duchesses. At the level of the second row of boxes are three small private boxes enabling the King to attend the performance in semi incognito. Enclosed with gilt bronze latticework screens and decorated with exquisite arabesques by Vernet the Younger, they communicate through a small oval room with the gallery leading to the state apartments.

Formerly the theatre had seating for more than one thousand, but today there is room for just over seven hundred spectators. The orchestra pit can accommodate eighty musicians.

78

79

As was usually the case with court theatres, the Opera could be transformed within twenty-four hours into a vast ballroom. A system of pulleys enabled the parquet floor of the stalls to be raised to the level of the amphitheatre and the stage, on which a new room was built, surrounded by practicable colonnades and adorned with a ceiling painted by Briard. This ingenious device, inaugurated for the full dress ball which ended the series of fätes organized for the future Louis XVI's wedding on 16 May 1770, was the work of the "stage hand" Blaise-Henri Arnoult, who was also responsible for the technical stage equipment. This was of exceptional proportions (13.50 m in width, 23 m in depth and 36 m in height), making it one of the vastest in France. Grand-scale operas requiring large crowd scenes could be staged, and changes of scenery occurred in sight of the audience.

The foyer, giving access to the amphitheatre, is embellished with statues by Pajou: *Apollo, Venus, Abundance* and *Peace, Youth* and *Health, Lyrical, Pastoral, Epic and Dramatic Poetry* (fig. 79).

The Opera, which Louis-Philippe had had repainted in red and which, in 1871, had been transformed to hold sessions of the National Assembly, was scrupulously renovated between 1952 and 1956 and restored to its original state. Thus it has become one of the most beautiful theatres in the world, illustrating once again Gabriel's intentions who, by uniting the fading graces of the Rocaille style with triumphant Neo-classicism, had wished, according to Patte "to give an idea of the progress achieved in the arts during the reign of Louis XV".

78
The Stage of the Opera

79
The Foyer at the Opera

The Private Apartments

Under this general title, the private apartments of the King, the Queen and the Dauphine, as well as three lodgings for courtiers, are grouped together here, and can be seen with a guide:

– the Inner Rooms and the Queen's Private Apartment, the Back Rooms belonging to the Dauphine;

– the King's Private Apartment, the apartments of the Marquise de Pompadour, of the Comtesse du Barry and of the Comte de Maurepas.

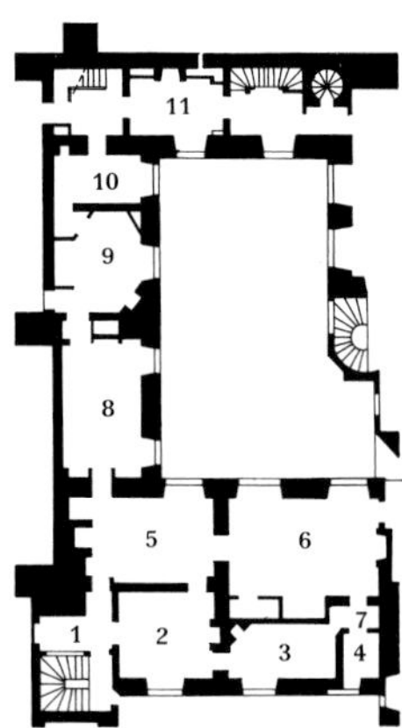

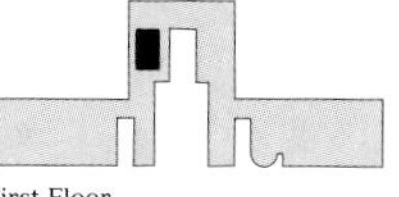

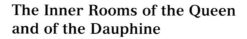

The Inner Rooms of the Queen and of the Dauphine

Conducted lecture tours

The visitor climbs the Queen's Staircase and enters the Guardroom; he then crosses the landing of the Fleury Staircase (called after the Duc de Fleury who, in the reign of Louis XVI, lodged in the attic above the Queen's State Apartment) and from there he enters the Queen's Inner Rooms.

The Queen's Inner Rooms

Originally the suite of the Queen's private rooms followed after her bedchamber in the New Château and communicated with a Small Apartment, called "convenience apartment" (appartement de commodité) situated in the Old Château, comprising three main rooms. When the Hall of Mirrors was built, these three rooms had to be pulled down and, at the death of Queen Marie-Thérèse, her Private Apartment was annexed to the King's.

Only three small rooms remained then: two of them, including an oratory, behind the Queen's Bedroom and a third one backing on to the Hall of Mirrors. In 1696, this room became a private boudoir for the future Duchesse de Bourgogne when she settled in the Queen's former apartment. In 1699, a "night apartment" was furnished near these small rooms for the Duc de Bourgogne, comprising a bedroom and another small room.

Marie Leszczynska had this night apartment joined to the Duchesse de Bourgogne's rooms to form new inner rooms which she had decorated and furnished with the most exquisite taste. Here she would retire to read and pray for several hours each day and in the evenings she liked to invite her close circle of friends and people renowned for their wit and intelligence. Scarcely anything remains of these arrangements, for Marie-Antoinette had the inner rooms completely redecorated and modernized to bring them up to fashion.

First we cross a small antechamber[1] communicating with the antechamber of the Great Dining Hall. It was from here that the Queen's personal guests were introduced into her presence by the chambermaids.

The Bathroom[2] (3.63 m × 3.45 m × 2.86 m) had two rooms added on, one for bathing[3] and the other with a privy[4]. The first of these rooms replaced Marie Leszczynska's oratory and still has six pictures commissioned by this Queen, of which one for the oratory, *The Conversion of Saint Augustine* by Charles-Antoine Coypel, and *The Five Senses* by Jean-Baptiste Oudry, for another room.

80

81

The library extension (5.27 m × 4 m × 2.97 m)[5] occupies the place where Marie Leszczynska's bathing room was situated. The bookcases contain calf-bound books and there is also on display a small silver-gilt salver with the arms of Marie-Antoinette, on which the lady-in-waiting would present the Queen with her handkerchief and gloves

The large inner or gold room (6.72 m × 4.52 m × 4.54 m)[6] first belonged to Marie Leszczynska and was installed in place of the Duc de Bourgogne's bedroom, but its present decor dates from 1783 (fig. 81): the beautiful panelling, carved by the Rousseau brothers from designs by Richard Mique, are a striking example of the "return to the antique", following the discovery of Pompei and Herculaneum. The rich furniture brought there by Marie-Antoinette has now disappeared with the exception of the gilt bronze "fire" which has been put back in the fireplace. Nevertheless the principal pieces of furniture had in fact served the Queen in other royal residences: the chest of drawers by Riesener comes from her bedroom at the Château de Marly, the seats from her apartment at the Tuileries and the gilt bronze chandelier probably comes from her apartment at the Château de St. Cloud. On the chest of drawers stand three precious Sèvres porcelain vases with a Chinese design, delivered to the Queen in 1775 (fig. 80).

It was in this elegant drawing room that Marie-Antoinette received her children and her friends, and where she played music with Grétry and sat for her portrait by Madame Vigée-Lebrun.

On the left of the chimneypiece a concealed door in the wainscoting leads to Marie Leszczynska's former Poets' Cabinet[7]. Here Marie-Antoinette had some charming panelling painted in natural colours and adorned with rustic scenes, which came from her mother-in-law, the Dauphine Marie-Josèphe de Saxe's back rooms (fig. 82).

82

80
Sèvres Porcelain Vases with a Chinese Decoration

81
The Queen's large Inner Room

82
Detail of Wood Panelling from one of Marie-Josèphe de Saxe's Rooms

The library[8] (5.06 m × 2.95 m × 4.26 m) (fig. 83) occupies the place of Marie Leszczynska's "laboratory" where she used to paint, tutored by Oudry. It was decorated for Marie-Antoinette, then still the Dauphine, as early as 1772, and slightly modified in 1779. Apart from the traditional decoration of the doors with fake bound books, it is worth noticing the adjustable shelves in the cupboards and the drawer handles in the shape of the imperial eagle, a reminder of the House of Austria. Morocco-bound books, stamped with the royal coat of arms, and a collection of lacquer work belonging to the Queen, are all displayed here.

The Sofa Room (le Cabinet de la Méridienne)[9] (fig. 84) (3.38mx 3.14mx 3.24m) is an octagonal room. The doors are placed in the diagonal cut-off corners, providing an independent access so that the chambermaids could pass from the bedroom to the library without disturbing the Sovereign. The mirrored alcove backing on to the bedroom wall contains a sofa where the Queen could rest in the daytime. Redecoration was done in 1781 from designs by Mique: the panelling carved by the Rousseau brothers and the bronzes affixed to the mirrors on the doors present sprays of roses, the emblems of married love and the dolphins are an allusion to the longed-for birth of an heir to the throne. The pedestal table in steel and gilt bronze with a top in petrified wood was offered to Marie-Antoinette by her mother the Empress Maria Theresa. The two armchairs were made for this room by Georges Jacob; the "grenadine" covering them has been rewoven from the original model that the Queen was later to replace with an embroidered fabric.

Beyond the Sofa Room are a Privy Room[10] and a Dressing Room[11], the latter being none other than the former private boudoir of the Duchesse de Bourgogne which has kept part of its wood panelling executed in 1701 for this princess. It was through this room connecting with her bedroom that Marie-Antoinette fled on the morning of 6 October 1789 to take refuge in the King's apartment.

Close by, a small staircase descends to the King's passage, the Dauphin's apartment and the Queen's private apartment. The Queen also used it to go to her small private rooms on the second floor.

Apart from a few orderly rooms reserved for the lady-in-waiting and the chambermaids, these small rooms consist of a boudoir, a dining room where the chimneypiece brought from the stucco library has been installed, and a billiard room, near which the staircase ends. The walls of the billiard room, now undergoing renovation, will be hung with a marvellous white satin, brocaded and rebrocaded, and this will also be used to cover the two couches by Georges Jacob (1784).

The visitor then goes back down the Fleury staircase and enters the back rooms of the Dauphine (see p. 124). He then

83

4

83
The Queen's Library

84
The Sofa Room

85

86

85
The Bedroom in the Queen's Private Apartment

86
Élisabeth Vigée-Lebrun
The Dauphin and Madame Royale, 1784

87
The Bathroom in the Private Apartment

walks along the corridor behind the Dauphine's inner room and the Dauphin's library, which links the princess's bedroom to the prince's large drawing room. From the Dauphin's bedroom and the second antechamber, he then reaches the lower gallery and enters the Queen's Private Apartment.

The Queen's Private Apartment

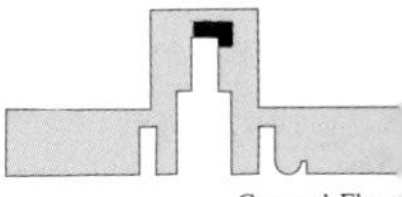

This was installed in 1784 for Marie-Antoinette in a portion of the former apartment of Madame Sophie who had died in 1782. This private appartment consisted of three main rooms and some minor orderly rooms. When the Queen left her State

87

Apartment on the first floor, she went along the King's Passage and down a small staircase leading to the former north bay of the marble vestibule.

The vestibule, which dated from 1679, had been partitioned off in 1769 at the request of Madame Sophie, in order to enlarge her apartment the main rooms of which had taken the place of the lower gallery. Two new rooms had been created in this way near the princess's bathroom: in the north bay, a lathe room and in the other two bays a library, its stucco walls painted with landscapes and ornamental foliage framed in fake marble. Fifteen years later this charming room became the pivot of Queen Marie-Antoinette's Private Apartment; demolished in the XIXth century, it has not been possible to restore it.

The bedroom (fig. 85) (7.80 m × 6 m × 4 m) was arranged on the spot where Madame Sophie had had her bathroom. The wall decoration has vanished with the exception of the fine mantlepiece in griotte marble enhanced with gilt bronzes. Most of the furniture however has been retrieved and put back in place: the chest of drawers and desk by Benneman, the dressing table by Riesener, seats by Georges Jacob, the "fire" by Gouthière. In the alcove lined with green damask hangs the portrait, painted in 1784 by Élisabeth Vigée-Lebrun, of the Queen's two eldest children, *The First Dauphin and Madame Royale* (fig. 86).

The stuccoed library communicated with the bathroom (6.40 m × 6.20 m × 3 m) (fig. 87). The wood-panelled decoration was perfectly in keeping with the purpose of this room: basins where swans are drinking, reeds, dolphins, shells, pearls, branches of coral, a lady's dressing table set, etc. The room was large enough to serve as bedroom cum bathroom: the bed, decorated with pearls and shells, came from Louis XVI's bathroom at Fontainebleau and was covered with a satin quilt embroidered with the intertwined monograms of the King and Queen; the pier table was made by Georges Jacob for Madame Adélaïde's bathroom at Versailles. Behind the wall at the end was the privy room and a stove to heat the bathroom.

For the visit of the rest of this apartment, see p. 148.

The Apartments of Madame du Barry, of Madame de Pompadour and of Monsieur de Maurepas

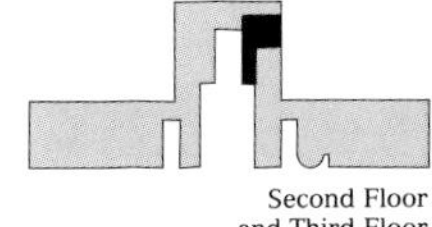

Conducted lecture tours

"Madame du Barry's apartment" corresponds in fact to a portion, no doubt the largest one, of Louis XV's Private Apartment. Although his favourite only lived here for five years,

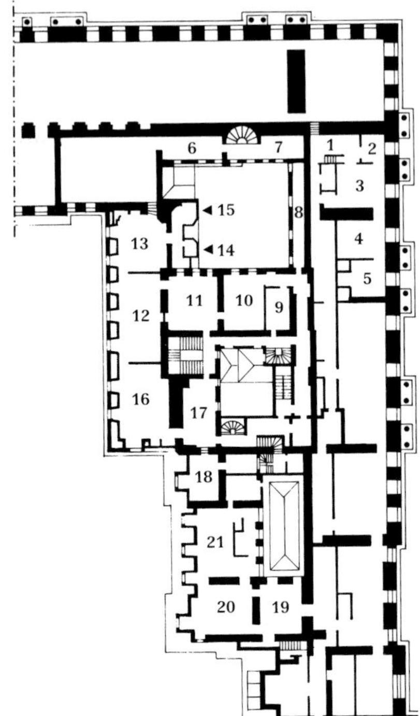

from 1769 to 1774, nevertheless she gave it her name, hence this over-simplified habit of calling it hers. If however we are to understand clearly the creation and transformation this lodging underwent, it is best to deal with it as part of the general history of the King's Private Apartment, which originated in Louis XIV's time.

As a complement to his State Apartment in the New Château and his "convenience apartment" in the Old Château, Louis XIV had indeed, as early as 1670, had a Small Apartment made in the attic above the Saturn and Venus Rooms. This small lodging, consisting of three rooms (an antechamber, a bedroom and a closet), disappeared in 1678, when the Hall of Mirrors was created. A few elements of the cornices do however remain below the roofs of the Gallery. It was immediately replaced by a new Small Apartment, arranged at the top of the Old Château at the far end of the Marble Court. This lodging also consisted of three rooms, and was reached by a small semicircular staircase at the back of the Hall of Mirrors. It in turn disappeared in 1701, during work on the King's first-floor apartment, but the staircase is still there.

As soon as Louis XV returned to Versailles in 1722, a workshop with a lathe was made for him on the level of the attics on the inner courtyard, near the semicircular staircase, where the boy King, then aged twelve, turned his hand to wood and ivory work. Four years later, Louis XV had a small library made on the other side of the staircase and a gallery at right angles on the north side of the courtyard, since named the "Deer Court" (la Cour des Cerfs), owing to the plaster stag heads which used to decorate it.

This was the start of a new Private Apartment that the King would never cease to enlarge and transform throughout his life to suit his needs and his whims. Louis XV had libraries, workshops, gamesrooms, summer and winter dining rooms, bathrooms, kitchens called "laboratories", aviaries and terraces laid out there, until, at the end, they occupied two storeys above that of the inner rooms.

This was the King's private domain, practically unknown to the courtiers, where he wanted to live the life of a simple individual, admitting only a few privileged friends. Not far from it was the apartment of his current mistress, first the Comtesse de Mailly, then the Duchesse de Châteauroux and finally the Marquise de Pompadour.

In September 1766, Louis XV lent the main rooms of his Private Apartment to his daughter-in-law Marie-Josèphe de Saxe, who had become a widow a few months earlier. This was intended as a provisional arrangement, while a new apartment was being made ready for the Princess on the ground floor of the central building. However, the Dauphine died on 13 March 1767 before being able to take possession of her permanent lodging.

Louis XV then retrieved these rooms for himself and ordered some transformations. Soon though, in 1769, he gave them to Madame du Barry. For, meanwhile, he had become a widower and having no further need for constraint, for the first time he did not hesitate to lodge his mistress in a part of his Private Apartment. The lodging was completely renovated and splendidly furnished for his favourite, who occupied it until the King's death on 10 May 1774.

Louis XVI allotted part of Madame du Barry's former lodging to his Principal Valet, Thierry de Ville d'Avray and the other part to the Duc de Villequier, First Gentleman of the Bedchamber. The new King merely kept for himself his grandfather's libraries, to which he added Physics, Chemistry and Geography rooms, as well as workshops for carpentry and lockmaking.

From here we go up the King's Grand Staircase leading on the first floor to the Inner Rooms. From the windows of the Dining Room of the Return from the Hunt (where supper parties were given after a day's hunting), the only façade of the Deer Court to have kept its former aspect can be seen, the others having lost their top floor in the XIXth century.

Next we go along a corridor the former decoration of which has disappeared; this was Louis XVI's Maproom (Cabinet des Plans), next to his "artillery" room, where the King kept his hunting equipment.

We then come to the Golden Cabinet with its charming wainscoting carved with dogs' heads, probably by Roumier. From there we reach the semicircular staircase leading to Louis XV's sixth bathroom, opening on to the Council Room.

A staircase goes straight up to the third floor. On the right of the landing, a glass door gives access to an extension of the library, which dates from Louis XVI and occupies the place of the Buffet Room of Louis XV's Summer Dining Room, which disappeared in 1755. A few steps lead down to the Great Library, established by Louis XV in 1755 above the Council Room, replacing Louis XIV's second Private Apartment. Here there is a flat-topped desk made for the Dauphin, the son of Louis XV, which Louis XVI later used right up until the Revolution. From this Library a staircase leads down to the Small Gallery.

We then return to the staircase, the last flight of which goes up to the attic rooms where Louis XVI's forge and his workshop for mechanics, lockmaking and clockmaking are still in place (not open to visitors). From there the King could reach an observatory and the roof garden above the Hall of Mirrors where, like Louis XV, he enjoyed walking about.

On the left of the staircase we enter a second extension of the library. The mirrored door near the window used to open on to Louis XVI's Physics and Chemistry Room, demolished in the XIXth century.

Before 1750 the library extension was the Marquise de Pompadour's bathroom. In those days, the room did not therefore communicate with the staircase, but was joined to the favourite's apartment which we now visit, leaving for a moment the King's Private Apartment.

The Marquise de Pompadour's apartment, with its magnificent view over the North ornamental garden and the forest of Marly, is situated in the attic over the King's State Apartment, right above the Mercury and Apollo Rooms. Its first occupants, from 1743 to 1744, were the Duchesse de Châteauroux and her sister the Duchesse de Lauraguais. After the former's death, Louis XV gave it to Madame de Pompadour who lived there from 1745 to 1750.

We pass through a Wardrobe Room[1] where the favourite's dresses were kept, above which was the bedroom of the chambermaid on night duty ("de veille"). On the left a few steps lead to the flattened dome of the War Room which Louis XV had surrounded with tiny rooms hung with different coloured damasks, which have since vanished.

From there we reach a small room[2] and then a reception room[3] which had once been Madame de Châteauroux's bedroom, before becoming that of Madame de Pompadour until 1748. The beautiful wood panelling was coated with a green and white Martin lacquer paint (*vernis Martin*). The fine furniture seen today dates from the XVIIIth century, but did not belong to Madame de Pompadour. Behind the alcove are a privy and a servant's room.

The next two rooms were originally only one, a reception room divided in 1748 to form an antechamber[4] and Madame de Pompadour's new bedroom[5], with wainscoting by Verberckt.

Beyond the bedroom there were two antechambers, no longer existing, one of which served as a dining room. Close by, the favourite had placed a "flying chair", a real little lift, worked with a wheel and a balance-weight.

In 1750, the relationship between Louis XV and Madame de Pompadour underwent a change; although she ceased to be his mistress, she remained nevertheless his friend and confident. She then left this apartment and settled on the ground floor of the Château, where the younger daughters of the King soon became her neighbours.

The visit of the King's Private Apartment continues after going back down the semicircular staircase to the second floor. On the landing at the right, one can glimpse through the glass door Louis XV's former lathe room, which Louis XVI had turned into a carpentry room[6].

The door on the left leads to a suite of about ten rooms altogether which, for forty years, was the main part of the the King's Private Apartment. Marie-Josèphe de Saxe stayed in these rooms for a while from 1766 to 1767 and later, between 1769 and 1774, the Comtesse du Barry, so that it is known today as Madame du Barry's apartment.

The first room is the former library installed by Louis XV in 1726[7]. In 1766, the Dauphine Marie-Josèphe had made it into her Wardrobe, and it subsequently served this purpose for Madame du Barry. After the latter left, Louis XVI turned it into a lathe room and gave it its present aspect.

From there we pass into a small gallery which Louis XV had also turned into a library[8]. He kept there, in particular, his collection of geographical maps and chronological tables, which were presented on sprung rollers and could be unrolled like a blind. Transformed by the Dauphine into a wardrobe, which was later used by Madame du Barry, it became once again a geographical gallery under Louis XVI. On the pier tables stood models of ships of the Marine Royale, globes and the first electric machines.

The two following rooms occupy the place of the library of Louis XV who, in 1751, transformed it into a dining room. In 1763, this was divided into two to make a new bathroom[9], its panelling painted in pale yellow with a blue Martin high gloss, and a small room[10] in pale yellow and lilac, which for some months was used as an inner room by Marie-Josèphe de Saxe.

The dining room[11], in green and white, was created in 1738, and the delightful fireplace and window bays (fig. 88) date from this period. Louis XV used it as his winter dining room, his summer one being on the floor above. From 1751 onwards, it served as an antechamber to the next dining room, before becoming, in 1763, the King's Bathroom. The Dauphine, who had made it into her bedroom, died there on 13 March 1767. Madame du Barry restored it to its original purpose as a dining room and the preceding room then became a Buffet Room.

Louis XVI attributed the three rooms we have just seen to Thierry de Ville d'Avray, his Principal Valet.

The following rooms are situated under the roof of the Old Château beside the Marble Court, which explains the width of the window recesses, for they are in fact dormer windows. Louis XV had them fitted out from 1735 onwards, at the time when he had started creating his inner rooms situated immediately below, which were to become the new bedroom, the Clock Room and the Angle Room.

The first two rooms formed only one at the beginning. It was the Small Gallery, lit by five windows and arched at one end. The wainscoting was painted then with a white and "gold-coloured" Martin lacquer paint and was the setting for nine

88

pictures representing hunting scenes of exotic animals, due to some of the most famous artists of the day: Lancret, Boucher, Pater, Van Loo, de Troy and Parrocel.

In 1766-1767 the Small Gallery served as the Dauphine's large drawing room. After her death, it was partitioned to form two drawing rooms: the hunting pictures were removed (they are now in the Amiens Museum) and a plainer wainscoting replaced the original wood panelling, though traces of this remain in the window recesses.

Two years later, the first drawing room became Madame du Barry's large boudoir[12] (fig. 89) and she had it gilded, together with the two adjoining rooms, and furnished it with two sofas and eighteen chairs in carved gilt wood. The griotte marble fireplace dates from the creation of the Small Gallery. It bears a terracotta bust of Madame du Barry after Pajou.

The favourite's bedroom[13] is the second room resulting from the partitioning of the Small Gallery and it has kept its arched end. Madame du Barry had a superb chest of drawers here, adorned with Sèvres porcelain panels and a poster bed, replaced today by a beautiful couch which belonged to Marie-Antoinette. The statuette of Venus, whose features are not without some resemblance to Madame du Barry, is attributed to Pajou. Behind the end wall are a privy[14] and the night chambermaid's bedroom[15].

A concealed staircase at the right of the chimney leads to the library (fig. 90) installed by Louis XV above the Council Room, not far from the semicircular staircase.

We retrace our steps to the Angle Room[16] which has a beautiful view over the Royal Court. First of all it was Louis XV's dining room and in his time there were two pic-

88
Madame du Barry's
Dining Room

tures, one *The Lunch of Oysters* by de Troy and the other *The Lunch of Ham* by Lancret (today they are at the Château de Chantilly). In 1738, after the winter dining room we have just seen had been created, this room was turned into a Gamesroom. The Dauphine transformed it into the Nobles' Room and Madame du Barry made it the Gamesroom once again. She had two chest of drawers placed there, one in lacquer and the other in Sèvres porcelain. Today we see a fine portrait of Louis XV in his later years, painted in 1773 by Vincent de Montpetit. A small heater was kept in a tiny closet under the sloping roof, where the King could warm up his coffee.

From here an antechamber[17] with pale yellow and white painted panelling leads to the King's Grand Staircase.

Three steps up is an enchanting library[18] which originally did not belong to this apartment; it had been installed in 1756 for Madame Adélaïde, above her inner room on the first floor. When, in 1769, the Princess moved to the ground floor to be with her sisters, Madame du Barry had the library given to her. The communicating door was then opened and an alcove containing a sofa was added. On the table stands Madame du Barry's copper parrot-cage strewn with porcelain flowers.

The next small apartment was fitted out in 1753, replacing the dome of the Ambassadors' Staircase and Louis XV's still-room. Situated above Madame Adélaïde's apartment, it was intended for her lady-in-waiting, the Duchesse de Beauvillier. From 1769 to 1774, it was occupied by Mademoiselle du Barry, the favourite's sister-in-law. When Madame du Barry departed, Louis XVI lodged the Comte de Maurepas here who had become his secret counsellor. In 1781, the apartment was

89

89
Madame du Barry's
Large Drawing Room

90
The Library

90

attributed to the Duc de Brissac, the colonel in charge of the Hundred Swiss Guards.

The apartment consists of three main rooms: an antechamber[19], a large drawing room[20] and a bedroom[21]. In the large drawing room a grisaille portrait of the Comte de Maurepas is seen, as well as a painted iron chest bearing the stamp of the Château de Compiègne and an elegant set of furniture by Boulard made for the Château de Versailles.

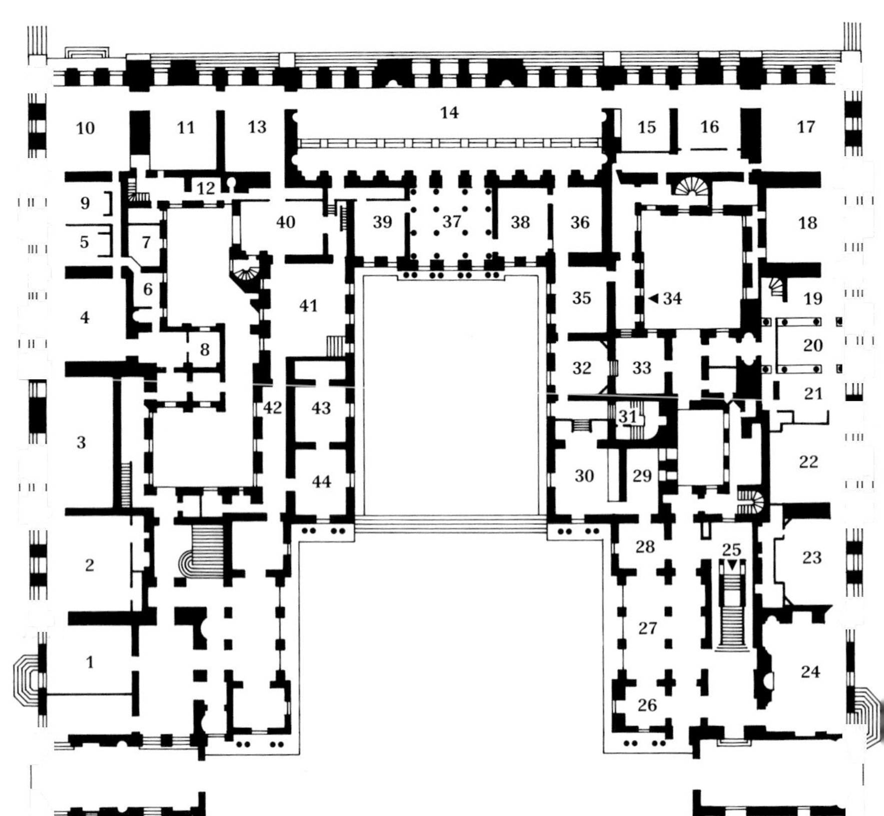

1
2
3
4
5
6
7
8
9
10
11
12
13
14
15
16
17
18
19
20
21
22
23
24
25
26
27
28
29
30
31
32
33
34
35
36
37
38
39
40
41
42
43
44

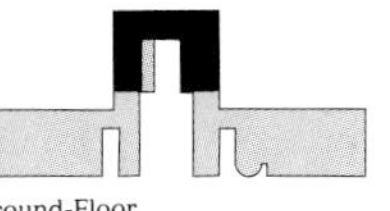

The Apartments of the Dauphin, of the Dauphine and of Mesdames

Conducted lecture tours

All these apartments are situated on the ground floor of the New Château, below the King's and the Queen's State Apartments. This was always one of the most important sectors of the Château, not only because of the nobility who inhabited it, but also owing to the luxurious decoration.

Louis XIV had had a sumptuous Bathing Apartment fitted out at the north-west angle, separated by a gallery from the double apartment situated in the south-west angle where Monsieur et Madame, the King's brother and sister-in-law resided.

In 1684, Monsieur and Madame went to live on the first floor of the South Wing and their apartments were allotted to their nephew, the Dauphin, called "Monseigneur", while his wife, Marie-Anne de Bavière had just taken possession of the Queen's apartment immediately above, which had become vacant on the death of Queen Marie-Thérèse.

Monseigneur was an indolent prince of limited intelligence, but a true lover of art, and his collections of pictures and jewels could almost rival the King's. In order to display them properly he had the two lodgings of Monsieur and of Madame made into one and added on two rooms, thus creating a vast apartment which he decorated with the most refined luxury, making it into one of the marvels of Versailles. When he died on 14 April 1711, the apartment was given to his eldest son, the Duc de Bourgogne, whose wife had occupied, since their marriage in 1697, the Queen's apartment where the Dauphine Marie-Anne had died in 1690. On the death of the Prince and the Princess in February 1712, Monseigneur's apartment was partitioned in order to lodge his third son, the Duc de Berry and his wife.

When the Court returned to Versailles in 1722, Monseigneur's apartment was reconstituted for the Regent, who was to expire here on 2 December 1723. The young Dauphin, son of Louis XV, occupied it from 1736 to 1745, at the time of his first marriage. He returned there with his second wife, Marie-Josèphe de Saxe and that is when the former apartment of Monseigneur was once again divided, forming two separate lodgings for the young couple who lived there until the death of the Dauphin on 20 December 1765.

The new Dauphin, the future Louis XVI, settled in his mother Marie-Josèphe de Saxe's former apartment, which was enlarged by annexing his father's library. His intention was to lodge his future wife, Marie-Antoinette de Lorraine, Archduchess of Austria, in the Queen's apartment which had remained vacant since the death of Marie Leszczynska on 24 June 1768, and which was being renovated. However, on the wedding day (16 May 1770), work had not finished and it was decided meanwhile to put the Dauphine Marie-Antoinette temporarily in her husband's father's former apartment, where she stayed for a few months before settling permanently in the Queen's apartment.

As soon as he came to the throne in 1774, Louis XVI took possession of the King's apartment on the first floor and those of the Dauphin and the Dauphine were allotted to his brother and to his sister-in-law, the Comte and Comtesse de Provence, who occupied them until 1787. In fact, at that time, they had to relinquish them for the Dauphin, Louis XVI's son, and his tutor, the Duc d'Harcourt. On the death of the young Prince on 4 June 1789, both apartments were given to his younger brother, the future Louis XVII, and to his sister, Madame Royale, who lived there until 6 October 1789.

The Bathing Apartment, symmetrical to the Dauphin's, was probably one of the most original of Louis XIV's creations. It consisted of five rooms decorated with marbles, pictures, sculptures and gilt bronzes: the Doric vestibule, the Ionic antechamber, the large drawing room, the bathing room and the bathroom.

In 1685, it was attributed to the Marquise de Montespan who hardly ever lived there. In 1691, it passed to the Duc du Maine, the legitimized son of the King and the Marquise, and then, after his marriage the following year, to his younger brother the Comte de Toulouse, who lived alone there until he in turn married in 1723, whereupon he left it to his wife and had a new apartment fitted out for himself, beyond the Doric vestibule, consisting of three main rooms, which, on his death on 1 December 1737, passed to his only son, the Duc de Penthièvre, who became the sole occupant until his marriage in 1744, when he shared it with his wife, Marie-Thérèse d'Este-Modène.

In 1750, the Duc and Duchesse de Penthièvre gave up their apartment to the Marquise de Pompadour who, until then had lived in the attic of the the King's State Apartment, two floors up. She undertook considerable renovations and had it enlarged, decorated and furnished with the greatest elegance. She died there on 14 April 1764. Two years later the apartment was given to Marie-Josèphe de Saxe, who had become a widow. However the Dauphine died on 13 March 1767, before being able to take possession of it. It then went to Madame Victoire and finally, in 1769, to Madame Adélaïde who lived there until 6 October 1789.

It was also in 1750 that the Comtesse de Toulouse ceased living in the former Bathing Apartment. For near on twenty-five years she had received an almost daily visit from Louis XV who appreciated his great-aunt's wit and virtue and showed great affection for her. The apartment then went to his son and daughter-in-law, but the Duc and Duchesse de Penthièvre had not long to enjoy it. Indeed, as early as 1752, Madame Adélaïde, Louis XV's eldest daughter, settled there for a few months, while waiting for the one on the first floor next to his that her father intended for her. After she left, her younger sisters, Mesdames Victoire, Sophie and Louise, occupied it, living together there until 1767. During the next two years its sole occupant was Madame Sophie who, in 1769, left it for her sister Victoire, who had left hers to Madame Adélaïde. Madame Sophie then settled in a new apartment created especially for her in part of the Lower Gallery, while Madame Louise occupied the other part. In 1770 Madame Louise finally left Versailles for ever to enter the Carmel Convent at St. Denis. A few years later Madame Sophie was able to enlarge her apartment so that it occupied the whole of the former Lower Gallery. She died there on 5 March 1782. Madame Victoire remained there with her sister Adélaïde and they left Versailles together on 6 October 1789.

On the eve of the Revolution, all these apartments counted among the most luxurious and elegant ones of the whole Château. Louis-Philippe had practically all of them demolished to create his "History Galleries" in 1837. However an important part of the decoration was preserved in the storerooms of the museum, so that it has been possible to restore them to the state they were in 1789, when the Château ceased to be inhabited and the evolution of its decoration came to a final standstill.

In these apartments, the XVIIIth-century collections, illustrating the reigns of Louis XV and Louis XVI, from 1715 to 1789, are presented, as also in the lodging of the Captain of the Guards next door on the ground floor of the Old Château.

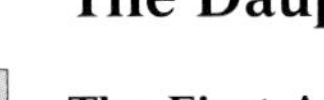

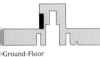

Ground-Floor

The Dauphine's Apartment

The First Antechamber[1]

(7.83 m × 9.94 m × 5.07 m)

This room corresponds to the site of a former two-storey chapel which stood here. The chapel was demolished in 1682 and then replaced by an apartment occupied successively by the Duchesse de Montpensier, called "la Grande Mademoiselle" (1692-1693), the First Chaplain of France (1693-1706) and the Grand Master of the King's Wardrobe (1706-1712). In 1712 this apartment was replaced by a Guardroom for the

Duc de Berry and on his death, on 4 July 1714, it became part of the Maréchal de Villars' apartment. In 1747 it was reduced to a third of its surface to form the Dauphine's first antechamber.

The pictures shown here evoke the coming to power and the coronation of Louis XV. Two portraits of the young king in particular, one painted in 1716 soon after his accession, by Hyacinthe Rigaud (fig. 91), the other in 1723 by Alexis-Simon Belle in which he wears the coronation regalia. Portraits of *Philippe d'Orléans, Regent of France,* by Jean-Baptiste Santerre, and of two unknown members of the Parlement by

91

92

Nicolas de Largillière. Two pictures by Pierre-Denis Martin represent *The King leaving the Parlement after exercising his Authority from the "lit de Justice" on 12 September 1715* (fig. 92) and *The Royal Procession after the Coronation, on 22 October 1722.*

The Second Antechamber[2]
(11.30 m × 9.98 m × 5.10 m)

It was here that the chapel was first supposed to be, before it was finally installed in the preceding room. Originally divided into four small rooms, this antechamber was part of the Grande Mademoiselle's apartment until 1693. It then became the vestibule of Monseigneur's apartment, and then of his eldest son, the Duc de Bourgogne. After being the Antechamber of the Duc de Berry from 1712 to 1714, it then became part of the Maréchal de Villars' apartment before being finally made, in 1747, the Dauphine's Second Antechamber.

On the overdoors are portraits of *Marie Leszczynska in royal Attire* and of an unknown duchess, as well as two flower paintings by Blain de Fontenay. On the fine sérancolin marble mantlepiece, which probably came from Marie Leszczynska's room on the first floor, stands a bust of *The Regent* by Jean-Louis Le Moyne (fig. 93).

93

•1
Iyacinthe Rigaud
ouis XV, 1716

•2
ierre-Denis Martin
he King leaving
ne "Lit de Justice",
2 September 1715

3
ean-Louis Le Moyne
hilippe d'Orléans,
egent of France,
715

94

An equestrian portrait of *Louis XV* by Jean-Baptiste Van Loo and Charles Parrocel in 1723. A charming portrait by Belle of the King's young cousin *Maria Anna Vitoria de Bourbon, Infanta of Spain*, daughter of Philip V, to whom he was fleetingly betrothed (fig. 95). Belle is also responsible for the portrait of *Bethisy's Children* (fig. 96).

The portrait of *Peter the Great* by Jean-Marc Nattier, recalls the time when the Tsar stayed at Versailles in May 1717. François Boucher painted the young *Louis XV on a pilgrimage to Cythera* and Parrocel has depicted *The Entry into the Tuileries Gardens of the Turkish Ambassador Mehemet Effendi, on 21 March 1721* (fig. 94).

95

96

7

The Large Drawing Room[10]
(15.17 m × 8.31 m × 5.12 m)

4
:harles Parrocel
'he Entry of
Aehemet Effendi into
he Tuileries Gardens,
1 March 1721

5
\lexis-Simon Belle
Aarie-Anne-Victoire
le Bourbon, Infanta
of Spain, 1723

6
\lexis-Simon Belle
Bethisy's Children,
716

7
The Dauphine's large
)rawing Room

Originally this room was divided into several small rooms to form the apartment of Mademoiselle, the eldest daughter of Monsieur, who became Queen of Spain in 1678. It was then given to the Marquise de Thiange, sister of the Marquise de Montespan, who occupied it until her death in 1693. The present room was then created, becoming Monseigneur's Guardroom. Once again partitioned in 1712 to make a bedroom and drawing room for the Duc de Berry, it resumed its function as Guardroom for the Duchesse du Berry, from the time she became a widow in 1714 until her death in 1719. It also served as the Regent's Guardroom, then as the Dauphin's, Louis XV's son, from 1736 to 1744, before becoming the large drawing room of his wife Marie-Josèphe de Saxe (fig. 97).

This is when it was adorned with carved gilt wood panelling, which unfortunately has vanished. It has been possible to copy it though from Gabriel's original drawings, as well as the frame of one of the five mirrors, and to put back under this mirror the original pier table. Above this hangs the barometer made for the Dauphin, the future Louis XVI, who was to occupy this apartment, which used to be his mother's, until he came to the throne.

The overdoors represent *Psyche and Love in a Chariot* and *Love leaving Psyche*. They were painted by Carle Van Loo for the apartment of the Dauphin's first wife, Marie-Thérèse-Raphaelle de Bourbon, in the South Wing.

Queen Marie Leszczynska is depicted here twice: at the moment of her marriage in 1725 by Jean-Baptiste Van Loo and holding her son the Dauphin on her lap, by Belle in 1729 (fig. 98). This picture is surrounded by portraits of the Queen's parents: Stanislas Leszczynski and Catherine Opalinska, King and Queen of Poland, by Jean-Baptiste Van Loo. The portrait of the banker *Samuel Bernard* is one of Rigaud's last masterpieces (fig. 99).

The Bedroom[4]

(9.67 m × 9.40 m × 5.04 m)

At first Monsieur's Guardroom, then that of Monseigneur, this room became an antechamber in 1693; in 1747, it was turned into the Dauphine's bedroom. Nothing remains of the rich decoration of this time, with the exception of the overdoors painted by Jean Restout representing *Psyche fleeing from the Anger of Venus* and *Psyche imploring Venus's Pardon*.

The *Portrait of the Dauphin* at the age of ten by Louis Tocqué and those of his sisters among which are those of *Madame Henriette as Flora* (1742) and *Madame Adélaïde as Diana* (1745), both by Jean-Marc Nattier.

The fine "Polish" style bed is by Nicolas Heurtaut and on the pier table between the windows is a model of a coach made by Chobert for the Dauphin.

98

99

00

101

102

8
lexis-Simon Belle
ueen Marie
eszczynska and the
auphin, 1729

9
lyacinthe Rigaud
amuel Bernard, 1726

00
he Dauphine's Inner
oom

01
ean-Baptiste Oudry
Vinter, 1749

02
ernard van
ysenburgh
he Dauphine's
loping Desk, 1745

The Inner Room[5]
(5.86 m 4.87 m 5.03 m)

For a long while this small room (fig. 100) and the following one were joined in one, first serving as an antechamber for Monsieur, then for Monseigneur, before becoming, in 1693, the latter's bedroom. It was also the Regent's bedroom, and then that of the Dauphin as a child, but was divided in 1747 to form an inner cabinet for the Dauphine and a retreat for the Dauphin. The young couple's apartments thus communicated through their most inaccessible rooms, preserving, to some extent, their marital intimacy.

Part of the charming decoration in natural woodwork with a Martin imitation lacquer finish has remained. It has been completed and it has also been possible to replace the overdoors representing the *Four Seasons,* painted especially for this room in 1749 by Jean-Baptiste Oudry (fig. 101).

Antoine Gaudreaux is responsible for the chest of drawers and Bernard Van Rysenburgh for the sloping desk (fig. 102).

These two admirable pieces of furniture were made in 1745 for the first Dauphine and were later used for the second.

On the right of the alcove, which formerly contained a sofa, a glass door provides access to the back rooms.

The Back Rooms[6]

These are visited during the conducted tour of the Queen's inner rooms.

These small rooms look out on to two inner courtyards, called "Monseigneur's Court" (or "Queen's Court") and "Monsieur's Court". Rearranged several times, they bear no trace of their original decoration, though the woodwork in one of them was removed by Marie-Antoinette to one of her inner rooms.

The back rooms were refurbished for the last time during the Restoration for the Duchesse d'Angoulême, formerly Madame Royale. Thus Louis XVI's daughter returned, twenty-five years later, to the apartment she had occupied in her childhood during the summer of 1789.

She had the former Sofa Room belonging to the Comtesse de Provence transformed into a bathroom[7], keeping though the delicate wood panelling put up in 1781. She decorated the six other small rooms with woodwork plainly moulded and painted in light colours. In the library[8] are four of the six corner cupboards made by Riesener for the Comtesse de Provence's dining room, which had occupied this site before.

The Dauphin's Apartment

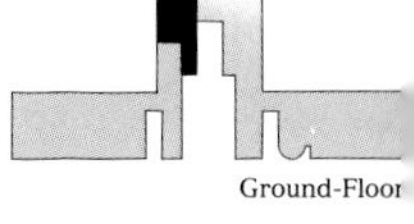

The Guardroom which led to the Dauphin's apartment is situated at the far end of the long suite of rooms. Thus the visit starts where it should normally finish.

The Library[9]

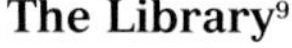

(6.99 m × 4.19 m × 5.05 m)

This graceful room served as a retreat and a study for Louis XV's son (fig. 103) and was later used by his own son, the future Louis XVI, when, as Dauphin, he lived in his mother's former apartment.

The panelling dates from 1755 and the angel-musicians in the cornice are a reminder that Louis XV's son enjoyed music, for he himself sung, played the organ and regularly took part in concerts of chamber music with his sisters. Four seascapes painted by Joseph Vernet (fig. 104) decorate the overdoors.

103

104

On the chest of drawers, made for this room by Criaerd, there is a Sèvres porcelain plaque representing the Battle of Fontenoy (11 March 1745) at which the Dauphin, then aged fifteen, was present. The flat-topped desk was made for Louis XV by Gaudreaux in 1744 and was later used by his son.

The Large Drawing Room[10]

(10.16 m × 10.11 m × 5.02 m)

Originally there were three rooms here: Monsieur's bedroom and drawing room and Madame's drawing room. They later served for Monseigneur who had them joined together in 1693 to make the one large room existing today (fig. 107). The decoration was renewed in 1747 for Louis XV's son, but only the chimneypiece and part of the wainscoting carved by Verberckt have been preserved.

To adorn the overdoors, the Dauphin had asked Nattier to portray his sisters Élisabeth, Henriette, Adélaïde and Victoire, with the attributes of the Four Elements. These pictures are today in the Museum of Sao Paolo (Brazil) and have been replaced by works of Charles-Joseph Natoire, brought from the princes' apartments, since vanished, at Versailles and Marly: *Telemaque on the Island of Calypso, Beauty kindling the Torch of Love, Diana resting* and *Bacchus and Ariadne.*

103
The Dauphin's Library

104
Joseph Vernet
Seascape, 1762

106

105

105
Jean-Marc Nattier
Madame Victoire,
1748

106
Jean-Marc Nattier
Madame Louise, 1748

107
The Dauphin's large
Drawing Room

107

108

109

108
Bernard van Rysenburgh
The Dauphin's Desk, 1745

109
Mancelle
Terrestrial and celestial Globe, 1781

The portraits of *Mesdames Adélaïde, Victoire* (fig. 105), *Sophie and Louise* (fig. 106) count among Nattier's most celebrated works. The last three were painted in 1748 at the Abbey of Fontevrault where the young princesses were brought up, and were offered by Louis XV to the Queen. The one of Madame Adélaïde was done the following year at the request of her elder sister, Madame Élisabeth, the Duchess of Parma.

The admirable flat-topped desk belonging to the Dauphin is the work of Bernard Van Rysenburgh (fig. 108). The seats by Georges Jacob come from Louis XVI's Gamesroom at the Château de St. Cloud. The celestial and terrestrial globe, enclosing a second one on which figure the emerged and underwater reliefs of the sea floor, was commissioned from Mancelle in 1781 by Louis XVI, who intended it for his son's education (fig. 109).

The Bedroom[11]
(10.11 m × 7.83 m × 5.20 m)

Formerly Monseigneur's Gold Room with a ceiling painted by Mignard, this is where Louis XIV's son displayed his collection of pictures. Later it became the Regent's study and he died here on 2 December 1723. Behind the end wall is a small room known as the "den" (le "Caveau").

In 1747 this room was enlarged and turned into a bedroom (fig. 110). Its entire decoration has been preserved: woodwork by Verberckt carved from drawings by Gabriel; a griotte marble chimneypiece with gilt bronze figures of Flora and Zephyr by Jean-Jacques Caffieri; overdoors painted by Jean-Baptiste Pierre representing *Juno asking Venus for her Belt* and *Juno deceiving Jupiter with Venus's Belt.*

On the mantlepiece is a marble bust of Marie Leszczynska attributed to Guillaume Coustou; in the alcove there are portraits by Louis-Michel Van Loo of the Dauphin's first wife, *Marie-Thérèse-Raphaelle de Bourbon,* Infanta of Spain, and her parents, King *Philip V* and Queen *Elisabeth Farnese.*

The Dauphin had commissioned a picture of a farm from Oudry, which is now in the Louvre. The copy exhibited here is due to Marie Leszczynska herself, for she was a pupil of this artist. She has signed it "Marie, Reine de France".

The beautiful library in red lacquer is the work of Van Rysenburgh (fig. 111); Marie-Josèphe de Saxe had one like it.

The alcove door covered with a curtain gives access to a staircase leading to the Queen's apartment, to a privy and to a bathroom[12] installed for the Dauphin, Louis XVI's son, in place of part of Monseigneur's "den".

The Second Antechamber[13]
(10.19 m × 7.02 m × 5.22 m)

Two thirds of this room correspond to Monseigneur's Mirror Room, one of the most sumptuous in his apartment. The intertwined monograms of the Prince and his spouse were inscribed on the inlaid parquet floor; the ceiling and walls were entirely covered with mirrors encased in frames inlaid with ebony, tin and copper reflecting the gems enriched with precious stones, the porcelain and rock-crystal placed on consoles of gilded wood. In 1747, the room was enlarged and its marvellous decoration disappeared, to be replaced by plain moulded panelling.

110

111

110
The Dauphin's Bedroom

111
Bernard de Rysenburgh
Red Lacquer Library, 1750

113

112

Here some of Jean-Marc Nattier's masterpieces are on display: the Queen *Marie Leszczynska in a Houserobe* (1748) (fig. 112), *Madame Élisabeth, Duchess of Parma in hunting Gear* (1760), her daughter *The Infanta Isabella* (1751), *The Dauphine Marie-Josèphe de Saxe* (1750), her eldest son *The Duc de Bourgogne* (1754) and *Madame Adélaïde tying Knots* (1756) (fig. 113). Between the windows hangs an enchanting sketch for the portrait of Madame Adélaïde disguised as Air, one of *The Four Elements* painted by Nattier for the Dauphin's Large Drawing Room.

The First Antechamber[40]
(8.60 m × 6.20 m × 5 m)

This room, lit by a large window looking on to Monseigneur's Court, gives access to the Dauphin's second antechamber. Here the visitor finds himself back in the apartment the main rooms of which he has already crossed.

The two small square windows also light indirectly the "King's Passage" which Louis XVI had made in 1775, so that his apartment communicated with that of the Queen. This is the passage she took to go to her Small Apartment. On the morning of 6 October 1789, Louis XVI rushed along it to fetch his children, while the Queen fled along the corridor on the first floor. The door on the left of the large window goes to a staircase leading to the King's second antechamber, called the Oeil-de-Boeuf Room.

Here are portraits of *Comte d'Angiviller*, Director of the King's Buildings, by Duplessis, *Maréchal de Castries* by Joseph Boze, and *Joseph Foulon*, Intendant General of the War and the Navy, who was hanged on the day of the Fall of the Bastille.

The Guardroom[41]
(11.20 m × 9 m × 5 m)

Installed in 1747, this was where the Grand Master of the King's Wardrobe had his apartment. It was then that the floor was lowered, together with that of the preceding room, to bring it to the same level as the other rooms in the Dauphin's apartment, so that this room is situated a little lower than the Marble Court reached by a flight of steps.

Above the fireplace there is a fine portrait of *Queen Marie-Antoinette* painted by Élisabeth Vigée-Lebrun in 1788 (fig. 114) and opposite, the portrait of the *Prince de Bauffrémont* by Adélaïde Labille-Guiard in 1791.

114

12
ean-Marc Nattier
ueen Marie eszczynska, 1748

13
ean-Marc Nattier
Iadame Adélaïde ring Knots, 1756

14
lisabeth Vigée-ebrun
ueen Marie-ntoinette, 1788

The Lower Gallery[14]

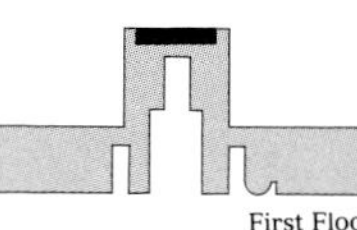

Built by Louis Le Vau in 1669, it consists in fact of two parallel galleries, separated by pillars supporting the springs of the arches and a stair tread compensating for the difference in level between the Old Château and the New Château. It is these galleries which provide a passage from the Marble Court to the gardens (fig. 115).

The main gallery, sometimes called the "peristyle" measures 36.60 m × 6 m × 5 m. It is covered by a three-centred arch and lit by nine bay windows which, originally were enclosed by gilt railings. They then supported a terrace of the same dimensions which vanished in 1678 when the Hall of Mirrors was created.

The Lower Gallery was demolished at the end of Louis XV's reign to form an apartment intended for his daughter Sophie. This apartment, greatly modified in Louis XVI's time, disappeared when the History Galleries were installed and it has not been possible to reconstitute it. The Lower Gallery has therefore been restored to its original state, so that the garden can be seen through the courtyard, which is what Louis XIV wanted. This is how Louis XV knew it for the greater part of his reign.

Work has revealed a decoration of trophies on the south wall, retained by draperies. In the niches between the windows are statues of *Apollo* by Jean Raon and *Diana* by Roger, executed in 1670 for this very spot. In the side alcoves a *Medici Venus* by Clérion can be seen, brought from the Bathing Apartment close by, and a *Flora* which once adorned the Comte de Toulouse's apartment.

115

116

117

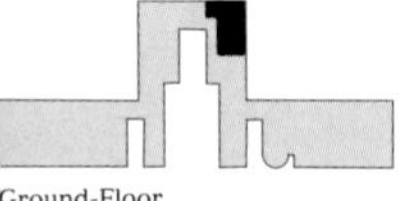

Ground-Floor

Madame Victoire's Apartment

This corresponds practically to the former Bathing Apartment; the decoration has almost entirely vanished.

The First Antechamber[15]

(8.00 m × 6.00 m × 5.10 m)

This is Louis XIV's former bathroom: the walls and floor were then covered with a mosaic of many-coloured marbles and a large octagonal bathing-pool in Rance marble, now in the Orangery, was placed here. First an inner room for the Comte de Toulouse from 1692 to 1724, then for the Comtesse de Toulouse from 1724 to 1750, and finally for Madame Adélaïde in 1752 and 1753, it became Madame Sophie's bedroom from 1755 to 1767. After this it was the Princess's First Antechamber until, in 1769, it was given to Madame Victoire.

Here are portraits of the *Comte d'Artois and his Sister Clothilde as Children* by Drouais, of the *Marquis de Marigny*, Madame de Pompadour's brother, by Tocqué (fig. 116) and a self portrait of *Louis-Michel Van Loo* (fig. 117). In this fine painting the artist, standing beside his sister, has depicted himself doing a portrait of their father Jean-Baptiste.

115
The Lower Gallery

116
Louis Tocqué
The Marquis de Marigny, 1755

117
Louis-Michel van Loo
Self Portrait

118

119

The other paintings evoke the life of the Princes of the Blood in the last years of Louis XV's reign. In *The Cup of Chocolate* (fig. 118), Jean-Baptiste Charpentier has represented the Comtesse de Toulouse with her son the Duc de Penthièvre and her grandchildren the Prince and Princesse de Lamballe and Mademoiselle de Penthièvre, the future Duchesse d'Orléans. Four charming paintings by Barthélemy Olivier recall the fêtes given by the Prince de Conti in his Château de l'Isle-Adam and in his Paris mansion in the Temple district. *The English Tea Party* is particularly worth noticing, in which young Mozart can be seen at the harpsichord (fig. 119).

Above the doors are portraits of two of Louis XV's ministers: the *Duc de Choiseul-Stainville* by Louis-Michel Van Loo and the *Duc de Choiseul-Praslin,* by Alexandre Roslin.

In 1756 Madame Adélaïde received this high-gloss chest of drawers made especially for her.

The Second Antechamber or Nobles' Room[16]
(7.73 m × 7.13 m × 5.10 m)

This used to be the bathroom with the floor and walls covered in marble. At the end, in an alcove framed in marble columns, was a sofa. It was from this time that shutters were added to the windows, beautifully decorated with dolphins and stalactite ornamentation.

This room then became the Comte de Toulouse's bedroom, then that of the Comtesse de Toulouse, after which it belonged to Madame Adélaïde and finally to Madame Victoire when she shared this apartment with her sisters Sophie and Louise. In 1767 the alcove was eliminated and the room became the Second Antechamber (fig. 120).

The wood panelling was probably done for Madame Victoire. The overdoors representing *The Fables of La Fontaine* were painted by Oudry for the Dauphin. Riesener's chest of drawers comes from the Nobles' Room belonging to the Comtesse d'Artois in the south wing. A Savonnerie screen after Blain de Fontenay, and a Chinaman clock with a Martin lacquer-like varnish completes the furnishing.

120

118
Jean-Baptiste Charpentier
The Cup of Chocolate, 1767

119
Barthélemy Ollivier
The English Tea Party with the Prince de Conti, 1766

120
Madame Victoire's Nobles Room

The Large Drawing Room[17]
(10.13 m × 10.10 m × 4.96 m)

This was first of all one of the large rooms in the Bathing Apartment, sometimes called the "Octagon Room", owing to the shape of the ceiling. At that time it was adorned with a painting by Houasse representing *Apollo and Daphne* and twelve figures in gilt *"métail"* symbolizing *The Months and the Signs of the Zodiac*. This lavish decor disappeared in 1763 at the request of Mesdames (Louis XV's daughters), and was replaced by an elegant decoration, a few traces of which still remain: the cornice, important fragments of the magnificent carved panelling by Verberckt and the fine griotte marble fireplace embellished with gilt bronzes (fig. 121).

The luxurious furniture was delivered in 1783 by Jacques Tilliard for the apartment of King Gustav III of Sweden, on the occasion of his stay at Versailles. The two small chests of drawers between the windows were made by Jean-François Leleu for the Duchesse de Bourbon's bedroom at the Palais Bourbon in Paris. *The Rape of Europa* clock is similar to the one adorning the mantlepiece at the time of Madame Victoire and the fire with lions comes from her drawing room at the Château de Bellevue. The Blanchet harpsichord is a reminder of the musical talent of this Princess who played "like a professional" and to whom the young Mozart dedicated, in 1784, his first six sonatas for harpsichord.

121

122

The portraits are of *Mesdames Sophie and Louise* by Drouais and of the *Duc and Duchesse de Parme*, while above the door are *Louis XV*, *Marie Leszczynska*, *Stanislas Leszczynski* and *Madame Infanta*.

The Bedroom[18]
(9.67 m × 9.13 m × 4.89 m)

This was the former Ionic antechamber in the Bathing Apartment, so-called because of the twelve marble columns decorating it. First the Second Antechamber of the Comte de Toulouse, then of the Comtesse de Toulouse, then of Madame Adélaïde and finally of the younger Mesdames, when in 1767 it became Madame Sophie's bedroom and in 1769 that of Madame Victoire (fig. 122).

The beautiful panelling is the work of Antoine Rousseau and the alcove hangings are in shadowed taffeta with the design of Madame Victoire's "summer furniture". In 1769 Péridiez finished making the two corner cupboards which were sold at the Revolution, when they went to Russia, then to England and were finally bought back in 1982.

The portraits are of *Madame Adélaïde* by Nattier, in 1758, of her brother *The Dauphin* and her sister-in-law *Marie-Josèphe de Saxe* by Jean-Baptiste Nivelon. The portraits of Mesdames Sophie and Louise, placed on the overdoors, are early copies by Drouais himself of his original pictures on display in the preceding room.

121
Madame Victoire's
large Drawing Room

122
Madame Victoire's
Bedroom

123

124

The Inner Room[19]
(6.80 m × 4.60 m × 5.02 m)

At the beginning this small elegant room formed a single room with the next two. It was the Doric vestibule of the Bathing Apartment, divided into three bays by two rows of Rance marble columns, which are still there behind the wainscoting. This vestibule was partitioned as early as 1724 to make two antechambers for the Comte and Comtesse de Toulouse. Her antechamber was in turn divided in 1767 to form this small drawing room and the library next door.

Antoine Rousseau was responsible for the admirable wood panelling, certain elements of which have been put back in place, together with the sérancolin marble fireplace (fig. 123). The chest of drawers made by Foullet arrived in 1768 for Madame Victoire's apartment. It bears an alabaster bowl which belonged to the Princess. The writing table was made by Levasseur for Mesdames at the Château de Bellevue.

The Library[20]
(7.76 m × 3.55 m × 2.42 m)

This used to belong to the next apartment until it was annexed to this one (fig. 124). It has a mezzanine floor on which the library extension is situated.

The cupboards contain books bound and stamped with the arms of Mesdames, a casket containing a collection of geographical maps which belonged to Madame Élisabeth, niece of Mesdames, some pieces of a coffee set in Sèvres porcelain with a Chinese decor, made for Madame Adélaïde in 1775, and a table bell in silver-gilt with the arms of Madame Victoire.

The small sloping desk was delivered to Madame Sophie or Madame Louise in 1760, on their return from Fontevrault Abbey. The chairs were part of Madame Victoire's furniture at the Château de Bellevue.

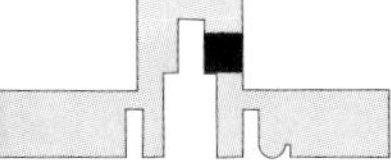
Ground-Floor

Madame Adélaïde's Apartment

Formerly this apartment was reached through an antechamber situated at the far end of the whole suite of rooms it contained. That is why we start our visit at the end of this series of rooms, contrary to the normal procedure.

The Inner Room[21]
(7.84 m × 4.60 m × 5.02 m)

This small room was created in 1724, by partitioning the Doric vestibule to serve as the Comte de Toulouse's Second Antechamber. Madame de Pompadour turned it into her private boudoir, decorating it with red lacquer panels. In those days the room was not so long and opened at the end on to a dark back room, at the top of Louis XV's private staircase.

The present arrangement dates from Madame Adélaïde, but only the carved panels above the doors still remain. They frame Jean-Baptiste Restout's paintings representing *The Four Seasons*, which came from the Château de Bellevue, where Mesdames resided (fig. 125).

123
Madame Victoire's Inner Room

124
Madame Victoire's Library

125
Madame Adélaïde's Inner Room

125

The chest of drawers, by Weisweiler, comes from the Comtesse de Provence's room in the south wing. The seats were made by Séné for the drawing room of the Duchesse d'Harcourt, wife of the tutor of Louis XVI's elder son. The terracotta statuettes are smaller copies of the statue of *Louis XV* and of the group of *Love embracing Friendship*, both made for the gardens of Bellevue. The oval portraits are those of Madame Adélaïde's nephews and nieces: *The Dauphin*, the future Louis XVI, and his brothers *The Comte de Provence* and *The Comte d'Artois*, all three by Louis-Michel Van Loo; his wife *The Dauphine Marie-Antoinette*; his sisters *Madame Clotilde* by Drouais and *Madame Élisabeth*.

The Bedroom[22]
(9.47 m × 8.95 m × 4.92 m)

This was the bedroom of the Comte de Toulouse from 1724 to 1737, then of the Duc de Penthièvre between 1737 and 1744, followed by the Duchesse de Penthièvre from 1744 to 1750. Then it became the Marquise de Pompadour's bedroom and she died here on 15 April 1764. It was meant to be the Dauphine Marie-Josèphe de Saxe's bedroom in 1766, but she died before being able to occupy it. Nevertheless, she lay in state on the bed here. From 1767 to 1769 it was Madame Victoire's bedroom and then, from 1769 to 1789, that of Madame Adélaïde (fig. 126).

127

126

128

The woodwork was probably made for the Dauphine in 1766, apart from the borders of the overdoors which may have been "leftovers" from the decoration of Madame de Pompadour's bedroom, used again to frame four pictures by Natoire of allegories of *Painting, Sculpture, Architecture* and *Music.*

In the alcove, its walls hung with a fabric resembling the "summer furnishing" of Madame Adélaïde, are portraits of *Louis XV* by Carle Van Loo and of *Mesdames Sophie and Louise* by Drouais. On the mantlepiece there is a fine bust of *The Dauphin*, Madame Adélaïde's brother, by Augustin Pajou (fig.127). The wonderful seating was made around 1770 by Nicolas-Quinibert Foliot and comes from the former Royal Furniture Store.

The Large Drawing Room[23]
(9.80 m × 7.80 m × 4.99 m)

Madame de Pompadour gave this room its present form and she had the fireplace in sérancolin marble installed. The rich panelling which adorned it has now completely vanished, but it has been possible to refit the cornice made for Madame Adélaïde (fig. 128). The small organ most likely belonged to this Princess, as well as the violon which "she played superbly".

Nattier had painted portraits of her elder sisters: *Madame Élisabeth, Duchesse de Parme* and *Madame Henriette playing the Bass-Viol* (fig. 129) and this one of Madame Adélaïde hung here. Above the door is a triple portrait of *Mesdames Victoire,*

126
Madame Adélaïde's Bedroom

127
Augustin Pajou
The Dauphin, Louis XV's Son,
c. 1765

128
Madame Adélaïde's Large Drawing Room

129

129
Jean-Marc Nattier
Madame Henriette playing the Bass Viol, 1754

130
The Hoquetons Room

Sophie and Louise by Drouais. On the mantlepiece stands a bust of *Madame Élisabeth*, the sister of Louis XVI and niece of Madame Adélaïde.

The Hoquetons Room[24]
(12.42 m × 8.75 m × 4.99 m)

This room was called "hoquetons" from the type of tunic worn by the Guards of the Grand Provost of the Royal Household, responsible for the maintenance of law and order within the Château. This room, where they were usually on duty, was given in 1672 a trompe-l'oeil decoration of trophies of arms and statues in the fake niches (fig. 130).

Madame de Pompadour had the room divided to make two antechambers which later served for the Dauphine, Madame Victoire and finally Madame Adélaïde, but which have not been restored.

Two statues stand in the recesses: a *Moor* in polychrome marble from the collections of the Borghese princes, and an admirable figure of a draped woman; the body is antique but the bronze head and arms are by Algardi, the celebrated XVIIth-century sculptor from Rome.

The staircase[25] , built by Louis-Philippe, has replaced the one which had enabled Louis XV to go straight down to his daughters' apartments. Together with the next rooms, it takes the place of the King's Grand Staircase, or Ambassadors' Staircase, built between 1678 and 1680. Covered with polychrome marbles and decorated by Charles Le Brun with allegorical pictures, this majestic staircase led to the King's State Apartment. In the reign of Louis XV, it was hardly ever used and the King had even had a small moveable theatre fitted up there. Its demolition in 1752 nevertheless deprived the Château of one of its most beautiful pieces of architecture. A very accurate model of it evokes its past splendour.

During Louis XVI's reign, the vestibule providing access to it and the small surrounding rooms were turned into a library and a lathe room for Madame Adélaïde, but they have not been restored.

The vestibule[27] is ornamented today with antique busts; in the first room[28] *Montesquieu* by Félix Lecomte, *Fontenelle* by Jean-Baptiste Le Moyne, *Voltaire* and *Diderot* by Jean-Antoine Houdon; in the second room are busts of the *Maréchal de Saxe* by Louis-Philippe Mouchy and *Dupleix* by Charles-Antoine Bridan.

The extraordinary clock on the theme of the Creation of the World was commissioned by Joseph-François Dupleix, director general of the French trading posts in India, who wished to offer it to an Indian prince: designed by Passemant, it was made in 1754 by the clockmaker Joseph-Léonard Roque and the bronzesmith François-Thomas Germain.

The following room[29] was formerly used as a warming-up room by the Captain of the Guards.

30

131

We may admire the magnificent portrait of *The Marquis de Sourches, Grand Provost of France* with his family, no doubt François-Hubert Drouais' masterpiece (fig. 131). Two pictures represent the wedding celebrations of the future Emperor Joseph II; in one of them three of his sisters are shown singing an opera by Metastasio and in the other, we recognize the Archduchess Marie-Antoinette, then aged ten, ballet-dancing with her brother Maximilian.

The extraordinary antique-style seats in carved mahogany are part of a set of furniture made by Georges Jacob around 1785 for Queen Marie-Antoinette's dairy at Rambouillet.

131
François-Hubert Drouais
The Marquise de Sourches and her Family, 1750

132
François-Hubert Drouais
Louis XV, 1773

133
Pierre Subleyras
Pope Benedict XIV, 1741

The King's Small Guardroom[30]
(9 m × 6 m × 2.85 m)

The main Guardroom of the King is found on the first floor at the entrance to his apartment. It protected the access to the King's Private Apartments. It was on leaving this room overlooking the courtyard that Louis XV was attacked and wounded by Damiens, on 5 January 1757.

On the mantlepiece stands a bust of *Louis Thiron de Crosne*, Lieutenant-General of the Police (1736-1794) sculpted by Augustin Pajou in 1788.

During the day, the lifeguards stored away their straw mattresses in the two closets on either side of five steps. On the right, at the top of these steps, the King's Grand Staircase[31] ended and this led to the King's inner rooms on the first floor and his Private Apartment on the second floor.

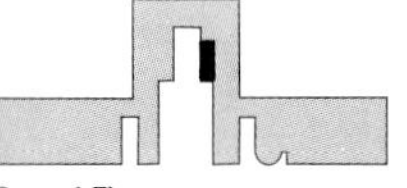

Ground-Floor

The Apartment of the Captain of the Guards

The important duties of the captain of the Lifeguards were assumed by four titularies, generally dukes and peers, who served in turn "by quarter" (for three months at a time). During his quarter, the current captain of the Lifeguards on duty occupied this lodging close to the small Guardroom.

The Large Drawing Room[32]
(6 m × 6 m × 4 m)

Some very fine portraits illustrating Louis XV's home and foreign policy have been assembled here: *The King at the End of his Life* by Drouais (fig. 132), *Pope Benedict XIV* by Pierre Subleyras (fig. 133), *The Dauphin in the Uniform of the regimental Colonel of the Dauphin-Dragons* by Alexandre Roslin (fig. 134), *The Prince of the Asturias*, future King Charles IV of Spain, by Raphaël Mengs, *The Abbé Terray* and *The Marquis de Marigny* by Roslin.

132

133

134

135

The Antechamber[33]
(6.40 m × 6.20 m × 4 m)

This room commemorates Louis XVI's accession to the throne. His portrait in royal regalia by Joseph-Siffrède Duplessis is surrounded by those of his brothers, the *Comte de Provence* and the *Comte d'Artois* by Drouais, and of his cousin the *Duc d'Orléans* by Callet. The three princes wear the robes of a knight of the Saint-Esprit Order. They are also seen in the large picture where Gabriel-François Doyen shows *The King receiving, on the Day after his Coronation, the Homage of the Knights of the Saint-Esprit, on 12 June 1775.*

136

134
Alexandre Roslin
The Dauphin in the Uniform of Colonel of the Dauphin-Dragons Regiment,
1765

135
Pompeo Batoni
The Bailli de Suffren,
1785

136
Joseph-Siffrède Duplessis
Louis XVI, 1776

137
Hubert Robert
The Gardens of Versailles, 1775

The Inner Cabinet[34]
(8 m × 2.40 m × 4 m)

This small room looks on to the Stag Court, around which the upper floors are occupied by the King's Small Apartment. The works exhibited here recall the decisive role played by France in the victory of the "insurgents" in the American War of Independence and the birth of the United States: portraits of *Louis XVI* by Callet, the *Bailli de Suffren* by Pompeo Batoni (fig. 135), the *Maréchal de Ségur* by Élisabeth Vigée-Lebrun; a bust of *La Fayette* by Houdon; gouaches by Van Blarenberghe representing *The Capture of Yorktown on 19 October 1781.*

The Bedroom[35]
(7.60 m × 6 m × 4 m)

This room is dedicated to the early years of Louis XVI's reign. There are portraits of *The King* by Duplessis (fig. 136), of *The Queen* by Gauthier-Dagoty, and of her sisters-in-law the *Comtesse de Provence* and the *Comtesse d'Artois*, and of the King's sister *Madame Clotilde* by Drouais. Hubert Robert's two famous pictures show *The Gardens of Versailles in 1775* (fig. 137) when Louis XVI ordered trees to be replanted. A picture by Francesco Casanova, the brother of the celebrated adventurer, represents *The Audience accorded to the Comte de Saint-Priest by the Sultan's Grand Vizir, on 13 March 1779.*

137

A gouache by Gautier-Dagoty shows *Marie-Antoinette in the Bedchamber of her State Apartment*; a canvas by Châtelet evokes the *Illumination of the Belvedere* at the Petit Trianon, on the occasion of a fête given by the Queen.

The next four rooms correspond to a Small Apartment that Marie-Antoinette had had arranged in 1784 in place of part of Madame Sophie's apartment (see p. 106).

The first room[36] has taken the place of several orderly rooms. The famous portrait of *Marie-Antoinette holding a Rose* was painted in 1784 by Élisabeth Vigée-Lebrun (fig. 138) to whom we also owe those of the *Duchesse d'Orléans* and of the *Comtesse de Ségur*. The portrait of *Madame Élisabeth*, the King's sister, is the work of Adélaïde Labille-Guiard (fig. 139), Madame Vigée-Lebrun's rival.

On the chest of drawers is a faithful copy of the necklace involved in the notorious "affair of the Queen's necklace". The visitor then passes to the upper part of the lower gallery. Copies of the celebrated statue of *The Dancing Fawn* stand in two opposite alcoves, one antique and the other of the XVIIIth century.

138

139

138
Élisabeth Vigée-Lebrun
Queen Marie-Antoinette, 1784

139
Adélaïde Labille-Guiard
Madame Élisabeth, 1788

140
The Marble Vestibule

40

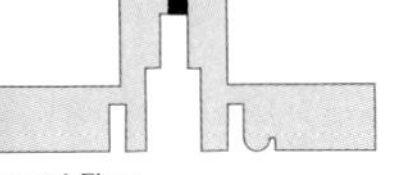
round-Floor

The Marble Vestibule[37]
(10 m × 8 m × 4.25 m)

Situated in the axis of the Château, beneath the King's bedroom, and opening on to the lower gallery, this vestibule was arranged in 1679 to ensure communication between the Marble Court and the gardens. It is adorned with sixteen columns and sixteen pilasters of Rance marble on a background of white veined marble (fig. 140).

In 1769, Madame Sophie, whose apartment occupied the site of the lower gallery, had part of the vestibule turned into a library. In 1784, this library became the central element of the Queen's Small Apartment. On the left it opened on to the bedroom[38] and on the right to the bathroom[39]. Both these rooms are shown to visitors during the conducted tour, as well as the Queen's inner rooms.

Returning to the upper part of the lower gallery, the visitor turns left, descends five steps and, leaving on his left a small staircase leading to the "King's Passage" on the mezzanine floor, he enters on the right the Dauphin's first antechamber.

The "History Galleries"

By creating a museum at Versailles in 1837, to commemorate "all the glories of France", Louis-Philippe wanted, by exalting their national history, to reconcile the French people sharply divided into four factions: the Legitimists who had remained faithful to Charles X, the Orleanists, partisans of the July Monarchy, the Republicans, attached to the ideals of the Revolution and the Bonapartists, nostalgic for the Napoleonic epic.

The conditions in which this new museum was created and its aims are recounted in the preface to the first catalogue. "To devote the former residence of Louis XIV to all the glories of France, to assemble therein all the great memories of our history, this was the immediate project conceived by His Majesty... The King ordered a search to be made in the Crown furniture stores and royal residences for all the paintings, statues, busts or bas-reliefs representing famous events or persons in our annals and at the same time, all the objets-d'art of a historical character... The same care was given to gathering together everything produced in the way of modern painting and sculpture. Yet all these collections were insufficient for His Majesty's project to materialize, for many great men or great events in our History were absent from this collection borrowed from diverse periods. The King filled this gap by commissioning from the most distinguished of our artists a considerable number of pictures, statues and busts intended to complete the magnificent ensemble of all the illustrations of France's history."

These commissions were no doubt the weak point in the royal plan, at least regarding the documentary value and historical accuracy of the works produced. That is why for the last one hundred years attempts have been made to weed out a certain number of indifferent copies or retrospective works. Henceforth only original documents are exhibited, that is to say, contemporary of the person or event to which they refer. The only exceptions to this rule are some of the pictures in the Crusades Room and the Battle Gallery which are significant examples of the approach to historical painting in the XIXth century.

These six rooms, together with some twenty more, devoted essentially to the First Empire and the July Monarchy, have kept their decoration chosen by Louis-Philippe. Thus they are especially interesting witnesses of the change in taste and of a particular moment in the history of museology.

The collections of the XVIIIth century are displayed in the princes' apartments which have recovered their original decoration. Everywhere else, efforts have been made to show the pictures and sculpture in a "palatial" setting, by a careful choice of wall hangings, furniture and objets d'art, thus avoiding any hiatus between the "History Galleries" and what remains of the former royal residence. The result is that a visit to these rooms, where portraits of the main figures of our history are exhibited, is the best way to prepare or complete the visit to the royal residence.

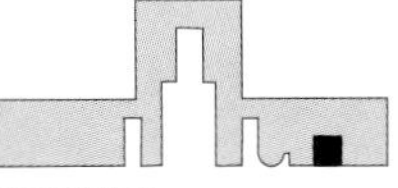

Ground-Floor

The Crusades Room

Conducted lecture tours (on request)

These five rooms were installed by Louis-Philippe on the site of several of the courtiers' apartments. They are reached through the ground-floor gallery in the North Wing, which is decorated with plaster casts of some of the gisants on the royal tombs in St. Denis Basilica.

The paintings in the Crusades Room were all commissioned by Louis-Philippe from the most celebrated historical artists of his day, to evoke the main episodes of the eight crusades. They are presented in a Neo-Gothic decor, rather incongruous at Versailles, but characteristic of the "troubadour" taste of the Romantic period. The window casements and the ceiling coffers bear the coats of arms of the most illustrious crusaders.

In the first room two pictures by Emile Signol represent *Crossing the Bosphorus in 1097* and *The Capture of Jerusalem on 15 July 1099*.

In the second room our attention is drawn to two works by Marius Granet: *Godefroy de Bouillon hangs the Trophies of Ascalon on the Arches of the Holy Sepulchre, in August 1099* and *The Chapter of the Order of the Templars held in Paris on 22 April 1147*.

The third room (fig. 141) has kept its original carved cedarwood door and the bronze mortar from the Hospital of the Knights of St. John of Jerusalem in Rhodes. These two remarkable mementoes, dating from the XVIth century, were offered to Louis-Philippe in 1836 by the Sultan Mahmoud II. Also displayed is the statue of *Philippe de Villiers de l'Isle-Adam, Grand Master of the Order of Malta*, which comes from the Temple Church in Paris. It was for this room that in 1840

141

Eugène Delacroix painted the famous *Entry of the Crusaders into Constantinople, on 12 April 1204,* today in the Louvre and replaced here by a copy. Among the other pictures worthy of notice are: *The Town of Ptolemais delivered to Philippe-Auguste and Richard the Lion-Heart, 13 July 1191,* due to Merry Blondel; *The Battle of Las Navas de Tolosa, on 12 July 1212,* by Horace Vernet; and *The Raising of the Siege of Malta in September 1565,* by Philippe Larivière.

In the fourth room we see two pictures by Rouget: *Saint Louis receives Envoys from the Old Man of the Mountain at Ptolemais in* 1251 *and* The Death of Saint Louis before Tunis on *25 August 1270.* In the fifth room there is a remarkable picture by Louis Gallait: *Baldwin, Count of Flanders, crowned Emperor of the Byzantine Empire at St. Sophia in Constantinople, 16 May 1204.*

On leaving the Crusades Room, the visitor finds himself face to face with the famous statue of *Joan of Arc,* the work of Princesse Marie d'Orléans, Louis-Philippe's second daughter.

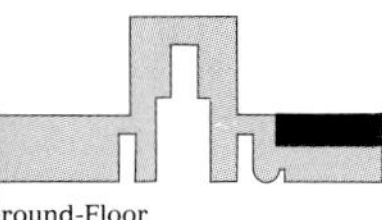

The XVIIth century Rooms

Unaccompanied visit

These rooms are situated on the ground and first floors of the North Wing, formerly called the New Wing, between the Chapel and the Opera. They look out on to the north ornamental garden and correspond to the apartments inhabited by members of the Royal Family and Princes of the Blood. These apartments were served by two galleries overlooking the inner courtyards and by a staircase in the centre of the wing; originally there were four on each floor, but they were reduced to three when the Opera was built.

They were demolished when the History Galleries were installed and practically nothing remains of the interior distribution and decoration, with the exception of two carved cornices in the sixth and seventh rooms. The central staircase likewise disappeared to make way for a room providing communication between the two groups of apartments. A new staircase was built in 1851 by the architect Questel at the far end of the suite.

The collections are displayed in chronological order and each room is devoted to a different theme.

The first eight rooms correspond to two apartments reached by two antechambers situated at each end and communicating through two small inner rooms. In the course of the XVIIIth century these two rooms were joined together to form a common antechamber for both apartments and their distribution was then reversed.

‹41
Ꞇhe Great Crusades
Room

‹42
Hermann Van der
Mast
*Ball given at the
Louvre to celebrate
the marriage
of the Duc de
Joyeuse*, 1581

142

The first room began as an antechamber and became an inner room when the distribution of the apartment was reversed. A few prints of the Château are on display.

The Wars of Religion and the Advent of the Bourbons

At first a large drawing room at the time of the Duc de Maine, this room later became the bedroom of this apartment.

The reign of Henri III is evoked mainly in three pictures: *Henri III received by the Doge Mocenigo at the Venice Lido, on 18 July 1574,* a sketch by Andrea Micheli, known as "Il Vicentino", for his picture in the Palace of the Doges (fig. 143); *Ball given at the Louvre on the Occasion of the Marriage of the Duc de Joyeuse in 1581,* attributed to Hermann Van der Mast (fig. 142); *Procession of the Army of the League, on 4 February 1593.*

The fine portrait of *Henri IV in Armour* (fig. 144) is framed by portraits of members of the royal family, among whom *Marie de Médicis,* and two small pictures representing two battles waged by the King.

Louis XIII appears, accompanied by allegorical figures of France and of Navarre, in a magnificent painting by Simon Vouet (fig. 145). Two sketches by Saint-Igny show *The King with Queen Anne d'Autriche on Horseback.*

143

143
Il Vincentino
Henri III received by the Doge Mocenigo at the Venice Lido, 18 July 1574

144
Artist unknown
Henri IV, 1610

145
Simon Vouet
Louis XIII between the Figures of France and of Navarre

144

145

The Reign of Louis XIII

This room began as a bedroom and later became a large drawing room.

The portraits are of *Louis XIII* on Horseback and the *Duchesse de Chevreuse as Diana*, both by Claude Deruet; *Cardinal de Richelieu* by Philippe de Champaigne; *The Dauphin*, the future Louis XIV, in the arms of his nurse; *The Dame Longuet de la Giraudière*, his first nurse; *Louis XIV on his Accession to the Throne, accompanied by his Brother the Duc d'Anjou and their Governess Madame de Lansac*. The bust of the young King is attributed to Jacques Sarrazin and his portrait is by an unknown artist (fig. 146).

Jansenism, Port-Royal and the Val-de-Grâce

Originally the inner rooms of two apartments stood here until the wall separating them was pulled down to form the present room which became a antechamber common to both lodgings.

The main figures of the Jansenist movement are represented here in a series of portraits, the most remarkable of which are: *Mère Angélique, Mère Agnès* (fig.147), *The Abbé de Saint Cyran* and the architect *Jacques Lemercier* (fig.148), all the work of Philippe de Champaigne. There are portraits of *Jacques Tubeuf*, Superintendant of Finance to the Queen Regent Anne d'Autriche, by Pierre Mignard and of *Pierre Séguier*, Chancellor of France. A small picture which comes from the Queen Mother's apartment at Val-de-Grâce Abbey, represents *Anne d'Autriche and her two Sons presented to the Trinity by Saint Benedict and Saint Scholastica*.

The Regency of Anne d'Autriche and the Peace of Westphalia

This room, which has preserved its carved cornice dating from the xviith century, was first a bedroom before becoming the great drawing room.

Round the equestrian portrait of the ten-year old *Louis XIV*, recalling his solemn entry into Paris, are those of *The Regent Anne d'Autriche* and *Cardinal Mazarin*. There is also the portrait of *The Grand Condé* by Juste d'Egmont, and several allegorical pictures among which an *Allegory of the Regency of Anne d'Autriche* by Laurent La Hyre painted in 1648, the very year in which the Peace Treaty of Westphalia was signed, bringing to an end the Thirty Years War.

The Royal Academy of Painting and Sculpture (1648)

This room was first a large drawing room and then a bedroom. It has kept its fine xviiith-century carved cornice.

The Royal Academy was founded in this same year of 1648 and we find here portraits of some of its founders: *Henri Testelin, Jean Nocret, Henri and Charles Beaubrun, Samuel*

146

147

148

146
Artist unknown
Louis XIV at the Time of his Accession to the Throne, 1643

147
Philippe de Champaigne
Mother Agnès Arnauld, 1662

148
Philippe de Champaigne
Jacques Lemercier, 1644

Bernard, Jacques Sarrazin, Philippe de Buyster and *Michel Anguier*. These portraits frame that of *The King* in his youth which adorned the Hall where the Royal Academy held its Sessions at the Louvre Palace.

The Peace of the Pyrenees (1659)

First of all an antechamber, this room was later made into an inner room.

The Peace of Westphalia had not put an end to hostilities with Spain. These were pursued for many years, marked by the alliance of France with Oliver Cromwell, the King's illness at Calais and the French victories at Valenciennes and Montmédy. A curious painted map recalls *The Siege of Valenciennes*, and an allegorical picture, attributed to Deruet and representing *The Judgment of Paris*, is an allusion to the peace settlement and Louis XIV's approaching marriage to his first cousin the Infanta Marie-Thérèse, the eldest daughter of the King of Spain, Philippe IV.

Louis XIV as a patron of the arts

This room occupies the site of the central staircase demolished at the command of Louis-Philippe to make it easier to visit the museum.

On either side of Jean Garnier's *Portrait of Louis XIV surrounded by the Attributes of the Arts, Sciences and Music* (fig. 149) are portraits of the most celebrated artists and writers of the day, in particular *Louis Lerambert* by Alexis-Simon Belle, *Louis Le Vau* and *André Le Nôtre* by Carlo Maratta (fig. 150),

149

Jules Hardouin-Mansart by François de Troy, and *Charles Couperin* by Claude Le Febvre.

The Creation of Versailles

This room contains a very important series of paintings (fig. 151) which enables us to follow all the transformations and embellishments carried out at Versailles from 1688 (Pierre Patel's picture) to 1722 (Pierre-Denis Martin's picture). The latter and those representing the Châteaux de Trianon, Marly, Fontainebleau and Meudon adorned the Princesse de Conti's dining room at the Château de Choisy. Four small paintings

49
ean Garnier
llegorical *Portrait of ouis XIV surrounded y the Attributes f the Arts, Sciences nd Music*, 1672

50
arlo Maratta
ndré Le Nôtre, 1678

51
harles Le Brun
he Second Conquest f Franche-Comté 1674), 1681

150

51

by Van der Meulen show the young King and his suite in front of the Châteaux de Versailles, Fontainebleau, St.-Germain and Vincennes.

This room and the two following ones take the place of an apartment which was always occupied by the Princes of the House of Conti.

The *Carrousel* of 1662

This famous *Carrousel* (tournament), which gave its name to a square in Paris, was organized by Louis XIV on 5 and 6 June 1662, in front of the Château des Tuileries, to celebrate the birth of the Dauphin which had occurred on 1 November 1661. The picture evoking this event here (fig. 152) gives a clear idea of the brilliant pomp of the Court of France in the early years of Louis XIV's personal reign.

On the wall hangings, reminiscent of the famous "Blue Room" at the Hôtel de Rambouillet, are portraits done by the Beaubrun brothers of the most famous beauties of the time. They flank two portraits, one of *Marie-Louise d'Orléans, Duchesse de Montpensier,* (called the "Grande Mademoiselle") *holding a Portrait of her Father, Gaston de France, Duc d'Orléans,* by Pierre Bourguignon, and the other by Antoine Matthieu of *Henrietta of England holding the Portrait of her Husband Philippe de France, Duc d'Orléans.*

152

153

154

The Royal Family around 1665

The portraits of *Louis XIV at the age of twenty-seven* by Charles Le Brun, of *Queen Marie-Thérèse* by Beaubrun, of the *Queen Mother Anne d'Autriche* by Nocret, of *The Prince de Condé and his Son the Duc de Bourbon* by Claude Le Febvre (fig. 153) surround a masterpiece by Le Brun, the preparatory drawing for his portrait of *Maréchal de Turenne* (fig. 154).

Amongst all these eminent characters we remark the elegant portrait of someone who has remained unidentified, but who passed for a long time as being the Superintendent Nicolas Fouquet.

152
Henri de Gissey
The Carrousel in 1662

153
Claude Le Febvre
The Prince de Condé and his son, the Duc de Bourbon, 1665

154
Charles Le Brun
Maréchal de Turenne, 1663

The Foundation of the Academy of Sciences (1666)

Originally this room belonged to an apartment which disappeared in 1768 when the Opera was built.

Testelin's great painting is the cartoon for a tapestry never woven, intended for the set on the *"History of the King"*. We see *Colbert presenting to Louis XIV the first Members of the Academy of Sciences.* In the background we catch a glimpse of the Observatory in the course of being built and, on the right, a map of the Deux-Mers Canal.

The fine portrait of *Jean-Baptiste Colbert,* by Claude Le Febvre (fig. 155) recalls the role played by the Minister in

155

the protection granted to the arts and sciences. His decisive action in favour of the reorganization and development of the Royal Navy is evoked in a picture representing *The Visit of his Son, the Marquis de Seignelay, to the Arsenal in Marseilles,* in November 1677.

We also remark the portrait by Philippe Lallemand of *Charles Perrault,* the author of the famous fairy-tales and one of the founder members of the Academy of Inscriptions and Humanities, as well as that of the *Cardinal de Bouillon, First Chaplain of France* by Jean-Baptiste Gaulli, called *"Le Baciccio".*

The Questel Staircase replaced in 1851 the Guardroom preceding the foyer of the Opera, situated at the level of the first landing. From this room a staircase led to a gallery on the first floor from which the King arrived.

The foyer door has a marble medallion on each side, representing *Louis XIV* and *Queen Marie-Thérèse*. On the first-floor landing there is a portrait of *The King, Protector of the Royal Academy*; it was painted in 1668 by Henri Testelin and intended to replace the one done twenty years earlier for the Session Hall of the Academy at the Louvre.

The War of Devolution and the Dutch War

This room is situated on the spot where the staircase linked the first-floor gallery behind the wall at the end to the Opera Guardroom.

156

The War of Devolution (1667-1688) was started by Louis XIV in support of the rights of succession of Queen Marie-Thérèse, née Infanta of Spain, to the Spanish Netherlands. The War of Holland (1672-1678) was waged to combat the threat of Holland's economic power.

Here are some of Adam Franz Van der Meulen's preparatory drawings for the great pictures intended to decorate the royal castles, a few of which are on display in this room and the next one. These sketches were also used by Charles Le Brun for the tapestries of the "History of the King" series.

The War of Devolution and the Dutch War (cont.)

This large room was once divided up and formed with the next one an apartment of three reception rooms.

The four pictures by Van der Meulen come from the Château de Marly (fig. 156). *The equestrian Portrait of Louis XIV* was painted by René-Antoine Houasse in 1672.

The bust of the Dauphin aged eighteen, by Coysevox, should be noticed, as well as that of *The King* by Jean Warin, placed on the Ambassadors' Staircase in 1678, the very year that the Peace of Nijmegen consecrated the victories of Louis XIV and the hegemony of France in Europe.

The bronzes placed in the angles are small copies of two marble groups commissioned for the gardens: *Pluto abducting Proserpine* by Girardon and *Boreas abducting Oreithyia* by Anselme Flamen.

155
Claude Le Febvre
Jean-Baptiste Colbert
1666

156
Adam-Frans van der Meulen
The Entry of Louis XIV into Arras, 30 July 1667

157

157
Nicolas Coustou
Jean-Baptiste Colbert
1708

158
Hyacinthe Rigaud
Martin Desjardins,
1683

159
Ferdinand Elle
Madame de Maintenon with her Niece, c. 1695

The Royal Households

The picture at the far end, the work of Etienne Allegrain, represents the *Château de St. Cloud* which belonged to Monsieur, the King's brother, and was destroyed at the end of the XIXth century. The other paintings come from the Hôtel of the Duc de Bourbon at Versailles and depict four of the most famous royal residences: *Vincennes, Trianon, Marly* and the *New Château of St.-Germain-en-Laye* where Louis XIV was born on 4 September 1638.

Fine busts of *Colbert* by Nicolas Coustou (fig. 157) and *Guillaume* de *Lamoignon,* First President of the Paris Parlement, by François Girardon. The hamadryad statue standing in the centre of the room is a replica in terracotta of the marble statue sculpted by Coysevox for one of the groves at Marly.

The Royal Academy of Painting and Sculpture

This room stands on the site of the central staircase of the wing.

An important series of portraits of artists can be seen, most of whom had taken part in decorating the royal châteaux. They are often presentation pieces (*"morceaux de réception"*) which new Academicians were obliged to offer to the Academy on their election. Part of this collection is today in the Louvre.

Next to the self-portraits of *Rigaud, Largillière* and *Antoine Coypel* are the following portraits: the sculptor *Martin Desjardins* (fig. 158), the iron-founders *Jean-Jacques and Jean-Baptiste Keller* by Rigaud; the artist *François de Troy* by Belle;

159

58

the sculptors *Jean Thierry* and *Nicolas Coustou* by Largillière; *François Giradon* by Gabriel Revel and *Guillaume Coustou* by Jacques-François Lyen.

La Marquise de Maintenon

The following rooms occupy the place of a double apartment: the first room, which used to open on to the gallery behind the wall at the end, was the antechamber of the first apartment.

The portrait of *Madame de Maintenon with her Niece* by Ferdinand Elle (fig. 159) and that of *Louis XIV holding the Plans for St. Cyr* both come from the Marquise's famous institution she had founded for the education of young girls of the nobility in reduced circumstances.

The portraits are of *The Dauphin* and of the *Marquis de Villacerf* by Pierre Mignard, of the *Comte de Pontchartrain* by Robert Le Vrac de Tournières and of *Mignard* by Hyacinthe Rigaud.

The Young Princes

Here we are in the main reception room of the apartment. The pictures exhibited are, for the most part, portraits by Pierre Mignard of *The King*, of *Madame de Maintenon*, of *Catherine Mignard*, the artist's daughter, and of two legitimized children of Louis XIV: *The Comte de Toulouse asleep* and *Mademoiselle de Blois blowing Bubbles* (fig. 160).

The room is dominated by one of Mignard's most celebrated works: a large picture representing *The Dauphin, his wife Marie-Anne-Christine de Bavière and their three Sons, the Duc de Bourgogne, the Duc d'Anjou and the Duc de Berry* (fig.162).

The Second Half of the Reign

This used to be the bedroom of the first apartment.

The Revocation of the Edict of Nantes (1685), *The Acceptance of the Will of Charles II, King of Spain* (1700) *and* The Congress of Baden (*1714*) are all evoked in these pictures, some of which are allegorical. Other paintings show scenes of the life at court: royal audiences, such as that of the *Prince Elector of Saxony at Fontainebleau* and that of *The Shah of*

160

161

Persia's Envoy, or the ceremony of the Royal Orders, with the badges on display in a showcase.

The most remarkable of all is the portrait of the *Marquis de Dangeau*, Grand Master of the orders of Saint Lazare and of Mount Carmel, by Hyacinthe Rigaud (fig. 161). The artist has succeeded in skilfully rendering the velvets and silks of the gorgeous costume, while expressing the fatuity and insignificance of the person himself.

The Princesses

Formerly this room was partitioned in length and breadth to form two inner rooms looking on to the gardens and several back rooms lit by the gallery on the other side of the wall at the end.

Portraits are assembled here of the Princesses whose beauty, grace and wit were to brighten Louis XIV's latter years: the King's two youngest daughters, the *Duchesse de Bourbon* and the *Duchesse de Chartres*, seen at the time of her marriage, by François de Troy; and the wife of his eldest grandson, the charming *Duchesse de Bourgogne*, in a large painting evoking the marriage ceremony on 7 December 1697, in the presence of the entire royal family.

162

160
Pierre Mignard
Mademoiselle de Blois, 1674

161
Hyacinthe Rigaud
The Marquis de Dangeau, 1702

162
Pierre Mignard
The Grand Dauphin and his Family, 1687

The Wars at the End of the Reign

This room used to be the bedroom of the second apartment.

The equestrian portrait of *Louis XIV* by Mignard is exhibited here, together with some portraits by Rigaud, that of the *King* and two masterpieces due to Largillière of the *Duc de Berry*, the King's third grandson (fig. 163) and of the *Comte du Puy Vauban*, the Marshal's nephew.

The famous portrait of *Louis XIV at the Age of sixty-eight*, a striking likeness done in wax by Antoine Benoist, is placed between the windows.

The Court of Versailles

This room occupies the place of the large drawing room and the antechamber of the second apartment.

Beside the portrait of the *Princesse de Conti*, eldest daughter of Louis XIV and a famous beauty, there is, above all, that of the King's sister-in-law, *Élisabeth-Charlotte de Bavière, Duchesse d'Orléans*, by Rigaud and opposite, that of his granddaughter *Marie-Adélaïde de Savoie, Duchesse de Bourgogne* (fig. 164) whose charm and elegance are skilfully caught by Jean-Baptiste Santerre.

163
Nicolas de Largillière
Charles de France, Duc de Berry, 1710

164
Jean-Baptiste Santerre
Marie-Adélaïde de Savoie, Duchesse de Bourgogne, 1709

165
Claude-Guy Hallé
The Audience granted to the Doge of Genoa, 15 May 1685, 1710

163

164

65

Antoine Coysevox is responsible for the bust of *Maréchal de Villars* and Nicolas Coustou for that of the *Marquis d'Argenson.*

The beautiful harpsichord, its case decorated with arabesques in the manner of Audran, is the work of Ruckers the Antwerp harpsichord-maker.

Claude-Guy Hallé has represented *The Audience granted by Louis XIV to the Doge of Genoa in the Hall of Mirrors on* 15 May 1685 *(fig.* 165). This large painting, a cartoon for a tapestry in the "History of the King" set, gives us a clear idea of the famous solid silver furniture which adorned the rooms in Versailles at the height of its splendour and enables us to imagine the long-vanished luxury of the State Apartments.

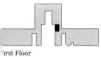

The XVIIIth century Rooms

'irst Floor

The collections of the XVIIIth century, illustrating the reigns of Louis XV and Louis XVI, from 1715 to 1789, are presented on the ground floor of the main building of the Château, in the apartments of the Dauphin, of the Dauphine and of Mesdames de France, as well as in the lodging of the captain of the Lifeguards.

The Hall of the States General

The Hall of the States General (fig. 166) is situated above the vestibule at the entrance to the museum. The only way in is by the Grand Staircase, and for this reason the Hall is not

166

included in the tour of the History Galleries. At the end of the *Ancien Régime*, this room served as a foyer for the theatre set up by Hubert Robert in 1786, in the well of the Grand Staircase which had not yet been completed. Louis-Philippe dedicated it to the history of the States General, from 10 April 1302 when they were convened for the first time by Philippe le Bel until 5 May 1789, when they met for the last time by order of Louis XVI. A frieze runs along the base of the vaulted ceiling in which Louis Boulanger depicts the procession of the deputies in the streets of Versailles, on the eve of the opening of this assembly which was to lead to the Revolution.

The Revolution, the Consulate and the Empire Rooms

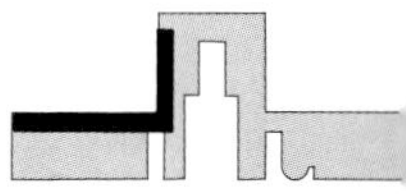

Conducted lecture tours

There are relatively few works here concerning the Revolution but, on the other hand, the Directory, the Consulate and the Empire are particularly well represented. Louis-Philippe having assembled in Versailles almost all the paintings

Napoléon had commissioned to celebrate his personal glory, the Napoleonic epic can be followed without interruption, with not a single important element missing, from the first campaign in Italy to the second abdication.

The collections are spread out in two groups of rooms which are visited in succession. The small and medium-sized works are exhibited in the attic called "de Chimay", above the Queen's State Apartment, and in the south attic along the arcade of the Battle Gallery; the large works are presented in the Coronation Room and on the ground floor of the south wing, beneath the Battle Gallery.

The Chimay and South Attics

We now go up to the Chimay attic taking the Queen's staircase and the stucco staircase prolonging it. From the tenth to the twenty-sixth room, the walls are hung with cotton fabrics copying the silk hangings commissioned by Napoléon for his various residences. Some of the furniture and objets d'art from the former imperial palaces accentuate the palatial character of this display.

166
The Hall of the States General

167
Jacques-Louis David
The Tennis-Court Oath, 1791

The Tennis-Court Oath

The painting covering the entire wall at the end is the only surviving portion of the huge picture intended to commemorate *The Tennis-Court Oath, 20 June 1789* (fig. 167) decorating the chamber of the National Assembly. Although unfinished, it remains nevertheless one of Louis David's great masterpieces.

A charming painting due to Hubert Robert evokes the *Fête of the Federation on the Champ-de-Mars, on 14 July 1790*,

167

while the picture by Jacques Berteaux represents the *Fall of the Château des Tuileries, on 10 August 1792*. The equestrian portrait of *Louis XVI* by Jean-Baptiste-Antoine Carteaux, shows the King as a constitutional monarch wearing the tri-coloured cockade.

The Cabinet of Drawings

The portraits of *Louis XVI* by Jean-Martial Fredou, of *Pierre-Ambroise Choderlos de Laclos* and of the composer *Etienne-Nicolas Méhul* by Joseph Ducreux, of *Mirabeau* and of *Robespierre* by Joseph Boze hang alongside the drawing by Jean-Michel Moreau representing *The First Session of the Assembly of Notables, on 22 February 1787* and David's preparatory drawing for the large painting of *The Tennis-Court Oath*.

Also by David is the portrait of *Marat assassinated* and designs for the "civic dress" of the Directory period. The *Battles of Lodi, Castiglione* and *Arcola* (10 May, 5 August and 17 November 1796) are represented in drawings by Carle Vernet.

The Convention

The room is dominated by David's famous painting representing *Marat assassinated in his Bath, on 13 July 1793*; it is an original reduced copy of the drawing we have just seen. Not far from here is the portrait of Marat's murderess, *Charlotte Corday*.

The tragic destiny of the royal family is eloquent in a portrait of *Louis XVI in Prison at the Temple*, painted during the Restoration by Henri-Pierre Danloux, and above all in two pastels due to Alexandre Kucharsky of the second Dauphin, the future *Louis XVII*, and *Queen Marie-Antoinette* (fig. 168). The latter, perhaps the most beautiful image of the sovereign, remained unfinished owing to the invasion of the Tuileries Palace on 10 August 1792.

A picture by Louis-François Lejeune represents the *Crossing of the Rhine at Düsseldorf by the French Army, on 6 September 1796*.

Society at the time of the Revolution

The fine portrait of the composer *Giovanni Paisiello* was painted in 1791 by Élisabeth Vigée-Lebrun, who also did that of the King of Poland, *Stanislas-Auguste Poniatowski*. Other portraits are of *Dominique Clément de Ris* and of his wife by Joseph-Benoit Suvée in 1795, and self-portraits of *Joseph Ducreux, Antoine-Jean Gros* and *Anne-Louis Girodet*.

Bagetti's watercolours

The topographer-engineer Giuseppe Pietro Bagetti followed General Bonaparte on his campaigns in Italy and Egypt

168

169

and brought back this valuable set of watercolours; their exceptional documentary interest is heightened by a poetical feeling for nature.

The Army of the Orient

These portraits of *Generals of the Army of the Orient* were drawn in charcoal by André Dutertre and their awkwardness does not deprive them of a certain charm.

The War at Sea

The portraits of *William Pitt* after Lawrence and of *Admiral Nelson,* as well as the bust of *Vice-Amiral Le Vassor de Latouche Tréville* by Jean-Martin Renaud recall the merciless struggle against France led by England, ruler of the seas. Jean-François Hue's painting represents the *Combat of the French Corvette* La Bayonnaise *against the English Frigate* The Ambush *on 14 December 1798.*

At the end of the room hangs the famous portrait of *General Bonaparte on the Bridge of Arcola* (fig. 169) which Gros exhibited at the *Salon* in 1801.

168
Alexandre Kucharsky
Queen Marie-Antoinette, 1792

169
Antoine-Jean Gros
General Bonaparte at Arcola, 1796

Society at the time of the Directory and emigration

Some sketches by François Gérard and Louis Gauffier evoke the elegant, carefree society during the Directory. In one showcase the sword of a member of the Directory is displayed, together with a magnificent shotgun made at the arms factory installed at Versailles by Boutet and offered to Barras by the City of Paris. The bust of *Jean-Marie Pichegru,* Commander General and the President of the *Conseil des Anciens* (upper body of the legislative Assembly), by François Masson in 1797.

Emigration is dealt with in the portraits painted by Danloux of the *Comte d'Artois,* Louis XVI's brother, and of his sons the *Duc d'Angoulême* and the *Duc de Berry,* and by two pastels portraying the *Prince de Condé,* head of the Princes' Army, and his grandson, the *Duc d'Enghien,* shot on 21 March 1804 in the moat at Vincennes. A drawing by Etienne Tafanelli depicts *The Meeting at Mittau, on 4 June 1799 of Louis XVIII with his niece Madame Royale*; and a picture by Jean-Claude Tardieu entitled *The Pretender presents the* "Rosière" *with a Wreath of Roses at Mittau.*

The First Italian Campaign

This room, situated above the Queen's bedroom, together with the three following ones, takes the place of a courtier's apartment. From the windows there is an incomparable view over the south wing, the south ornamental garden, the Swiss Pool and the hills of Satory.

Round the bust of *Bonaparte* by Charles-Louis Corbet are some paintings depicting the main feats of arms of this military expedition which was to ensure the young General's reputation: *The Battle of Lodi on 10 May 1796 by Lejeune; The Battle*

170

171

of Rivoli on *14 January 1797* by Louis-Albert Bacler d'Albe (fig. 170); *The Surrender of Mantua on 2 February 1797* by Hippolyte Lecomte; *The Fall of Ancona on 9 February 1797* by Didier Boguet; and *General Bonaparte receiving Prisoners on the Battlefield* and *An Army Hospital* by Nicolas-Antoine Taunay.

The Egyptian Expedition

Lejeune's pictures recall three of the main victories of this campaign: the *Battle of the Pyramids on 21 July 1798, The Battle of Mount Tabor on 16 April 1799* and *The Battle of Aboukir on 25 July 1799*. François-Henri Mulard painted *General Bonaparte giving a Sabre to the military Chief of Cairo*, and Taunay, *General Bonaparte at the Battle of Nazareth in April 1799*.

70
ouis-Albert Bacler
'Albe
he Battle of Rivoli,
4 January 1797

71
ndrea Appiani
eneral Desaix, 1800

A fine portrait of *General Desaix* by Andrea Appiani (fig. 171) is worth seeing. As for *Charles Letourneur*, he has been represented by Jean-Baptiste Desoria in his offical attire as member of the Directory.

The Second Italian Campaign

The famous episode of *Crossing the St. Bernard Pass* is evoked in several pictures, among them that of Taunay which deserves particular attention, owing to its romantic character.

One of David's most celebrated works shows *The First Consul crossing the Alps on 20 May 1800* (fig. 172). The General had asked David to present him as "a serene figure on a fiery steed".•David made five versions of this work; the one pre-

172

sented here is his personal copy which he kept in his atelier until his death, after which it belonged to Napoléon III. The picture is reproduced on one of the Sèvres porcelain vases placed in the corners of the room.

The Entry of the French Army into Naples, on 21 January 1799 was painted by Jean-Jacques Taurel, *The Battle of Marengo, 18 June 1800* is due to Lejeune and *The Entry of the French Army into Genoa, on 24 June 1800* is by Jean-François Hue.

The preparation for the invasion of England is told in *The Visit of Napoléon to the Encampment at Boulogne in July 1804* by Hue and in *The Distribuion of Crosses of the Légion d'Honneur at Boulogne, on 16 August 1804* by Philippe-Auguste Hennequin. A third picture, representing *A Naval Battle*, by Louis-Philippe Crépin, is exhibited in the next room.

173

The Consulate

This period is evoked in two large pictures: *The Agricultural Show in Lyon, on 26 January 1802* by Nicolas-André Monsiau (fig. 173), imbued with a very delicate sense of colour, and *The Entry of the First Consul into Antwerp, on 18 July 1803* by Mathieu Van Brée.

As for the portrait of *Jean-Baptiste Belley*, deputy of St. Domingue, this is one of the most beautiful works of Girodet (fig. 174).

174

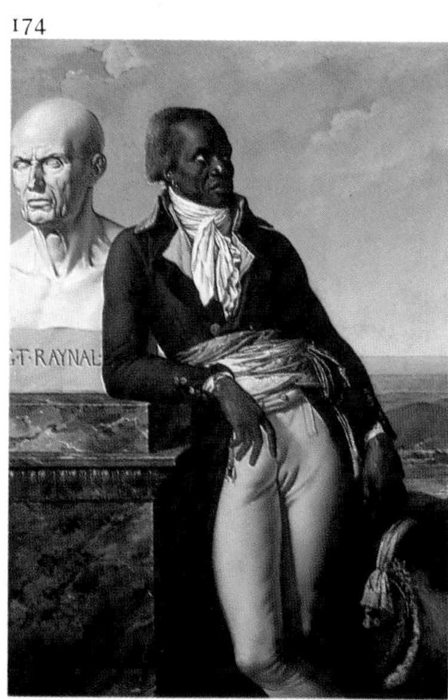

172
Jacques-Louis David
The First Consul crossing the Alps, 20 May 1800

173
Nicolas-André Monsiau
The Agricultural Show in Lyon, 26 January 1802, 1808

174
Anne-Louis Girodet
Jean-Baptiste Belley, 1797

The Second Cabinet of Drawings

Two fine gouaches by Jean-Baptiste Isabey recall *The Visit of the First Consul to the Sévène Brothers' Factory at Rouen on 2 November 1802* and *The Visit of the Emperor to the Oberkampf Factory at Jouy on 20 June 1806.*

The Signing of the Concordat between France and The Holy See by the First Consul, 15 July 1801, is evoked by Gérard; *The Signature by the Pope, 15 August 1806* was done in the same year by J.B. Wicar.

Five drawings by David are studies for the huge pictures of the *Coronation* and the *Distribution of Eagles* we saw in the Coronation Room. A drawing by Innocent-Louis Goubaud represents *The King of Rome at Notre-Dame on 10 June 1811*.

A few steps lead to a passage beyond the Coronation Room where engravings after drawings by Isabey, taken from the *Coronation Book*, are displayed.

175
Jacques-Louis David
Pope Pius VII, 1805

176
Robert Lefèvre
Pauline Bonaparte, Princess Borghese, 1806

177
François Gérard
Maréchal Murat, 1804

The Imperial Family

The portrait of *Pope Pius VII* (fig. 175), in which David reveals rare psychological insight, is surrounded by those of most of the members of the imperial family: *Napoléon I* by Gérard and *The Empress Joséphine* by François-André Lethière, both in coronation robes; the Emperor's father, *Charles Bonaparte*, painted retrospectively by Girodet; his mother, *Madame Mère* by Gérard; his uncle *Cardinal Fesch* by Charles

175

Meynier; two of his brothers, *Joseph, King of Spain* by Wicar and *Jérôme, King of Westphalia* by François Kinson; his three sisters *Elisa, Grand Duchess of Tuscany* by Lethière, *Pauline, Princess Borghese* by Robert Lefèvre (fig. 176), *Caroline, Queen of Naples* by Élisabeth Vigée-Lebrun; his brother-in-law *Joachim Murat* by Gérard (fig. 177); and his sister-in-law *Marie-Julie Clary, Queen of Spain* by Lefèvre.

Busts of *Louis*, King of Holland, by Pierre Cartellier, of *Joseph*, of *Jérôme*, of *Elisa*, of her husband *Félix Bacciochi* and of *Camille Borghese*.

The Third Coalition (1805)

This room is just above the 1792 Room.

The pictures evoke the campaign in 1805 which ended with the brilliant victory at Austerlitz: *The Surrender of Ulm, on 20 October 1805*, by Berton and Thévenin; *Napoléon enters Münich*, on *24 October* by Taunay; *Napoléon visiting a Bivouac before the Battle of Austerlitz on 1 December* by Lejeune.

The pictures representing *The Emperor interviewing the Duke of Württemberg and the Prince of Baden* were commissioned to decorate the Trianon Gallery.

Portraits of *Maréchal Ney, Duc d'Elchingen*, by Meynier, and of *Maréchal Bernadotte, Prince of Pontecorvo*, by Kinson. A fine bust of *Prince Eugène*, son of Joséphine, by Pierre Chinard (fig. 178).

177

76

178

The Campaigns of Prussia and Poland (1806-1807)

This room takes the place of the dome of the Princes' Staircase.

A campaign lasting three weeks, marked by the victories at Jena and Auerstädt, wiped out the Prussian army and opened the gates of Berlin to Napoléon, where he made his entry on 26 October 1806; this event is commemorated in Meynier's picture, whereas that of Marie-Nicolas Ponce-Camus recalls the *Visit of the Emperor to the tomb of Friedrich II.*

178
Pierre Chinard
Prince Eugène, 1806

179
Louis Ducis
The Terrace of the Château de St.-Cloud

180
François Gérard
Madame Bonaparte, 1808

181
François Gérard
Madame Récamier, 1805

179

The following winter finds Napoléon in Poland, where he receives *An Embassy from the Shah of Persia,* recalled in a painting by Mulard. The victories at Eylau, Danzig and Friedland put an end to the war. The Emperor and Tsar Alexander I meet at Tilsit. Napoléon returns to France and a picture by Louis Ducis shows him with his nephews and nieces on *The Terrace of the Château de St. Cloud* (fig. 179).

Three paintings commissioned for the Trianon Gallery recall *Interviews of the Emperor with the former Elector of Mainz, now Prince Primate, and with the Grand Duke of Würtzburg;* as well as *The Entry of Napoléon into Dantzig on 25 May 1807.*

The portraits of the *Maréchal* and of the *Maréchale Lefebvre, Duc and Duchesse de Dantzig* are worthy of attention.

The room is adorned with three Sèvres porcelain vases, one with a tortoiseshell background and the other two with a blue background.

Sketches by Gérard

This room and the following ones are situated at the level of the arcade in the Battle Gallery and above the Stone Gallery continuing it.

Here the major part of the precious collection of François Gérard's sketches is presented. In fact they are not so much preparatory sketches, but rather smaller copies made by the artist himself of his great portraits, now dispersed in museums and private collections. Gérard always kept these small pictures in his atelier. On his death in 1837, his widow sold them to Louis-Philippe for the museum at Versailles.

180

181

Much freer in treatment than the final pictures (these "sketches" prepared respectively for the portrait of *Murat*, already seen, and for those of the *Empress Marie-Louise* and of *Regnaud de Saint-Jean d'Angely*, which we shall see later, can be compared with the definitive versions), these paintings have the charm and vivacity of improvisation. They form, in any case, an unrivalled gallery of portraits of the elegant society and of the Court from the Directory to the Restoration: *Madame Bonaparte at Malmaison* (fig. 180), *Madame Récamier* (fig. 181, now at the Musée Carnavalet), *The Emperor and the Two Empresses*, the brothers, sisters, brothers-in-law and sisters-in-law of Napoléon, the ladies of the imperial court, sovereigns of allied or enemy countries, the marshals and ministers.

The 1808 Room

A large picture that Gros had left unfinished represents *Napoléon decorating some Artists at the Salon in the Louvre, on 20 October 1808*: the Emperor is seen presenting awards to Gros, the Empress Joséphine and Queen Hortense, David, Girodet, etc.

Gros also painted the two equestrian portraits of Jérôme, King of Westphalia and his wife Catherine von Württemberg. Busts of *Napoléon* (fig. 182) and *Joséphine* by Houdon, and of *Prince Eugène*, son of the Empress and Viceroy of Italy, by Giovanni-Battista Comolli.

The Administration of the Empire

In his portrait (fig. 183) by Robert Lefèvre, the Emperor is surrounded by most of his ministers, particularly *Comte Daru, Minister of State*, by Gros, *Savary, Duc de Rovigo, Min-*

182

183

ister of the General Police, by Lefèvre, and *Comte de Montalivet, Minister of the Interior*, by Regnault.

A picture by Goubaud represents *The Deputation of the Roman Senate offering its Homage to Napoléon on 16 November 1809*. The scene takes place in the Throne Room of the Tuileries Palace, Louis XIV's former bedroom. Two Sèvres porcelain vases with a chrome green background stand on each side. On the right is a portrait of *Jérôme and Catherine, King and Queen of Westphalia*, by Kinson.

The Austrian Campaign (1809)

The two large paintings represent *The Last Moments of Maréchal Lannes at Essling, on 22 May 1809*, by Florent Bourgeois and *Napoléon ordering a Bridge to be thrown across the Danube at Ebersdorf to allow him to cross over to the Island of Lobau, in June 1809*, by Ludovico Venuti. Other pictures evoke *Crossing the Bridge of Landshut, on 21 April*, by Louis Hersent, *The Fall of Ratisbon, on 23 April*, by Charles Thévenin, and *Napoléon bivouacking on the Battlefield of Wagram, on the Night of 5 to 6 July*, by Adolphe Roehn.

Portraits of *Maréchal Lannes, Duc de Montebello*, by Jean-Charles Perrin, and of *Maréchal Oudinot, Duc de Reggio* by Lefèvre.

182
Jean-Antoine Houdon
Napoléon I, 1808

183
Robert Lefèvre
Napoléon I, 1806

The Empress Marie-Louise and the King of Rome

The Battle of Ebersberg, 4 May 1809 was painted by Taunay and *The Bombardment of Vienna, on 11 and 12 May* is the work of Bacler d'Albe. These two events brought about the fall of Vienna.

The following year Napoléon married the Archduchess Marie-Louise; the wedding scene is depicted in several paintings, in particular *The Imperial Retinue arrives in the Tuileries Gardens, on 2 April 1810* (fig. 184) by Etienne-Barthélemy Garnier who has succeeded in rendering in great detail the splendour of the costumes, uniforms and carriages, as well as the *Religious Wedding Ceremony in the Square Salon of the Louvre*, by Georges Rouget. Two paintings by Van Brée recall the sovereigns' visit to Antwerp, a month after the marriage.

The famous portrait of *The Empress holding the King of Rome in her Arms*, by Gérard (fig. 185) is framed by two charming little pictures: *The King of Rome* by Gérard and *The Empress gazing at her Son asleep*, by Joseph Franque.

Portraits of *Comte Regnaud de Saint-Jean d'Angely* (fig. 186) who attended the council meeting at which the dissolution of the Emperor's first marriage was decided (this painting in sober colours is of one of Gérard's principal masterpieces), of *Maréchal Berthier, Prince of Wagram and of Neufchâtel*, who represented *Napoléon at the marriage by Proxy in Vienna*, by Jacques-Augustin Pajou, and of *Madame Mère*, grandmother and godmother of the King of Rome, by Lefèvre.

184

85

186

187

84
tienne-Barthélemy
arnier
he Imperial Retinue
rrives in the
uileries Gardens,
April 1810

85
rançois Gérard
he Empress Marie-
ouise with the King
f Rome, 1813

86
rançois Gérard
omte Regnaud de
aint-Jean d'Angely,
808

87
obert Lefèvre
aron Vivant Denon,
808

Literature, the arts and sciences

Three large paintings portray: the poet *Jacques Delille*, by Danloux, the manufacturer *François-Bernard Boyer-Fonfrède and his Family* by François-André Vincent; and *Alexandre Lenoir*, who saved a great number of ancient monuments from destruction during the Revolution, by Pierre-Maximilien Delafontaine.

Among the other portraits, we remark above all those of the following people: *The Vicomte de Chateaubriand* by Girodet, *The Baroness de Staël*, after Gérard, and their friend, *Madame Récamier*, by Eulalie Morin; *Vincent Arnault*, Perpetual Secretary of the French Academy by Vincent, *Madame Arnault* by Regnault; the poet *Jean-François Ducis*, by Gérard; *The Baron Vivant Denon, Director General of Museums* (fig. 187), and the architect *Charles Percier*, by Lefèvre; the musi-

188

cians *Pierre-Joseph Zimmermann* by Gros and *André-Ernest-Modeste Grétry*, by Lefèvre; *The Marquis de Laplace*, mathematician and astronomer, by Paulin Guérin; *Antoine-Auguste Parmentier* by François Dumont; the *Comtesse Regnaud de Saint-Jean d'Angely* by Appiani.

The Spanish War (1807-1813) and the Russian campaign **(1812)**

The long, cruel war in Spain is the subject here of many pictures: *The French Army crossing the Sierra de Guadarrama in December 1808*, by Taunay; *The Battle of Somo-Sierra, 30 November 1808*, the *Assault on the Monastery of San Engracia at Saragossa*, 8 February 1809, the *Battle of Chiclana, 5 March 1811*, the *Battle of Guisando, 11 April 1811*, all four by Lejeune; *The Defence of the Castle of Burgos, in October 1812* by François-Joseph Heim.

On the other hand, the Russian campaign, which was to toll the knell of the Empire, is represented by only two paintings, one of which is *The Battle of the Moskova on 7 September 1812* by Lejeune fig. 188.

Portraits of *Général Duroc, Duc de Frioul, Grand Marshal of the Imperial Household*, by Gros, *Maréchal de Marmont, Duc de Raguse* by Paulin Guérin, *Lieutenant Général, Comte de Ségur* by Gérard, *Baron Dominique Larrey, Chief Surgeon of the Imperial Guards* by Guérin.

188
Louis-François Lejeune
The Battle of the Moskova, on 7 September 1812 (detail)

189
François-Dominique Milhomme
General Lazare Hoche, 1808

The End of the Empire

The two official portraits of *Napoléon* and *Marie-Louise* by Lefèvre date from 1812. They are surrounded by those of *Général and Comtesse Walter* by Lefèvre and by *Général and Comtesse Legrand* by Gros.

Saying Farewell at Fontainebleau is shown in a reduced copy of Horace Vernet's famous picture. Ambroise-Louis Garneray painted the *Return from the Island of Elba, 28 February 1815*.

Busts of *Tsar Alexander I* by Lorenzo Bartolini and the *Empress Marie-Louise* by Paolo Triscornia.

The Napoleonists (*"Napoléonides"*) in exile

The bust of *Napoléon* wreathed in laurels is surrounded by portraits of *Louis, ex-King of Holland*, painted in Rome in 1815 by Carl-Christian Vogel, of *Louis and his eldest Son Napoléon-Louis* after Wicar, of *Charlotte Bonaparte*, daughter of Lucien, by Jean-Pierre Granger, and of *Prince Federico Bacciochi*, second son of Elisa, by Barbara Krafft in 1819.

The visitor descends to the ground floor by the Provence Staircase, so called because, on the eve of the Revolution, it led to the apartments of the Comte and Comtesse de Provence, Louis XVI's brother and sister-in-law.

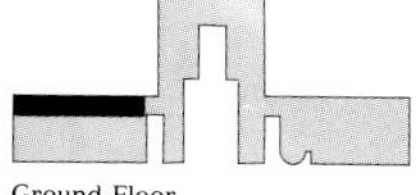
Ground-Floor

Ground floor rooms in the South Wing

General Hoche

This room is devoted to Lazare Hoche, born in Versailles on 24 June 1768. A sergeant in the French Guards in 1789, he defended Louis XVI when the Château was invaded on 6 October, before becoming one of the most brîlliant military chiefs of the Revolution. He died at the age of twenty-nine on 19 September 1797.

The statue, executed in Rome in 1808 by François-Dominique Milhomme (fig. 189), represents him nude as a hero of Antiquity, holding in his hand a "volumen" (scroll); it is then as peacemaker rather than as conqueror that he is shown here. Yet the armchair on which he is seated is adorned with a Victory between the figures of the Rhine and the Moselle which were the scenes of his most glorious feats of arms.

The four bas-reliefs, sculpted in 1799 by Simon-Louis Boizot, were intended to ornament a commemorative monument at Weissenthurm. They represent *The Attack on the Lines at Wissembourg, 26 December 1793, The Battle of Neuwied, 18 April 1797, The Fall of Fort Penthièvre at Quiberon, 21 July 1795* and *The Pacification of the Vendée in 1796*.

The visitor now crosses the lower gallery of the South Wing and reaches the Princes' Staircase. This gallery is adorned with statues and busts representing famous figures of the Revolution and the Empire. We remark in particular the statues of *Général de Custine* by Moitte, *Pichegru* and *Louis Bonaparte* by Cartellier, *Joseph Bonaparte* by Delaistre, *Prince Eugène* by Ramay, *Portalis* by Deseine, *Général Cafarelli* and the *Consul Lebrun* by Masson, *Tronchet* and *Général Dugommier* by Chaudet.

In the middle of the gallery, facing the centre vestibule, stands a statue of *Minerva* by Cartellier, that Louis-Philippe had placed in one of the recesses of the Hall of Mirrors. The doors on either side lead to the Congress Room, built after 1875 to house the Chamber of Deputies, while the Senate was to sit at the Opera House. In fact it has never served for anything else but meetings of the Congress, when the Senate and the Chamber hold a joint assembly, formerly to elect the President of the Republic, today to revise the Constitution.

Before reaching the Princes' Staircase, the visitor enters on the left the suite of rooms devoted to the Revolution, the Consulate and the Empire, occupying the ground floor of the south wing, where the large-sized pictures are exhibited. These rooms have kept the decoration chosen by Louis-Philippe, in particular the ornamental panels of historical scenes inscribed in gold grisaille arabesques, placed near the windows.

The first six rooms correspond to two apartments in which, during the *Ancien Régime*, the princes of the House of Condé usually resided. It was in one of these that King Gustav III of Sweden stayed when he visited Versailles in May 1784.

The First Italian Campaign (1796)

Colonel Rampon defending the Redoubt of Monte Legino, on 10 April 1796 by René Berthon; the *Assault on the Castle*

190

190
Hippolyte Lecomte
Attack on Madame Bonaparte's Carriag[e] on the Banks of Lak[e] Gardia, 1806

91

191
Anne-Louis Girodet-Trioson
The Revolt in Cairo, 21 October 1798, 1810

of Cossaria, 13 April by Taunay; the *Death of Général Causse at Dego on 16 April* by Mulard.

The *Attack on Madame Bonaparte's Carriage on the Banks of Lake Gardia, in August 1796* by Hippolyte Lecomte (fig. 190); *Général Augereau on the Bridge of Arcola, 15 November* by Thévenin; the *Battle of Arcola, 17 November,* by Bacler d'Albe.

The Battle of the Pyramids

The Italian Campaign ended with the *Peace Preliminaries signed at Leoben on 17 April 1797,* depicted here by Lethière.

The Expedition to Egypt began with the *Entry of Général Bonaparte into Alexandria, 1 July 1798,* commemorated in Guillaume-François Colson's painting. In the picture opposite, Gros shows *Bonaparte haranguing the Army before the Battle of the Pyramids, on 21 July.*

The Revolt in Cairo

The dramatic violence of the *Revolt in Cairo, 21 October 1798,* the celebrated picture by Girodet-Trioson (fig. 191) contrasts with the tranquil lyricism and the Orientalism of *Pardoning the Cairo Rebels on 23 October 1798* by Pierre-Narcisse Guérin.

Général Kléber succeeds Bonaparte at the head of the Army of the Orient but, on 14 June 1800, he is assassinated by a fanatic. His portrait by Antoine Ansiaux, is surrounded by those of *Six Egyptian Sheiks,* painted by Michel Rigo.

The busts of *Général Joubert* and of *Julien,* Bonaparte's aide-de-camp, are both due to Boizot.

The Consulate

The coup d'Etat of 18 Brumaire an VIII (9 November 1799) provoked the fall of the Directory and the advent of the Consulate. This is evoked in François Bouchot's painting representing *Général Bonaparte at the Council of the Five-Hundred at St. Cloud, 19 Brumaire* (10 November).

A few months later came the victory of Marengo; in the *Death of Général Desaix at Marengo, 14 June 1800*, Jean Broc, a pupil of David, paints one of the most faithful and moving portraits of the First Consul.

Four years later, the Empire is proclaimed and one of the first ceremonies presided over by the new Emperor is the *First Distribution of Crosses of the Légion d'Honneur in the Invalides Church, 14 July 1804* depicted here by Jean-Baptiste Debret.

The Proclamation of the Empire (18 May 1804)

Owing to the size of certain pictures, it has been difficult to exhibit them in chronological order.

Georges Rouget, one of David's best pupils, was responsible for the painting showing *Napoléon, in the Gallery at the Château de St. Cloud, receiving the Senatus-Consult who proclaims him Emperor of the French*; around the Emperor we see the Empress Joséphine, her daughter Hortense and her sister-in-law Caroline and, among the senators, Talleyrand and Lacépède.

The coronation takes place in Notre-Dame in Paris on 2 December and, on 8 December, *Napoléon receives in the Louvre the Deputies of the Army after his Coronation*. Gioacchino Serangeli has situated the scene in one of the rooms of the former summer apartment of Anne d'Autriche, which has become the Antiquity Gallery, and at the end the famous group *Laocoon*, from the Vatican, can be seen.

War however soon broke out again and *Napoléon haranguing the 2nd Corps of the Grand Army from the Bridge of Lech near Augsburg on 12 October 1805* is represented in Claude Gautherot's picture.

The Third Coalition (1805)

Napoléon rendering Homage to misfortunate Courage, in October 1805, by Debret. *Maréchal Ney gives back their Flags, found in the Arsenal at Innsbruck, to the Soldiers of the 76th Infantry Regiment, on 7 November* by Meynier, *The Surprise Attack on the Bridge over the Danube on 14 November* by Guillon-Lethière.

92

The Napoléon Vestibule

The Doric architecture of this vestibule, situated in the centre of the wing, has barely changed since Louis XIV; the bas-reliefs above the doors date however from Louis-Philippe.

Statues of *Napoléon I* by Ruxthiel in 1836 and of the *Empress Joséphine* by Vital-Dubray in 1857.

The following rooms correspond to two apartments occupied in Louis XIV's time by two of his daughters, the Princesse de Conti and the Duchesse de Bourbon and, at the end of the *Ancien Régime* by the Children of France and their governess.

The Victory of Austerlitz (2 December 1805)

Napoléon receiving the Keys of the City of Vienna, 13 November 1805 by Girodet; *Napoléon issuing Orders before the Battle of Austerlitz, 2 December* by Carle Vernet (fig. 192) and the *Interview between Napoléon and the Emperor Francis I at Sarutschitz, 4 December* by Gros.

Between the windows stands the vase commemorating the battle of Austerlitz, made in 1806 at the Sèvres Manufactory. It is an imitation of the Greek vases with red figures on a black background.

92
:arle Vernet
Iapoleon issuing
)rders before the
ßattle of Austerlitz,
December 1805,
808

The Fourth Coalition (1806-1807)

The Senate receives the Flags taken at Elchingen, 1 January 1806, by Jean-Baptiste Regnault; *Napoléon receives Deputies from the Senate at the Royal Palace in Berlin, 19 November* by René-Théodore Berthon; and, on the end wall, *Napoléon on the Battlefield at Eylau, 9 February 1807*, a copy by Jean-Baptiste Mauzaisse of Gros's picture exhibited in the Louvre.

The Interview at Tilsit (July 1807)

Napoléon receives the Queen of Prussia at Tilsit, 9 July 1807 by Nicolas Gossé; *Napoléon decorating a Soldier of the Russian Imperial Guards, 9 July* by Debret; and *The Emperor and the Tsar taking Leave of each other at Tilsit, 9 July* by Serangeli.

The Spanish War (1808) and the Fifth Coalition (1809)

Two dramatic scenes evoke the capitulation of Madrid: *The Ultimatum, 3 December* by Carle Vernet and *The Surrender of Madrid, 4 December* by Gros.

A few months later, the Austrian campaign began, which was to lead to the fall of Vienna. It is depicted here by Meynier: *Napoléon visiting the Wounded on the Island of Lobau on the Danube, after the Battle of Essling, 23 May 1809.*

The Imperial Court

Two pictures relate episodes of the Austrian campaign: *Napoléon haranguing the Bavarian and Württemberg Troops at Abensberg, 20 April 1809* by Debret; and *Napoléon wounded during the Assault on Ratisbon, 23 April* by Gautherot.

The splendour of the court at the Tuileries Palace is evoked in the large picture at the end of the room and by the sumptuous furniture.

193
Jean-Baptiste Regnault
The Wedding of Prince Jérôme and Princess Catherine of Württemberg, 22 August 1807, 181[illegible]

193

194
Jacob-Desmalter
Stand in the
Emperor's large
Drawing Room in the
Tuileries, 1813

195
Antonio Canova
Pope Pius VII, 1805

Jean-Baptiste Regnault painted the *Wedding of Prince Jérôme to Princess Catherine de Württemberg, 22 August 1807* (fig. 193). The Emperor is seen with the Empress Joséphine and all the members of the imperial family.

The three stands in ebony and gilt bronze, with figures of War and Peace applied on silvered plaques (fig. 194), were made in 1812 by Jacob Desmalter for the Emperor's large drawing room at the Tuileries Palace where, since the preceding year, two great torches in engraved bronze by Thomire stood. The bust of *Pope Pius VII* by Antonio Canova (fig. 195) also adorned this large room.

The Birth of the King of Rome and the Court of Elisa

The Marriage of Napoléon and Marie-Louise, Archduchess of Austria, on 2 April 1810 by Georges Rouget, is a considerably enlarged copy of the small picture we have already seen. It was Rouget too who painted the *Birth of the King of Rome, 20 March 1811*, or rather the moment when *Napoléon presents his Son to the Grand Dignitaries of the Empire. Elisa, Grand Duchess of Tuscany and her Court* appear in the great picture painted in 1813 by Pietro Benvenuti (fig. 196). The scene takes place in Florence – the Cathedral is visible in the background – and Canova presents the bust of the Princess which he had just finished, a copy of which is on display close to the painting.

The Marengo Room

We have already explained that the huge dimensions of certain pictures sometimes prevented Louis-Philippe from respecting their chronological order. This is the case in particular with the room installed in the former apartment of the governess to the Children of France and entirely devoted to the events of 1800.

The Crossing of the Great St. Bernard Pass by the French Army on 20 May is depicted by Thévenin, and the *Death of Desaix at Marengo on 18 June* by Regnault.

A large picture by Carle Vernet of the *Battle of Marengo* occupied the entire end wall; unfortunately it has been removed and replaced by a staircase leading to the apartment of the president of the National Assembly, which is none other than that of the Comtesse de Provence, Louis XVI's sister-in-law.

This staircase is at present flanked by the portraits of *The First Consul* by Jean-Baptiste Greuze painted in 1801 and by that of his brother-in-law *Charles-Emmanuel Leclerc*, Pauline Bonaparte's first husband, commander in chief of the army in Saint Domingue, by Kinson.

196

Opposite hangs a copy made by a pupil of David of the portrait of *Bonaparte crossing the Alps,* of which we have already seen one of the originals.

The beautiful Sèvres porcelain vase with bronzes by Thomire evokes the marriage of Napoléon to Marie-Louise; unfortunately though, the Emperor's face was obliterated during the Restoration. The four candelabras in metal plate painted to imitate malachite come from the Château de Saint-Cloud.

Once again the visitor crosses the Hoche Room, and goes along the whole length of the gallery as far as the Princes Staircase, leaving by the Princes Peristyle. Turning left he comes to the gardens. If though he wishes to continue the visit of the History Galleries, he should take the covered passage on the right, cross the Royal Court and enter by the vestibule which will take him straight to the Chapel Vestibule.

The XIXth Century Rooms

Second Floor

These rooms are devoted to the Restoration, the July Monarchy, the Second Empire and the Third Republic. Situated in the north wing they are divided into two groups: the first group comprises seven rooms on the first floor (called the African, Crimean and Italian Rooms) reserved for large canvases: these rooms are at present being renovated and are therefore closed to the public. In the other group, situated on the attic floor, small and medium-sized paintings are exhibited in twenty-one rooms (visit with guide on special request).

Access to the north attic floor is by the Questel staircase, at the extremity of the north wing.

197.

96
ietro Benvenuti
'lisa, Grand Duchess f Tuscany and her 'ourt, 1813

197
Horace Vernet
King Louis-Philippe I and his Sons in front of the Château de Versailles, 1846

198

199

200

198
Hippolyte Lecomte
Interview between Louis XVIII and Princess Caroline of the Two Sicilies, 15 June 1816, 1817

199
Louis Ducis
Louis XVIII watches the Return of the Army from Spain, 2 December 1823, 1824

200
Louis-François Lejeune
Entry of Charles X into Paris, 6 June 1825, 1825

201
François Gérard
The Duc and Duchesse de Berry and their Children, 1820

202
Antoine-Jean Gros
The Duchesse d'Angoulême, 1817

The Restoration

The pictures evoke happy and tragic events of the Restoration period: the *Interview of Louis XVIII with Princesse Caroline of the Two Sicilies in the Forest of Fontainebleau on 15 June 1816* by Hippolyte Lecomte (fig. 198); *Last moments of the Duc de Berry, 14 February 1820* by Alexandre Menjaud; *Louis XVIII watching from the central Balcony of the Tuileries Palace the Return of the victorious Army from Spain, 2 December 1823* by Ducis (fig. 199); *Charles X arriving at Notre-Dame, on his offical Entry into Paris, 27 September 1825* by Gosse; *Entry of Charles X into Paris after his Coronation, 6 June 1825* by Lejeune (fig. 200); *Laying the Foundation Stone of the Monument to Louis XVI, 3 May 1826* by Joseph Beaume.

The Royal Family

An important series of portraits of members of the Royal Family and the Princes of the Blood are assembled in his room: *Louis XVIII* by Guérin; *Comte d'Artois as Colonel General of the Carabineers,* the *Duc and Duchesse de Berry and their Children* (fig. 201), *Charles X in his Coronation Robes,* all four pictures by Gérard; the *Duc d'Angoulême* by Kinson, the *Duchesse d'Angoulême* by Gros (fig. 202); *Louis-Philippe, Duc d'Orléans and his two elder Sons, the Duc de Chartres and the Duc de Nemours* by Louis Hersent; the *Duchesse d'Orléans* after Gérard; *Mademoiselle and the Duc de Bordeaux* by Hersent.

201

202

Military expeditions during the Restoration

The Spanish Expedition is evoked in the *Capture of the Entrenchments before El Corogna, 15 July 1823* by Lecomte and the *Battle of Puerto de Miraverte, 30 September* by Eugène Lami. The Greek Expedition is conjured up, particularly in the *Naval Battle of Navarino, 20 October 1827* by Ambroise-Louis Garneray and the Algerian expedition in the *Attack on Algiers from the Sea, 29 June 1830* by Théodore Gudin.

The political world and the literary and artistic circles

A remarkable collection of portraits grouped around that of the *Duchesse de Berry* by Thomas Lawrence (fig. 203) ena-

203

204

205

206

bles us to recall to memory the most celebrated politicians, writers and artists of the first half of the century. Particular attention should be paid to *Lamartine* by Gérard (fig. 204), *Royer-Collard* by Géricault, *Paul-Louis Courier* by Ary Scheffer, *Alexis de Tocqueville* by Chassériau (fig. 205); *Casimir Périer* by Hersent, *Lamennais* by Paulin Guérin, *Lacordaire* by Louis Janmot, the *Baron Gérard* by Lawrence, *Charles Baudelaire* by Emile Deroy, *Manuel, Stendhal,* etc.

Les Trois Glorieuses

The events of the July Revolution on 27, 28 and 29 July 1830, which was to cause the end of absolute monarchy and the abdication of Charles X, are evoked here in several pictures, among them the *Storming the Hôtel de Ville, on 28 July* by Amédée Bourgeois (fig. 206); *Attack on the Barracks on the Rue de Babylone, on 29 July* by Jean-Abel Lordon; *Arrival of the Duc d'Orléans at the Palais-Royal, on the evening of 30 July* by Jean-Baptiste Carbillet after Horace Vernet.

203
Thomas Lawrence
The Duchesse de Berry, 1825

204
François Gérard
Alphonse de Lamartine, 1831

205
Théodore Chassériau
Alexis de Tocqueville, 1850

206
Amédée Bourgeois
Storming the Hôtel de Ville, 28 July 1830, 1830

August 1830

Two paintings by François-Joseph Heim show the *Delegates from the Chamber of Peers and the Chamber of Deputies presenting the Duc d'Orléans with the Act summoning him to the Throne* and *The 1830 Charter, at the Palais-Royal on 7 August 1830*. A work by Gosse recalls the *Visit of Queen Marie-Amélie to those wounded during the July Insurrection, at the Bourse Ambulance Station on 25 August*.

Political and military events

The National Guard celebrating the King's Birthday in the Courtyard of the Palais-Royal, on 6 October 1830 by François

Dubois; *The National Guard bivouacking in the Courtyard of the Louvre during the Trial of Charles X's Ministers, on the Night of 21-22 December* by Jean Gassies; *Louis-Philippe refuses the Belgian Crown offered to his Son the Duc de Nemours, on 17 February 1831* by Gosse; *The Surrender of the Dutch Garrison of Antwerp Citadel, on 24 December 1832* by Eugène Lami; *Fieschi's Attempt to assassinate the King, 28 July 1835* by Eugène Lami.

Portraits of *Louis-Philippe* by Horace Vernet and of *Queen Marie-Amélie accompanied by her two younger Sons, the Duc d'Aumale and the Duc de Montpensier* by Hersent.

Louis-Philippe I and his Family

Portraits of the royal family have been grouped together in this room, including those of *The King, the Queen,* their five sons, the *Duc d'Orléans, Duc de Nemours, Prince de Joinville, Duc d'Aumale and Duc de Montpensier* with their wives, their three daughters, *Princesse Louise, Princesse Marie and Princesse Clémentine,* with their husbands, and finally, *Madame Adélaïde,* the King's sister. All these portraits are due to Franz-Xavier Winterhalter or to his atelier, with the exception of the one of the *Duc d'Orléans,* painted by Jean-Dominique Ingres.

Our attention should focus above all on those of *The King* (fig. 207), *The Queen* (fig. 208), *Madame Adélaïde, The Duchesse d'Orléans holding her eldest Son, the Comte de Paris, in her*

207

208

209

Arms, and of the *Duc de Nemours* and the *Duc de Montpensier* by Hersent.

Weddings and Baptisms of the Princes

A series of pictures commemorate some happy events in the family life of Louis-Philippe: *Marriage of Princesse Louise to Léopold I, King of the Belgians, at the Château de Compiègne, on 9 August 1832* by Court; the *Marriage of the Duc de Nemours to the Princess of Saxe-Coburg-Gotha at the Château de St. Cloud on 27 April 1840* by Philippoteaux; the *Baptism of the Duc de Chartres in the Tuileries Chapel on 14 November 1840* by Marius Granet; the *Baptism of the Comte de Paris at Notre-Dame on 2 May 1841* by Hippolyte Sebron; the *Marriage of the Duc de Montpensier to the Infanta Marie-Ferdinande in Madrid on 10 October 1846* by Karl Girardet. Another work by Granet should be mentioned, that of *Louis-Philippe conferring the cap on the Cardinal de Cheverus in the Tuileries Chapel, 10 March 1836*. Among the portraits exhibited, that of the *Duc d'Orléans*, eldest son of Louis-Philippe, is one of Ingres's masterpieces (fig. 209). Those of the *Princesse de Joinville* and of the *Comte d'Eu*, eldest son of the Duc de Nemours, by Winterhalter, as well as the charming picture of the *Comte de Paris and the Duc de Chartres in the Park at Claremont in 1849* by Alfred de Dreux, are all worth admiring.

07
ranz-Xavier
Vinterhalter
ing Louis-Philippe I,
839

08
ranz-Xavier
Vinterhalter
ueen Marie-Amélie,
842

09
ean-Auguste-
ominique Ingres
erdinand-Philippe
'Orléans, Duc
'Orléans, 1843

The Policy of National Reconciliation

Louis-Philippe, anxious to reconcile the French in the cult of their past history, made two positive decisions: to create the Museum at Versailles dedicated to "all the glories of France", and to organize the return of Napoléon's ashes.

The first of these resolutions is recalled here in several paintings, among which: *Louis-Philippe visiting the Battle Gallery, 10 June 1837* by Heim; *the Royal Family in front of the Statue of Joan of Arc in the Galleries at Versailles, in 1839* by Auguste Vinchon; *Louis-Philippe and Marie-Amélie visiting the great Crusades Hall in the Company of the King and Queen of the Belgians, in July 1844* by Prosper Lafaye. Portraits of *Charles-François Neveu*, responsible for transforming the Château into a museum, by Hersent, and *Marius Granet*, first curator of the Museum as such.

The return of the ashes is conjured up by the *Transfer of the Remains of Napoléon I on Board the* Belle-Poule, *15 October 1840* by Eugène Isabey, and by the *Funeral of the Emperor Napoléon, 15 December* by Jacques Guiaud.

The "Entente cordiale"

The improved relations with England, the "entente cordiale", are marked by two visits to France by Queen Victoria and the reception of Louis-Philippe into the Order of the Garter.

The Queen of England's first visit is depicted in several paintings by Eugène Lami: *Arrival at Le Tréport on 2 September 1843; Arrival at the Château d'Eu; Reception in the private Drawing Room at the Château d'Eu, 3 September* (fig. 210);

210

211

212

210
Eugène Lami
Reception for Queen Victoria in the private Drawing Room at the Château d'Eu, 3 September 1843, 1843

211
Edouard Dubufe
Empress Eugénie, 1854

212
Edouard Dubufe
Princess Mathilde, 1861

Concert given in the Guise Gallery, 4 September; the *Charabanc Ride, 3 September*. Isabey also represents *Louis-Philippe conducting Queen Victoria aboard the Royal Yacht in Le Tréport Bay, 7 September 1843* and, a year later, *Louis-Philippe disembarking at Portsmouth, 8 October 1844*.

Portraits of *Queen Victoria, Prince Albert*, the *Duchess of Kent*, the Queen's mother, and *Louis-Philippe wearing the Garter*, all four by Winterhalter.

The Second Empire

The revolution of February 1848 is evoked in a painting by Adolphe Leleux, *The Watchword*, and the Second Republic with two works by Ary Scheffer, the portraits of *Lamartine* and of *François Arago*.

The Second Empire is brought to life again in the portraits of the imperial family: *Napoléon III* and *Empress Eugénie* by Winterhalter, *The Empress* (fig. 211) and *Princesse Mathilde* (fig. 212) by Edouard Dubufe. The splendours of the court are evoked in the famous painting by Jean-Léon Gérôme commemorating the *Reception of the Siamese Ambassadors in the Ballroom at the Château de Fontainebleau, 27 June 1861* (fig. 213). Literature and the arts are present in the portraits of *Alfred de Musset* by Charles Landelle and *Charles Gounod* by Ary Scheffer, and in two pictures: *The Dames-Sociétaires of the Comédie Française in 1855* by Faustin Besson and the *Rehearsal of the "Flute Player" in the Atrium of Prince Napoléon's Pompeian House, in 1861* by Gustave Boulanger.

213

The Italian Campaign (1859)

The Battle of Montebello, on 20 May was painted by Philippoteaux, while Eugène Guiraud has depicted the *Triumphal Return to Paris of the Army from Italy, 14 August.*

Portrait of *Napoléon III* by Hippolyte Flandrin in 1861 (fig. 214).

Poland subdued

In this small room the busts of some of the most celebrated people of the XIXth century have been assembled. They surround the statue sculpted by Antoine Etex in 1841, which is a moving *Allegory of the Subjugation of Poland.*

The Mexican Expedition and the War of 1870

The Mexican Campaign is depicted in two paintings by Jean Adolphe Beaucé : *The Fall of San Xavier Fort, 29 March 1863* and *the Expeditionary Corps enters Mexico, on 10 June.*

214

The Franco-Prussian War is conjured up in a remarkable series due to Alphonse de Neuville which includes the *Battle of Champigny, 2 December 1870* (fig. 215) and *Bivouac outside Le Bourget, on 21 December.*

215

213
Jean-Léon Gérôme
Reception of the Siamese Ambassadors in the Ballroom at the Château de Fontainebleau, 27 June 1861, 1864

214
Hippolyte Flandrin
Emperor Napoleon III, 1861

215
Alphonse de Neuville
Battle of Champigny, 2 December 1870, 1881

The Third Republic

Benjamin Ulmann has immortalized the session on 16 June 1877 of the Chamber of Deputies at Versailles, during which Thiers was hailed as the *Liberator of the Land.*

Léon Bonnat is the author of some fine portraits of *Cardinal Lavigerie, Victor Hugo* (fig. 216), *Thiers, Comte de Montalivet* and *Léon Gambetta,* which count among his most significant works. His manner is in striking contrast to that of Jean-François Raffaelli's painting of *Georges Clemenceau making a Speech at an Election Campaign Meeting in 1885.*

The End of the Century

Marcel Baschet has done a painting of *The Critic Francisque Sarcey at his Daughter Madame Adolphe Brisson's House in 1893.* The Franco-Russian alliance is mainly recalled in two large pictures: *Arrival of the Russian Fleet at Toulon, 13 October 1893* by Paul Jobert, and *Review at Bétheny in Honour of Tsar Nicolas II, 21 September 1901* by Albert Dawant.

216

217

218

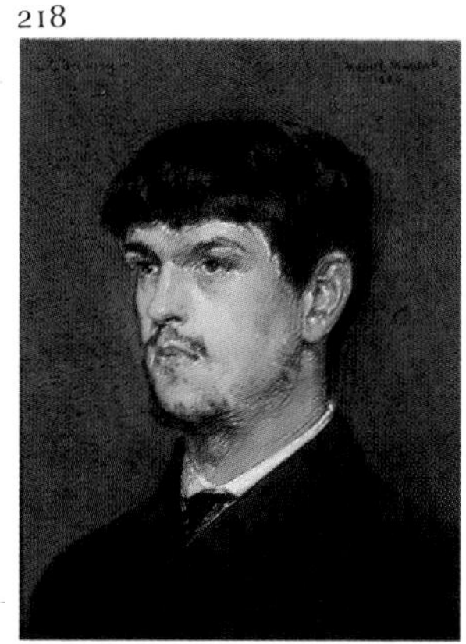

Portraits of *Alexandre Falguière* and *Alexandre Dumas the Younger* by Bonnat, of *Gabriel Fauré* by Ernest Laurent, of *Stéphane Mallarmé* by Auguste Renoir (fig. 217) of *Joris-Karl Huysmans* by Jean-Louis Forain and of *Claude Debussy* by Baschet (fig. 218).

The "Great War"

The History Galleries end by evoking the First World War with portraits of *Maréchal Foch* by Jean Patricot, of *Albert I, King of the Belgians* by Isidore Opsomer, of *President Raymond Poincaré* by Baschet and of *Georges Clemenceau* by François Cogné, together with a painting by Herbert A. Olivier representing *The Supreme Interallied Council in Session at the Palais de Trianon at Versailles, in July 1919*.

16
éon Bonnat
ictor Hugo, 1879

17
uguste Renoir
téphane Mallarmé,
890

18
larcel Baschet
laude Debussy, 1885

The Gardens

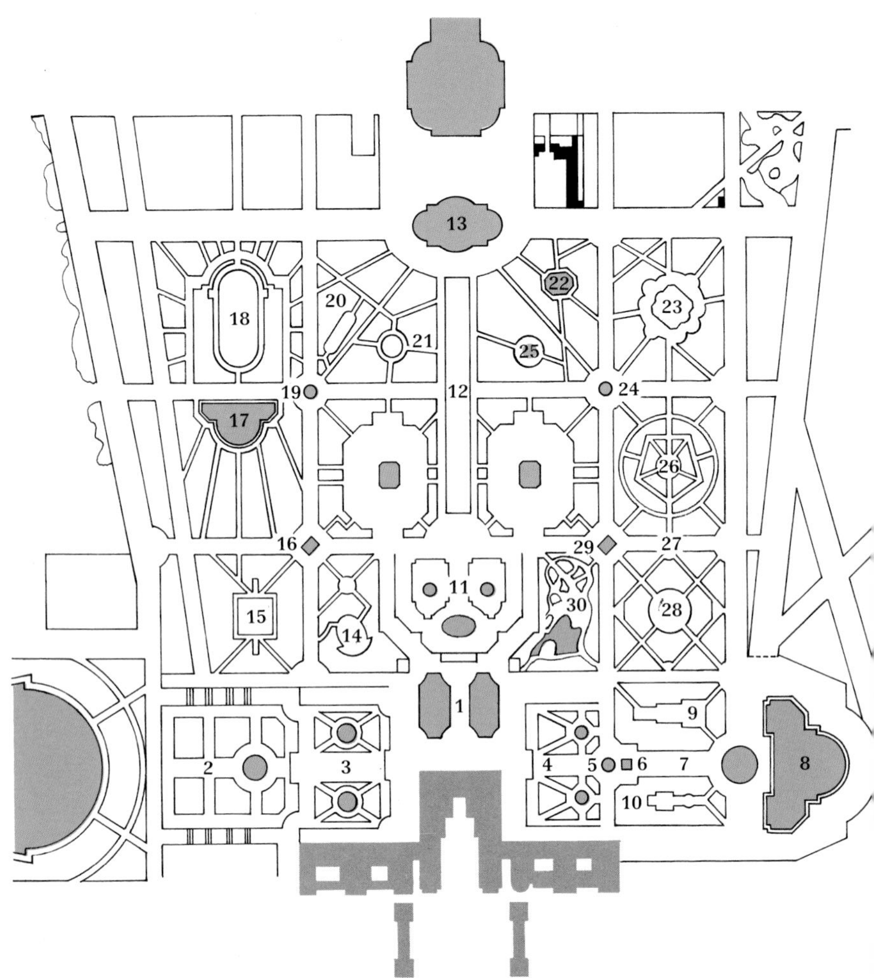
13
22
23
18
20
21
25
12
19
24
17
26
16
29
27
11
15
30
28
14
1
9
2
3
4
5
6
7
8
10

Before the Revolution the royal estate of Versailles covered more than 8 000 hectares. Surrounded by a 43-km long wall with twenty-two gates, it consists of three distinct areas:

– the gardens, comprising ornamental flowerbeds, lawns and wooded groves;

– the Small Park including, among others, the Swiss Pool, the Grand Canal, the Menagerie and Trianon estate;

– the Great Park, reserved for hunting, which took in many villages (fig. 219).

Split up at the Revolution with a large part of it confiscated, today the domain is reduced to 815 hectares corresponding to the gardens and a portion of the former Small Park.

The gardens are adorned with over three hundred statues and terms, busts and vases, in marble, bronze or lead, making them the most important outdoor museum of sculpture in the world.

Among the statues there are about twenty original antiques and some thirty copies from the antique executed by pupils of the French Academy in Rome; all the rest are original works due to the greatest sculptors of their day. Some of these statues, damaged by pollution or vandalized, have been

219
Boileau
Plan of the Gardens
of Versailles, 1744

219

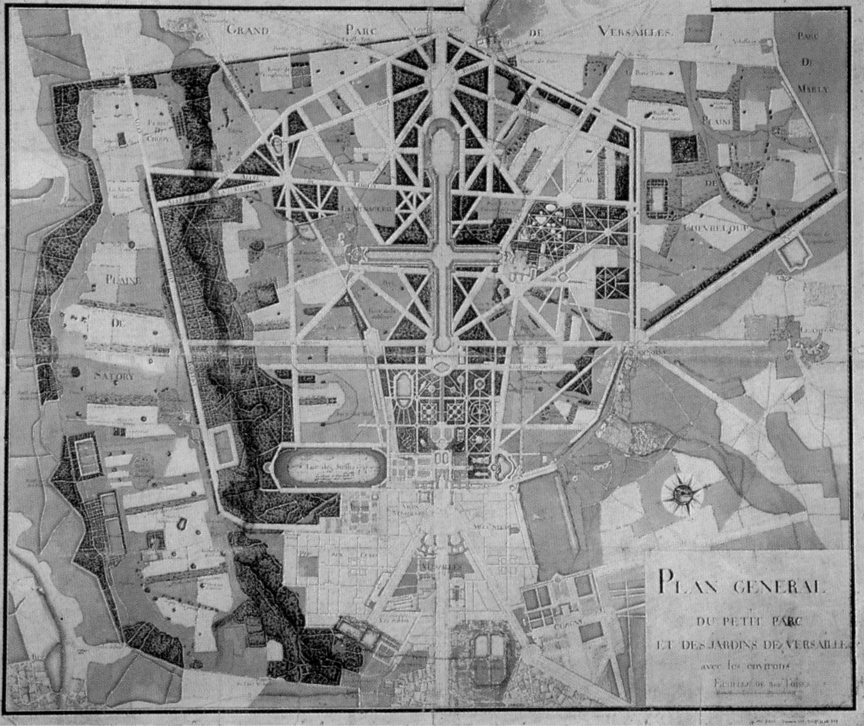

removed for safety to the galleries of the Great Stable; they have been replaced by plaster casts.

Generally the sculptures are placed around the ornamental gardens and along the Royal Avenue. They can be seen every day from sunrise to sunset, though some of them adorn groves which are usually closed to the public; these are of course only accessible to visitors on the days when the great fountains are playing and the groves are open.

The gardens are usually reached through the Princes' Passage, or else via the North Passage.

220

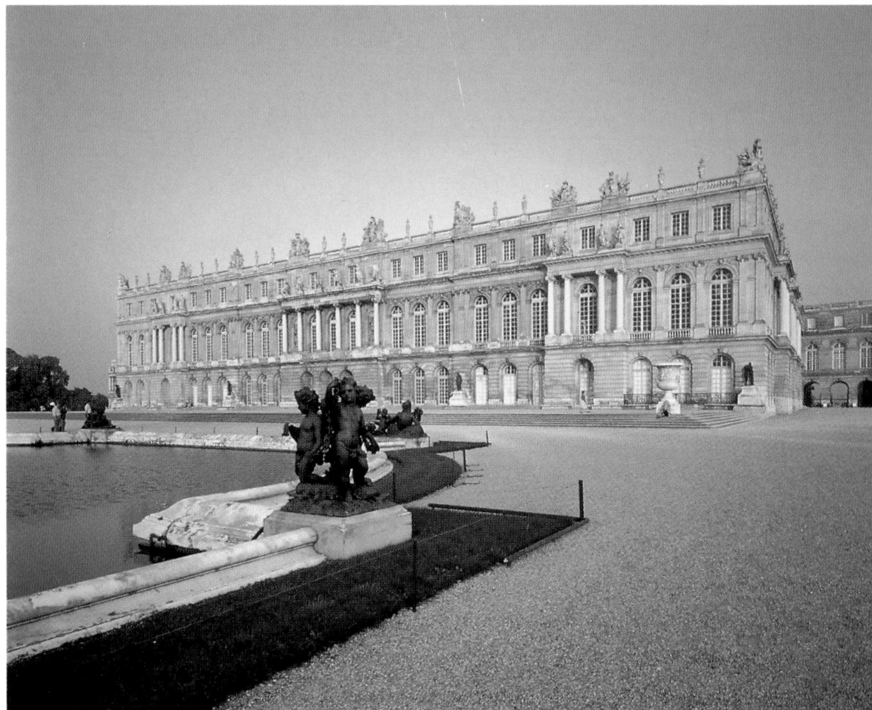

The Ornamental Gardens and the Royal Avenue

The Water Garden[1]

This stretches in front of the main central body of the Château at the foot of the Hall of Mirrors.

Originally it consisted of five principal basins with sweep-saw curved rims and bore a large sculpture group. Four of these groups represent "ravishments" symbolizing *The Four Elements* and twenty-four statues represent *The Four Parts of the World, The Four Seasons, The Four Hours of the Day, The Four Elements, The Four Poems* and *The Four Temperaments of Man*, in short, everything in the universe influenced by the course of the sun. Thus the myth of Apollo, which has inspired the decoration of the State Apartments, also provides the main theme for that of the gardens, thereby ensuring an organic link between the inside and the outside of the Château and emphasizing the perfect homogeneity of the Versailles iconography.

Here again, it was Charles Le Brun who supervised the work of the sculptors, providing them with preparatory drawings from which they were to draw inspiration. In particular he indicated which symbols should characterize the different allegorical figures, after having searched for models in the *Iconologia* of Cesare Ripa.

However, this "Great Order of 1674" took twenty years to materialize so that, when the sculptures were delivered, they were no longer placed according to the original scheme which had been radically transformed in the meantime. The groups were spread out: two of them adorned the Orangery Garden[2] (today they are in the Louvre), the third one was put in the Colonnade Grove and the fourth one was never made. As for the statues, they were distributed on either side of the Latona Steps and along the arbours enclosing the North Garden, without taking notice of their significance. The aesthetic point of view prevailed henceforth over the allegorical and symbolical programme.

In 1683 the Water Garden acquired its present aspect, when the South Wing was completed and the construction of the North Wing gave the façades of the Château their final appearance (fig. 220).

The façade of the main building is adorned on the ground floor with four bronze statues, cast by the Keller brothers after famous antiques: *Bacchus, Apollo, Antinous and Silenus*. At

:20
'he Water Garden

221

the angles of the terrace there are two wonderful marble vases, decorated with motifs similar to those used in the War and Peace Rooms just above: at the north, *The War Vase* by Coysevox (fig. 221) and at the south *The Peace Vase* by Tuby.

In front of the terrace are two long rectangular basins with marble rims adorned with bronze statues: groups of children in the corners and on the sides; reclining figures which harmonize perfectly with the immensely long, uninterrupted, horizontal, frontal line of the Château. Their beautiful faces, their elegant shape, the delicate chiselling and the quality of the bronze casting, also due to the Keller brothers, all make this monumental ensemble one of the great masterpieces of XVIIth-century statuary.

On the longer sides eight water nymphs can be seen, and on the shorter sides, the artist has evoked the Kingdom of France by introducing the allegorical figures of its four great rivers, each accompanied by its main tributary: opposite the *Peace Vase* we find *The Loire* and *The Loiret* rivers by Regnaudin and opposite the *War Vase*, *The Garonne* and *The Dordogne* by Coysevox; at one end are *The Seine* (fig.222) and *The Marne* by Le Hongre and at the other, *The Rhône* and *The Saône* (fig. 223) by Tuby.

The visitor then walks as far as the flight of steps leading to the South Garden[3] which is surrounded by groups of *Children mounted on Sphinxes*, a charming creation of Jacques Sarrazin for the children, and of Louis Lerambert for the sphinxes (fig. 224). On either side, on a marble tablet, are twelve bronze vases, cast after models of Claude Ballin. At the end of the perspective, beyond the Swiss Pool, one catches a

221
Antoine Coysevox
The War Vase, 1684

222
Etienne Le Hongre
The Seine, 1687

223
Jean-Baptiste Tuby
The Saône, 1687

224
Jacques Sarrazin and
Louis Lerambert
Sphinxes with Children, 1660-1668

222

223

224

225

226

glimpse of the equestrian statue of *Louis XIV* by Lorenzo Bernini, transformed by Girardon into *Marcus Curtius*; this is a plaster cast but the original is now kept in the Great Stable.

Retracing his steps the visitor passes in front of the reclining figure of *Ariadne asleep*, a copy by Van Clève of the famous antique in the Vatican Museum. He then reaches the *Daybreak Fountain* adorned with *Animals fighting* by Jacques Houzeau and flanked by statues which were part of the "Great Order": *Water* by Pierre Legros (fig. 225) and *Spring* by Laurent Magnier; at right angles is *Dawn* by the Marsy brothers.

On arriving at the top of the Latona Steps, the visitor has before him the magnificent perspective around which the whole symbolical lay-out of the gardens turns, based on the myth of Apollo: at the foot of the steps, *Latona with her Children Apollo and Diana*, symbolizing Day and Night; at the end of the perspective, *Apollo's Chariot rising from the Waves to start its Course across the Firmament*; on the right, in a wooded grove is *Apollo visiting Thetis*.

The visitor should now turn round to gaze at the whole extent of the immense façade of the Château which with the two wings at right angles to the central building measures 570

227

225
Pierre Legros
Water, 1681

226
Martin Desjardins
Diana or the Evening Hour, 1680

227
Etienne Le Hongre
Air, 1680

metres. The statues placed on the avant-corps are almost all connected with the solar myth. In the centre are *Apollo* and *Diana,* flanked by the figures of the *Twelve Months;* in the niches there are *Nature* and *Art.* At right angles to the south side, statues symbolize *Comedy, Music* and *Dancing,* as well as *Flowers* and *Fruits;* those at the front of the south wing evoke the *Muses, Arts* and *Sciences.* At right angles to the central building, towards the north, certain statues depict *The Pleasures of the Table,* others *Aquatic Divinities;* those on the north wing represent *Poems,* the *Muses; Sciences, Arts* and *Seasons.*

The visitor next passes in front of the *Evening Fountain;* adorned with *Animals fighting* by Corneille Van Clève and flanked by statues of *Diana or the Evening Hour* (fig. 226), a replica by Martin Desjardins of a celebrated antique statue, and of *Venus or the Hour of Midday* by Gaspard Marsy (plaster cast). At right angles near the Latona Steps is *Air* by Etienne Le Hongre (fig. 227), perhaps the most beautiful of all the statues produced for the "Great Order".

228

228
Drouilly
The Heroic Poem,
1680

229
François Girardon
The Pyramid
Fountain, 1679

230
François Girardon
The Bath of Diana's
Nymphs, 1679

The North Garden[4]

Leaving the *Evening Fountain*, the visitor goes past five statues belonging to the "Great Order": *Europe* by Pierre Mazeline, *Africa* by Sybraique and Cornu, *Night* by Raon, *Earth* by Massou and *The Pastoral Poem* by Pierre Garnier. Where the paths next meet there are terms executed after drawings by Mignard, representing *Ulysses* by Magnier, *Isocrates* by Granier, *Theophrastus* by Simon Hurtrelle, *Lysias* by Dedieu and *Apollonius* by Mélo. Next there is a new set of statues which were part of the "Great Order": *Autumn* by Thomas Regnaudin, *America* by Gilles Guérin, *Ceres or Summer* by Hutinot, and *Winter* which is one of Girardon's great masterpieces. Beyond the Pyramid Fountain are *The Satirical Poem* by Buyster, *Asia* by Roger, *The Phlegmatic* by Lespagnadelle and *The Heroic Poem* by Drouilly, portrayed with the features of Louis XIV (fig. 228).

The visitor retraces his steps to the Pyramid Fountain[5], an elegant work by Girardon (fig. 229), who is also responsible for the fine bas-relief of *The Bath of Diana's Nymphs*[6] (fig. 230) which forms the principal element in the decoration of the following basin. *The Choleric* by Houzeau and *The Sanguine*

229

230

by Jouvenet, flank the entrance to the Water Avenue[7] which leads to the Basin of Neptune.

This avenue and the amphitheatre at the end are bordered by twenty-two fountains, each composed of a marble basin supported by a group of three children in bronze; these groups which go in pairs are due to Legros, Le Hongre, Lerambert, Mazeline and Buirette.

The Basin of Neptune[8] did not receive its sculpted decoration until the reign of Louis XV; in the centre, *Neptune and Amphitrite* by Sigisbert Adam; on the right, *The Ocean* by Le Moyne; on the left, *Proteus* by Bouchardon who also did the two dragons. At the end of the perspective is the fine Baroque group of *The Fame of the King* by Domenico Guidi.

From the *Basin of Neptune* the visitor can go straight to Trianon, but for those who wish to continue the tour of the gardens and, eventually, of the groves, it is necessary to go back along the Water Avenue as far as the Water Garden, passing once again between the Three Fountains Grove on the right[9] and that of the *Triumphal Arch* on the left[10] , where only the group of *France Triumphant* by Coysevox and Tuby remains. Walking round the *Bath of Diana's Nymphs* and the Pyramid Fountain, the visitor passes between the Mermaid Basins to reach the steps leading to the Water Garden. These steps are flanked by two bronzes: *Chaste Venus* by Coysevox and the *Knife-Grinder* after an antique statue. The marble tablet is adorned with fourteen bronze vases after Ballin.

The L'atona Garden[11]

From the Water Garden we arrive either by a few steps adorned with marble vases, or by two sloping paths bordered by statues. These are mostly copies after the antique, among which those particularly worth attention are, on the left, *The Callipygian Venus, Apollo of the Belvedere* and *The dying Galathea* from the Capitol; on the right, *Antinous of the Belvedere, The Medici Bacchus, Hercules Commodus* and the beautiful *Nymph with a Shell.* Among these antique statues are some original contemporary works: on the left, *The Lyric Poem* by Jean-Baptiste Tuby and *Fire* by Drossier; on the right, *The Melancholic* by La Perdrix.

The Latona Basin (fig. 231) represents the mother of Apollo and Diana protecting her young children from the insults of the Lycean peasants and imploring Jupiter to avenge her; Jupiter turns her persecutors into toads and lizards. All these works are due to the Marsy brothers who found their inspiration in Ovid's *Metamorphoses*. An allusion can be supposed here to the turbulent Fronde uprising and the Regency of Anne d'Autriche, the mother of Louis XIV.

The ornamental garden is bordered by a series of marble terms; from left to right, *Circe* by Magnier, *Plato* by Rayol; *Mercury* by Van Clève, *Pandora* by Legros, *The River Achelous*

231

232

231
Gaspard and Balthazar Marsy
The Latona Basin,
1670-1689

232
Antoine Coysevox
Castor and Pollux

by Mazière, *Hercules* by Leconte, a *Bacchant* by Dedieu, a *Fawn* by Houzeau, *Diogenes* by Lespagnadelle and *Ceres* by Poultier.

The Royal Avenue or Green Carpet[12]

This monumental avenue leads to the Basin of Apollo's Chariot and is extended by the perspective of the Grand Canal.

At the entrance where Louis XIV had placed some works by Pierre Puget, now in the Louvre, four groups are seen which are copies from the antique: on the left, *Castor and Pollux* (fig. 232), *Arria and Poetus,* both by Coysevox; on the right, *Laocoon and his Sons,* by Tuby, *Papirius and his Mother*

233

by Carlier. In quincunx on either side of the Royal Avenue stand sixteen marble terms, fourteen of which were executed after drawings by Nicolas Poussin.

The Royal Avenue is bordered on both sides by six monumental vases and six statues, among which, on the left, *Fidelity* by Lefèvre, *The Venus from Richelieu* by Legros, an *Amazon* by Buirette and *Achilles at Scyros* by Vigier; on the right are *Deceit* by Leconte, *The Medici Venus* by Fremeri, *Cyparissus* by Flamen and *Artemisia* by Lefèvre and Desjardins.

The Royal Avenue ends in a half-moon round the Basin of Apollo[13]; the group of *Apollo on his Chariot* (fig. 233) was done by Tuby after a drawing of Le Brun. On either side of the half-moon stand one group, four terms and a statue: on the left, *Ino and Melicerta* by Garnier, *Pan* by Mazière, *Spring* by Arcis and Mazière, *Bacchus* by Raon, *Pomona* by Le Hongre and an antique *Bacchus*; on the right, *Aristaeus seizing Proteus* by Sébastien Slodtz, *Syrinx* by Mazière, *Jupiter* by Clérion, *Juno* by Clérion, *Vertumnus* by Le Hongre and *Silenus bearing the Child Bacchus* (antique).

Two avenues, each bordered by six statues, lead to a railing separating the gardens from the Small Park. The avenue on the right, alongside the former buildings of Little Venice, leads to Trianon.

The Wooded Groves

As the groves are only open when the great fountains are playing, the route suggested is planned so that the visitor can follow each stage of this magnificent spectacle. It can be combined with a visit to the ornamental gardens and to the Royal Avenue.

Approaching from the Water Garden and the Latona Garden, the visitor turns left to walk through the South Groves. On reaching the Basin of Apollo, he turns back towards the Château and crosses the North Groves.

The Ballroom[14]

Louis XIV sometimes held balls in this grove decorated with rock-gardens and shells (fig. 234) and the guests danced on a central marble platform, now vanished. Eight vases and eight torchères in gilt lead, due to Houzeau, Leconte and Massou, accentuate the atmosphere of an open-air drawing room by evoking the silver furniture in the Hall of Mirrors.

The Queen's Grove[15] replaced in 1775 the Labyrinth with its thirty-nine fountains adorned with multicoloured lead groups representing *Aesop's Fables*. Large fragments of this decoration are preserved today in the Great Stable.

The visitor passes in front of the Basin of Bacchus, or of Autumn[16], the work of Marsy and bears left to the Mirror

234

:33
'ean-Baptiste Tuby
\pollo's Chariot, 1671

:34
'he Ballroom

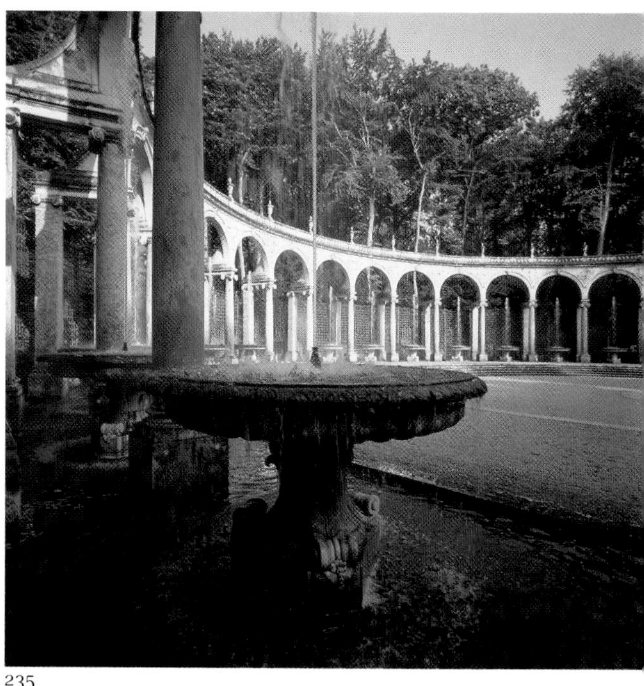

235
The Colonnade

235

Basin[17] embellished with two vases and four antique statues: a *Vestale, Apollo, Venus* and another *Vestale.*

From there he enters the King's Garden[18] , designed at the time of Louis XVIII, where the Basin of the Royal Isle had stood. At the end of the garden are copies of two famous antique statues: the *Farnese Flora* by Raon and the *Farnese Hercules* by Cornu.

Returning to the Basin of Saturn or of Winter[19], the work of Girardon, he arrives at the Sweet-Chestnut Trees Room[20] containing two antique statues: *Antinous* and *Meleager*, surrounded by eight busts.

The Colonnade[21]

This wooded grove was planted in 1684 under the supervision of Jules Hardouin-Mansart (fig. 235). The carving on the arcade spandrels, representing young satyrs, fawns, nymphs, naiads and bacchants, was entrusted to the finest sculptors: Coysevox, Regnaudin, Mazière, Van Clève, Leconte, Le Hongre, Lespingola, Degoullons, Granier, Flamen, Cornu and Magnière.

In the centre, Louis XIV had placed *Pluto abducting Proserpine*, symbolizing *Fire*. This masterpiece of Girardon is now safely installed in the galleries of the Great Stable and has been replaced here by a plaster cast.

On arriving at the bottom of the Royal Avenue, the visitor walks round the Basin of Apollo and bears right to reach the Enceladus Grove[22]: the figure of the giant attempting to climb Mount Olympus is due to Marsy. From there he goes to the Obelisk Basin[23] and then to the Basin of Flora or Spring[24], the work of Tuby.

The Domes Grove[25]

This grove owes its name to two marble pavilions which have disappeared, though the place where they stood is marked out on the ground. Elements of the decoration of these pavilions are exhibited in the Great Stable.

The central shallow basin and the bas-reliefs on the balustrade are the work of Girardon and his atelier.

Eight statues represent, from left to right: *Arion* by Raon, a *Nymph* by Flamen, *Leucothoe* by Rayol, *Daybreak* by Legros, *Acis* by Tuby, *Dawn* by Magnier, *Galathea* by Tuby and *Amphitrite*, which is a modern copy of the original statue by Michel Anguier, now kept in the Louvre.

The visitor goes back to the Basin of Flora and walks round the Star Grove[26] adorned with statues of *Apollo* by Coustou, *Mercury* and a *Bacchant*. The delightful Children's Basin[27] was created in 1710 by Hardy, who used lead from the Porcelain Trianon attics.

The Green Circle Grove[28] has supplanted the Water Theatre, which was no doubt one of the most enchanting groves in Versailles. It shelters statues, most of them antique: *Hadrian, Health*, a *Dancing Fawn, Pomona, Ceres and Ganymede*. The visitor walks in the direction of the Basin of Ceres or Summer[29], the work of Regnaudin, to reach the Apollo Baths.

The Apollo Baths[30]

The romantic atmosphere of this grove contrasts sharply with that of all the others. It was laid out from 1776 onwards, according to Hubert Robert's plan to accommodate three marble groups from the Thetis Grotto, built in 1665 on the site of the present Chapel Vestibule (fig. 236). This grotto, entirely lined inside with shells, rocks, crystals, corals and mother-of-pearl (fig. 237) was demolished when the North Wing was built.

The statues of *Acis and Galathea*, standing today in the Domes Grove, adorned the vestibule of the Grotto. The three groups illustrate the moment when the sun, having ended its glorious course across the firmament, descends into Thetis's marine grotto. Originally this could have been an allusion to Louis XIV retiring from the fatigues of power at Versailles. The *Sun Horses*, in the care of tritons, are the work of Guérin on the right, and of Marsy on the left. The main group showing *Apollo served by Thetis's Nymphs* (fig. 238) is due to Girardon and Regnaudin; it is one of the finest masterpieces of XVIIth-

236

237

century French sculpture rivalling here the most celebrated groups of Antiquity.

On leaving the Apollo Baths, the visitor takes the direction of the Pyramid Fountain and walks down the Water Avenue, round the Dragon and Neptune Basins until he finds himself in front of *The Fame of the King*. This is the best spot from which to watch the final apotheosis of the great fountains playing.

238

36
ean Le Paultre
'he Thetis Grotto
exterior), 1665

37
ean Le Paultre
he Thetis Grotto
nterior), 1665

38
rançois Girardon
nd Thomas
enaudin
pollo served by
hetis's Nymphs,
672

Trianon

Veüe et perspectiue de l'Entrée du Trianon de Versailles
1 Maison du Concierge

239

Veüe et Perspectiue de Trianon du côté du Jardin

240

239
Adam Pérelle
The Porcelain
Trianon, from the
Courtyard Side, 1670

240
Adam Pérelle
The Porcelain
Trianon, from the
Garden Side, 1670

History

Trianon is the name of a small village the origins of which go back to the Middle Ages. In 1660 Louis XIV bought the lands surrounding it and added them to his estate at Versailles. In 1663 he demolished the houses and relodged the inhabitants nearby. In 1667 Notre-Dame Church disappeared in its turn.

In 1670 Louis Le Vau was put in charge of building on this site a "house where one could take refreshments", as Saint-Simon put it. Indeed, at a time when the Château de Versailles was being enlarged, the King wished perhaps to save some traces of the intimate character of the castle he had known in his youth.

Work went on apace; according to Félibien "this palace was thought to have arisen by enchantment for, begun only at the end of the winter, it was completed in the spring, appearing to have emerged from the ground together with its accompanying garden flowers". It was these very flowers which were the principal luxury of Trianon: there were arbours of jasmine, orange-trees planted straight into the ground and ornamental gardens where each day new combinations of colours and scents were arranged.

The buildings consisted of a main pavilion for the King and Queen and four small pavilions intended for the preparation of soup, entrées, roasts, sweetmeats, jams, etc. The walls were lined with blue and white tiles and this delicate harmony of colours was repeated in the interior decoration and the furniture, hence the name of the "Porcelain Trianon" given to this charming creation (fig. 239 and 240).

This decor, which claimed to evoke some Chinese pagoda, was however fragile and the tiles, cracked by the frost, had to be renewed every year. Moreover the King's taste changed and he relinquished the fantasies of his youth. The result was that the "Porcelain House" was replaced in 1687 by the "small palace of marble and porphyry with delicious gardens" described by Saint-Simon and still greatly admired today.

Louis XIV came to Trianon for short visits to rest from the fatigue of the responsibilities of the realm and the constraint of court etiquette. He was accompanied by the royal family only and a minimal number of servants. The Princes of the Blood had to ask permission to come and sup here.

Louis XV, in the early days of his reign, seems to have shown little interest in Trianon. He gave it to the Queen who sometimes lodged her father, King Stanislas, there. From 1750 onwards though, the King brought new life to this domain. He had a new apartment fitted up and, being a great lover of botany, he created an experimental garden where the gardener, Claude Richard, attempted to acclimatize exotic species and Bernard de Jussieu tried out for the first time his new classification of plants.

In order to be able to work amidst his flowers and greenhouses, Louis XV ordered Ange-Jacques Gabriel to build the French Garden Pavilion, complete with a small dining room called the Cool Room, and the new Menagerie where different selected species of domestic animals were bred. In 1763 the King asked Gabriel to erect a new pavilion vast enough to provide accommodation, which is known today as the Petit Trianon.

Louis XVI gave the domain to Marie-Antoinette, who replaced the botanical garden with a landscape garden scattered with "factories" and completed in 1783 by the small houses of the Hamlet. The Queen allowed only the royal family and some close personal friends here; she dismissed all protocol and adopted the mode of gracious living of the country nobility. Nevertheless, on exceptional occasions she did organize some brilliant fêtes, in honour of her brother Joseph II and of King Gustav III of Sweden.

The Revolution deprived the Grand and the Petit Trianon of their furnishings. Napoléon had them refitted and often came here with the Empress Marie-Louise. Though Louis XVIII and Charles X hardly ever came, Louis-Philippe enjoyed staying here with the royal family. The Empress Eugénie dedicated the Petit Trianon to the memory of Marie-Antoinette, assembling pieces of furniture some of which could well have belonged to the Queen.

At the present time, the Grand Trianon has been completely renovated to welcome chiefs of state on official visits.

The Palais de Trianon or Grand Trianon

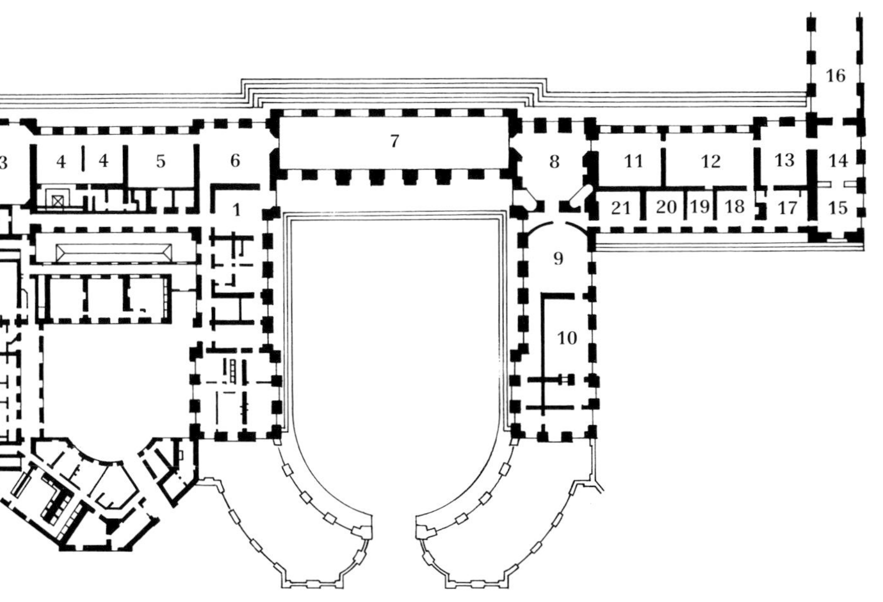

This small palace has been planned to resemble a "French mansion" standing between a courtyard and a garden, but its architecture is more in the Italian style: a single storey covered with a flat roof concealed by a balustrade. Formerly this was adorned at regular intervals with reclining figures, groups of children and vases, which unfortunately have all disappeared. The façades in light stone, delicately carved with climbing flowers are punctuated by Languedoc marble pilasters (fig. 241).

The courtyard is enclosed on the outer side by a ha-ha and very low railings which do not spoil the view. The left-hand side wing hides the Kitchens Court and the one on the right, the King's Garden. The main building, improperly called the "peristyle" by Louis XIV himself, is in fact a "loggia" opening on to the garden through a colonnade. This peristyle ensures communication between the two groups of buildings, one at the south and the other, a far more important one, at the north.

241

The garden front is surprisingly long and assymetrical (fig. 242). On the north side, there is even a perpendicular wing enclosing a gallery which juts forward. This unusual disposition is due to the need to protect the flowers in the upper ornamental garden from the cold. This wing is prolonged at right angles by a second building disappearing beneath the trees, thus bearing the name of Trianon-sous-Bois.

As Trianon's original furniture was dispersed at the Revolution, the present fittings, with a few exceptions, date back to the First Empire. The paintings, on the other hand, are mostly those that Louis XIV himself had commissioned for the decoration of the palace.

The South Buildings

Approaching from the peristyle along the south wing on the courtyard, the visitor enters a small vestibule on the right. In the pavilion situated on the left of the vestibule is the former apartment of Madame Adélaïde, Louis-Philippe's sister.

Besides the King's former Kitchens, transformed today into guest rooms for the people accompanying visiting heads

'42

of state, the South Buildings contain an apartment which was occupied in turn by Louis XIV from 1691 to 1703, by his son the Dauphin ("Monseigneur") from 1703 to 1711, by Queen Marie Leszczynska in 1740 and, in the XIXth century, by Madame Mère (Napoléon's mother) in 1805, the Empress Marie-Louise from 1810 to 1814 and Queen Marie-Amélie from 1830 to 1848.

After crossing the entrance hall where tickets are sold, the visitor enters a room situated on the site of some service rooms[1] . There is *A View of the North Parterre in the Gardens of Versailles* painted by Etienne Allégrain for the Gardens Room. The seats come from the Château de St. Cloud.

The door on the right at the end opens on to the first antechamber of the King's former apartment, normally reached through the peristyle, but for the sake of convenience, the visit follows the normal succession of rooms in a reverse order. Thus the visitor takes the corridor leading to the last room in the apartment: the Boudoir.

The Boudoir[2]

Originally the double door did not exist and the door on the right was the only means of communication between the Boudoir and the neighbouring Mirror Room. The door on the left of the fireplace was opened up by Louis-Philippe to link the boudoir to the apartment the King had had installed in place of the former kitchens of Louis XIV.

.41
'ierre-Denis Martin
'rianon Palace, 1722

:42
'rianon Palace:
;arden Front

243

The fine "triumphal arch" desk was made in 1796 by the Jacob brothers for the Paris mansion of Madame Bonaparte, the future Empress Joséphine, and brought to Trianon in 1809. The seats upholstered in abricot "gourgouran" (Indian silk) came from the Empress Marie-Louise's boudoir at the Petit Trianon.

The Mirror Room[3]

This beautiful room, with a wonderful view over the Grand Canal, is Louis XIV's former large study, where the King met with the members of the Council; the decoration of mirrors encased in wooden frames carved with garlands of flowers dates from his time (fig. 243).

The Empress Marie-Louise made it into her study and had a piano, an easel, a sketching table, a work table, a pouch table and a "letterbox" table delivered to furnish it.

Two small temples in semi-precious stones stand on the pier tables; they belonged to the dinner-table set offered to Napoléon by King Charles IV of Spain.

The beautiful fleur-de-lis chandelier dates from 1817. The torchères in gilt bronze are modern copies of two made by Thomire for the Emperor's large study at the Palais des Tuileries.

244

245

243
The Mirror Room

244
The King's Bedroom

245
Charles Le Brun
Saint John the Evangelist, 1690

The Bedroom[4]

The decoration of columns and woodwork delicately sculpted with the emblems of Apollo dates from 1700 and makes this room one of the most beautiful in the palace (fig. 244). In the Empire days, it was partitioned to form a smaller bedroom and a drawing room; today it has been restored to its original size.

The picture representing *Saint John the Evangelist* is the work of Charles Le Brun (fig. 245). The flower paintings on the overdoors, by Monnoyer and Blain de Fontenay, have replaced Claude le Lorrain's pictures which hung here in Louis XIV's day.

The balustrade in front of the bed, the linen chests and the seats were made for the Empress Marie-Louise, as well as the dressing table, the basin and the water jug, the Sèvres porcelain breakfast set, the clock and the vases on either side. The rest of the furniture was brought for Queen Marie-Amélie, the chest of drawers and the bed in particular. The latter, executed for Napoléon's bedroom in the Tuileries Palace, was also used by Louis XVIII who died there. It has been enlarged and the head was altered when it was brought to Trianon.

The Sèvres porcelain vase on the chest of drawers shows Napoléon in the gardens of the Château de Sans-Souci at Potsdam.

The Chapel Room[5]

At the beginning this room was a chapel. Transformed into an antechamber in 1691, when Louis XIV settled in this part of the palace, it has nevertheless kept its original purpose. Indeed the door at the end opens on to a recess containing an altar; once mass had been said, the door was shut again (fig. 246). The decoration though is still a reminder of this use: a cornice with alternating bunches of grapes and ears of corn evoke the eucharistic wine and bread, and pictures representing *Saint Mark and Saint Luke the Evangelists.*

The portraits of *Louis XV* and *Marie Leszczynska* by Jean-Baptiste Van Loo recall the times when the Queen stayed at Trianon.

246

246
The Chapel Room

247
The Peristyle

247

In the Empire days, this room became the Empress's main drawing room. It was then that the tea table made by Martin was brought here, its revolving top adorned with marquetry representing the signs of the Zodiac.

The Antechamber[6]

This is the former Lords' Room which became the King's first antechamber, then that of the Empress.

The large table was made by Félix Rémond in 1823; its teak top, 2.77 m in diameter, is supported by an elm pedestal. The two pier tables come from the Château de St.Cloud and the seats from the Château de Meudon.

Above the fireplace is a picture painted by Delutel for the Château de St. Cloud; it is a small copy of Mignard's painting of *Monseigneur and his Family*. *The Birth of Adonis* and *Venus, Love* and *Adonis* were painted in 1688 by François Verdier for Trianon-sous-Bois.

The Peristyle[7]

Originally this "loggia", wide open on to the garden, was enclosed on the courtyard side by a wall with french windows. A few years later these windows were taken away to accentuate the transparency of the building; but the earlier disposition is still visible on the courtyard front in the window

248

splays where the fillister to which the wooden frame was fixed can still be seen (fig. 247).

In 1810 Napoléon had glass installed on either side of the peristyle to make communication between his apartment and that of the Empress easier. It was in this newly formed vestibule that Maréchal Bazaine (responsible for the capitulation of Metz during the Franco-Prussian War) was tried between October and December 1873 by a military tribunal presided over by the Duc d'Aumale. The glass panes were dismantled in 1910.

248
The Round Room

The North Buildings

More important than those at the south, they contain several apartments and a gallery linking them to the Trianon-sous-Bois wing.

The Round Room[8]

This vestibule provides access to Louis XIV's apartment which he occupied from 1688 to 1691, when he moved to the one we have just visited. At the time of the Empire this suite of rooms formed the Emperor's Great Apartment, or State Apartment.

The design of the Corinthian columns dates from Louis XIV, just as the pictures by Verdier do, representing *Juno and Thetis* and *Boreas abducting Orithyia* and the overdoors by François Desportes depicting *Flowers and Fruits of America* (fig. 248).

The two wooden drum casings at the end date from 1750; the one on the left houses a small staircase going up to the mezzanine floor and in the vestibule on the right there used to be an altar, so that the Round Room could be turned into a chapel.

The door in between formerly opened on to the theatre where, on 17 September 1697, the opera *Issé* by Destouches was created. In 1703 this theatre disappeared to make way for the third and last apartment of Louis XIV, consisting of four main rooms: an antechamber, a bedroom, a private study and a large drawing room.

In 1750 Louis XV transformed this apartment into reception rooms. The antechamber became the gamesroom[9]; it acquired the arched shape it has today and new panelling was installed, as well as the magnificent violet breccia marble fireplace, still here. The bedroom and private study were joined together to make a dining room[10] and the large drawing room became the Buffet Room where stood two marble wine coolers, now in the gallery.

Napoléon had Louis XV's Gamesroom turned into a private drawing room and the furniture he ordered for it has remained here until today.

Louis-Philippe once again had these reception rooms turned into an apartment for his son-in-law and daughter, the King and Queen of the Belgians.

The Music Room[11]

This is the former antechamber of Louis XIV's first apartment where the King's supper was held. The wood panelling is among the oldest in the palace and on the overdoors we can see the shutters of the tribunes where the musicians played during the meal.

Napoléon made this room the Drawing Room of the High Dignitaries of the Court and Louis-Philippe turned it into a Billiard Room. The chairs are upholstered in Beauvais tapestry made especially for this room; the fine pedestal table and the tea fountain did not arrive until the Second Empire.

The pictures representing *Mars* and *Pallas* come from the Games Antechamber and the Chamber of Sleep.

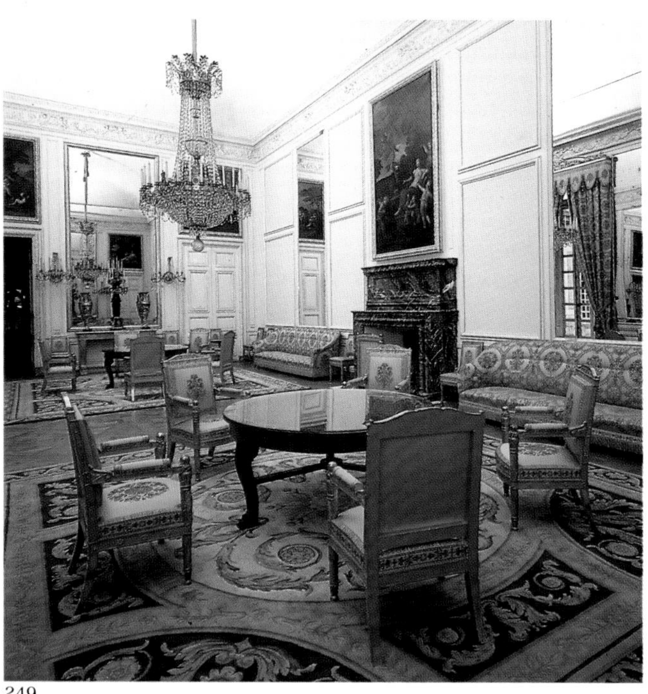

249

250

249
The large Drawing Room

250
The Malachite Room

The Large Drawing Room[12]

Originally there were two rooms here: the Games Antechamber and the Chamber of Sleep, which in Empire days became the Drawing Room reserved for the High Dignitaries of the Court and the Princes' Drawing Room. Louis-Philippe had them joined into one to form the Large Drawing Room where the royal family gathered in the evening (fig. 249).

Above the fireplace is a picture by Bon de Boulogne of *Venus and Mercury*; on the overdoors are *Nature and the Elements* by Bon de Boulogne, *Venus and Adonis*; *Venus, Hymen and Love* and *Jupiter changed into a Bull* by Louis de Boulogne. All these paintings, except for the last one, come from the Games Antechamber. On either side of the fireplace there is a picture by Verdier brought from Trianon-sous-Bois: *Venus retaining Adonis* and *Argus with Io changed into a Heifer.*

Brion's rich furniture is covered with a yellow "cannetillé", woven with gold and silver thread, brocaded in blue with a fleur-de-lis pattern and there are also two couches and two lacquer pedestal tables. The two "family" tables around which the Queen and the Princesses would sit have numbered drawers in which each Princess could lock away her work and keep the key.

The Malachite Room[13]

This used to be Louis XIV's Sunset Room (fig. 250) which was later made into a bedroom for the Duchesse de Bourgogne. It was for her that the mirrors with frames surmounted by a carved gilt crown were put up. Of the original decoration only the cornice and two fine pictures by Charles de La Fosse remain: above the fireplace, *Apollo visiting Thetis* and on the overdoor, *Clytia changed into a Sunflower.*

In Napoléon's time, the room became the Emperor's Drawing Room and was richly furnished by Jacob-Desmalter with gilded wooden seats upholstered in crimson damask fringed with gold brocade and above all a set of furniture the principal ornamentation of which was in malachite offered by the Tsar Alexander I: two ebony sideboards, a shallow basin and two candelabras, all embellished with gilt bronzes.

The Cool Room[14]

This rooms looks north, hence its name. Napoléon used it as his Council Room and Charles X took leave of his ministers here, after holding his last council meeting on 31 July 1830.

The magnificent carved wood panelling with flame ornaments and garlands of flowers dates from Louis XIV, as well as the pictures: above the fireplace, *Flora and Zephyr* by Jean Jouvenet who also painted the overdoors representing *Spring* and *Winter*; between the windows is *Vertumnus and Pomona* by Nicolas Bertin and on the side walls, four *Views of Versailles* by Jean-Baptiste Martin (fig. 251).

The furniture dates from the First Empire and consists of filing cabinets by Jacob-Desmalter, a regulator by Lepaute, a barometer-thermometer by Bailly and seating upholstered in Beauvais tapestry.

The Springs Room[15]

This room owes its name to the Garden of Springs which it used to overlook. It was a small wood where several springs gushed forth, forming streams which meandered between the trees. This charming creation by Le Nôtre disappeared in Louis XVI's time.

The room was the antechamber to Madame de Maintenon's apartment and its woodwork dates back to 1713. The

251

252

picture above the fireplace representing *Cyane, Proserpine's Friend, changed into a Fountain,* is the work of René-Antoine Houasse who also painted *Alpheia and Arethusa* and *Narcissus*. The *Views of the Gardens at Versailles* are due to Pierre-Denis Martin and those of the *Gardens at Trianon* are by Charles Chastelain (fig. 252).

Napoléon chose this room for his topographical cabinet and had the large desk installed. The mahogany pier table incrusted with ebony and pewter comes from the Palais de l'Elysée. The door on the left of the fireplace leads to Madame de Maintenon's former apartment, which later became the Emperor's Private Apartment.

The Gallery[16]

This gallery, intended to protect the flowers of the upper garden from the cold, is lit by eleven windows on the south and five only on the north. The sculpted decoration, particularly the groups of children surmounting the mirrors, is the work of Lespingola, Gautier and Legay. The pictures represent some *Views of the Gardens at Versailles and Trianon* as they were in the days of Louis XIV. These documents are very precious for the groves they depict have mostly disappeared

251
The Cool Room

252
The Springs Room

253

253
The Gallery

or have been transformed. Twenty-one of these paintings are the work of Jean Cotelle, two are by Allégrain and one by Jean-Baptiste Martin (fig. 253).

At the beginning the alcoves contained sofas; Louis-Philippe had Languedoc marble and gilded lead wine-coolers brought here from the Buffet Room of Louis XV.

The chandeliers, pier tables, benches and stools date from the First Empire.

It was in this gallery that, on 4 June 1920, the Peace with Hungary was signed.

The Garden Room

This has six windows opening on to the small quincunx and the perspective of the Grand Canal. The pictures by Louis-Philippe Crépin represent *The Torrent, Hunting* and *Fishing*.

At the time of Louis XIV, gymnastic equipment was kept here and in Napoléon's day there was a billiard table. The present furniture comes from the Palais de l'Elysée, except for two pedestal tables made for the Empress Marie-Louise at the Hamlet of the Petit Trianon.

The door on the left of the chimney leads to the Trianon-sous-Bois wing.

Trianon-sous-Bois

This right-angle wing contains several apartments on two floors, decorated with finely carved woodwork. In the reign of Louis XIV, the King's sister-in-law, "Madame", his nephew the Duc de Chartres, the future Regent with his three daughters, the Duchesse de Chartres, the Duchesse de Bourbon and the Princesse de Conti, lived here. Peter the Great lodged here with his suite in May 1717. Under Louis-Philippe, Trianon-sous-Bois was occupied by the King's younger sons.

The first room is the former Billiard Room of Louis XIV; in those days it was decorated with a series of pictures by Houasse illustrating the myth of Minerva. Louis-Philippe had it transformed into a chapel where, on 17 October 1837, his second daughter, Princesse Marie, was married to the Duke of Württemberg. The Trianon-sous-Bois wing is at present reserved for the head of state and is not open to visitors.

The Emperor's Private Apartment

Conducted lecture tours

Composed of five rooms with french windows opening on to the former King's Garden, Trianon-sous-Bois was made by joining part of the erstwhile apartment of Madame de Maintenon - where Stanislas Leszczynski stayed on his visits to Trianon - and the Private Apartment installed in 1750 for Louis XV.

Napoléon occupied it for the first time in December 1809 following his divorce from Joséphine. In the days of Louis-Philippe, the King's younger daughters, the Princesses Marie and Clémentine, lived here.

The furniture dates from the First Empire, but most of the pictures were already in place at the time of Louis XIV.

The Antechamber[17]

This was the former East Room which was used as a drawing room by Madame de Maintenon. In 1812 it was shortened to accommodate a staircase leading to the mezzanine floor and it then became the office of the Emperor's secretary.

The walls are hung with a damask the colour of "the soil of Egypt", with a green and poppy-red border. The following pictures are displayed: *Juno and Flora* by Bon de Boulogne; two paintings of *Zephyr and Flora,* one by Noàl Coypel and the other by Michel Corneille and *Apollo receives his Bow and Arrows from Mercury* by Noàl Coypel.

The Private Study[18]

This is the former Rest Room which had been Madame de Maintenon's bedroom. Partitioned in the XVIIIth century into several small rooms, this one recovered its full size in 1813 when it acquired its present-day aspect (fig. 254).

The filing cabinets were made by Jacob-Desmalter and the clock by Bailly. The chairs had been used by the First Consul at the Château de St. Cloud and the pedestal table comes from the Palais de l'Elysée.

The following pictures are seen on the walls hung with green damask bordered in gold brocade: *Apollo and the Sybil* and *Apollo and Hyacinth* by Louis de Boulogne; *Apollo visiting Thetis* by Jean Jouvenet; *Apollo crowned by Victory* and *Apollo resting* by Noël Coypel.

254

255

254
The Emperor's
Private Study

255
The Emperor's
Bedroom

The Bathroom[19]

This is where the Private Apartment fitted up in 1750 for Louis XV starts. This had been the retiring room which Napoléon made into a bathroom.

The walls are hung with white cotton damask which also covers the gondola seats. The bath is concealed behind a bench upholstered in green cloth.

The Bedroom[20]

Once Louis XV's bedroom created in 1750 in place of a staircase and part of the next room (fig. 255).

The walls are lined with brocaded moiré on a lemon background, edged with silver brocade on a lilac background. The chest of drawers and the mahogany desk embellished with gilt bronzes were delivered by the dealer Baudouin. The Athenian, or Empire-style basin, consists of a mahogany and gilt bronze support and a basin in Sèvres porcelain.

La Salle du Déjeun - Breakfast Room[21]

Originally this room and half of the preceding one formed the Buffet Room, communicating with the antechamber (now the Music Room) where Louis XIV supped. It is surmounted by a musicians' gallery. Its present size dates from Louis XV who used this room as his large study. The decoration and furniture were made for Napoléon who turned it into his Breakfast Room.

The walls are lined with a plain blue and white damask surrounded by a golden yellow border, which has also been used to cover Jacob-Desmalter's seats. The variegated marble, jasper and lapis-lazuli clock in the shape of a temple was made out of pieces from Charles X's table centrepiece. It is flanked by two Sèvres porcelain vases decorated with landscapes. The oriental alabaster bowl was confiscated from an emigrant; during Empire days it was placed on one of the pier tables in the gallery. The pedestal table, its band adorned with muses dancing, was brought here by Princesse Marie.

Noël Coypel's picture representing *Nymphs proffering a cornucopia to Amalthea* came from Trianon-sous-Bois.

The Breakfast Room communicated with the Emperor's "Family Room", Louis XV's former Gamesroom.

256
Plan of the Trianon Gardens

The Gardens of Trianon

Returning to the peristyle the visitor crosses the upper parterre, descends to the lower parterre and turns left towards the stone balustrade dominating the Horseshoe Basin flanked by two flights of steps (fig. 256). Thus he finds himself in the axis of the secondary branch of the Grand Canal at the end of which, in Louis XIV's time, stood the Menagerie, now vanished.

He then walks round the Flat-Bottom Basin adorned with dragons by Hardy, reflecting the peristyle. From there he perceives the perspective of green lawns, once embellished with marble statues and vases. Then he comes to the Water Buffet (fig. 257) built by Jules Hardouin-Mansart and adorned with figures of *Neptune*, *Amphitrite*, lions, tritons and a bas-relief of *The Triumph of Thetis*. Crossing the Sweet-Chestnut Tree Garden, he reaches the amphitheatre, or Antiquity Room,

256

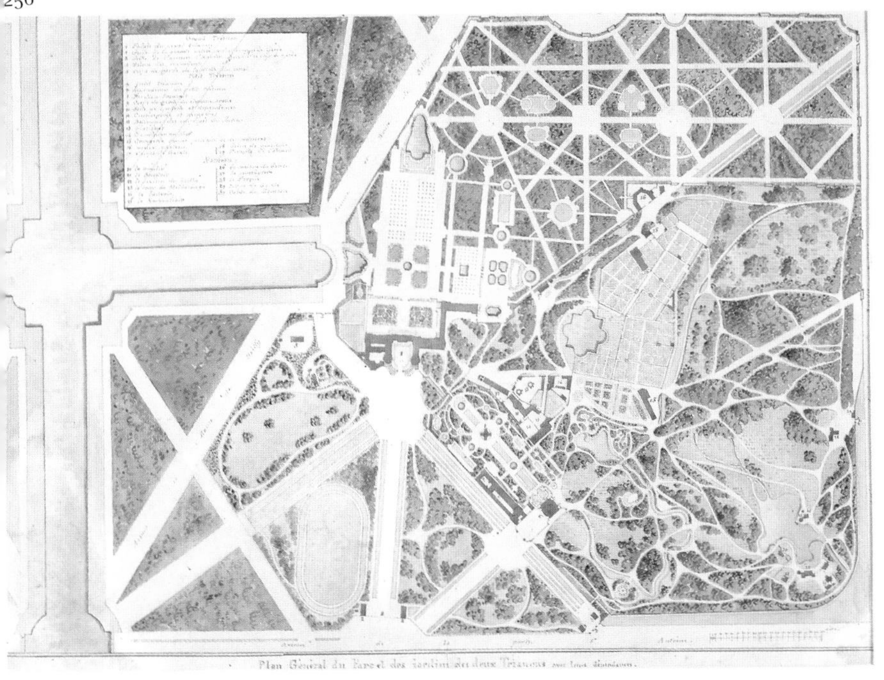

257

housing a series of busts imitating the antique and surrounding that of *Alexander*: the *Nymphs* on the basin are due to Hardy and both vases are the work of Robert le Lorrain.

Going down a majestic flight of steps towards the Trianon-sous-Bois wing, he crosses a lawn which has taken the place of the Springs Garden and reaches the King's Garden, at the entrance to which is a fountain by Marsy, brought from the Water Theatre, one of the groves which has disappeared from the gardens of Versailles.

257
The Water Buffet

The "New Trianon" or Petit Trianon

Approaching from the King's Garden, the visitor crosses a small bridge ordered by Napoléon but renovated at the end of the last century.

The new Trianon began with the creation, in 1750, of a botanical garden which Louis XV entrusted to the charge of Claude Richard. The King took a passionate interest in the astonishingly varied and numerous scientific experiments carried out there. Attempts were made to acclimatize the coffee plant, the fig tree and pineapple; China asters, geraniums and strawberries were cultivated; tropical trees were planted; studies were made on the reasons why corn rotted and the way to prevent this.

Hothouses were built to protect the most fragile plants, particularly tropical ones brought back, at the King's request, by the fleet commanders of the Royal Navy from their far-distant voyages.

In the botanical garden, Bernard de Jussieu applied for the first time the principles of his new system of classification.

Twenty-five years later however, after the death of Louis XV, all these scientific activities were abandoned, the flowerbeds and hothouses were destroyed and the precious botanical collections were sent to the King's Garden in Paris, the present-day Jardin des Plantes. In their place, Queen Marie-Antoinette had a landscape garden laid out, scattered with "factories" in the "Anglo-Chinese" style then in vogue.

From the beginning the botanical garden had been extended by a small garden "à la française", embellished with four basins decorated with groups of children symbolizing the *Four Seasons*. At the bottom of this garden there is a charming building, the Pavilion of the French Garden which, like all the "factories" of the Petit Trianon, can only be visited with a guide (information obtainable at the Grand Trianon).

The French Garden Pavilion

Built in 1750 by Ange-Jacques Gabriel, this pavilion is a model of Rocaille architecture: a plan designed round a central cross of St. Andrew; mascarons on the french windows representing the *Seasons*; a balustrade at the roof enlivened by groups of children and vases of flowers (fig. 258).

The interior consisted of a circular drawing room, its windows alternating with doors leading to four small rooms:

258

a boudoir, a warming-up closet, a kitchen and a wardrobe. The woodwork in the drawing room, now gilded, used to be painted in green and white; the bas-reliefs carved by Verberckt represent children playing at hunting, fishing and gardening; eight Corinthian columns support a cornice where ducks, pigeons, swans, cocks and hens are treated in a naturalist style, an allusion to the New Menagerie nearby (fig. 259).

Louis XV, after his long walks through the botanical gardens and his visits to the hothouses, liked to stop here to arrange his herb collection, or to take a cup of milk with strawberries.

The French Garden Pavilion is on an axis with the Cool Room on one side, and with the New Menagerie on the other. At the end of the ornamental garden, where today the Château du Petit Trianon stands, there used to be a portico with trellis work screening the greenhouses from view.

259

The Cool Room

This is a small summer dining room and the walls used to be covered with lattice work and surmounted by vases, also in a lattice design.

The interior, paved with marble, was formerly adorned with wood panelling carved by Verberckt, painted white and green; the two main panels are now found in one of the rooms of the French Garden Pavilion.

The New Menagerie

This elegant building is called "new" to distinguish it from Louis XIV's Menagerie. It housed a sheepfold, a cowshed, a dairy, hen runs and an aviary and carefully selected domestic animals were bred here.

The thatched roofs of Louis XIV's former Ice-Houses can be glimpsed behind the Menagerie.

258
The French Garden Pavilion (exterior)

259
The French Garden Pavilion (interior)

The Château du Petit Trianon was built to enable Louis XV to make lengthy stays in his favourite domain. Begun in 1763 it was completed in 1768. A comparison with the French

260

Pavilion shows how rapidly the style of Ange-Jacques Gabriel had evolved, passing, in the space of thirteen years, from a Rocaille architecture to a pure Classical style (fig. 260).

Built to a square plan, it lies on a basement - owing to the different levels of the ground this is only visible on two sides - the main floor and the attic. The four façades are all different. The largest one, looking on to the French Garden, bears traces of the influence of Andrea Palladio, the great Venetian architect of the xvith century. Its harmonious proportions and delicate ornamental sculpture make it without doubt the gem of French Neo-Classical architecture.

The Chapel

The architecture of this chapel is simple but refined.

The high altar is surmounted by a picture painted by Joseph-Marie Vien in 1774 representing *Saint Louis and Marguerite de Provence paying a visit to Saint Thibault*: the holy man gives the royal couple a spray of lilies, the eleven flowers symbolizing their future descent.

Outside steps leading to the Chapel provide direct access to the royal tribune.

260
Façade of the Petit Trianon overlooking the French Garden

261
The Queen's Theatre

The Theatre

In the XVIIIth century the theatre played an important part in "château life". Marie-Antoinette wanted therefore to have one too and commissioned her architect, Richard Mique, to build it in 1780.

Outside it is very plain, with the exception of the entrance porch with Ionic columns supporting an ornamental front bearing a *Cupid* sculpted by Deschamps. He was also responsible for the bas-reliefs of *Muses* which decorate the vestibule and foyer.

The auditorium is relatively small for, apart from the royal family, the Queen invited only her personal guests and some of her retainers. The decoration however is particularly exquisite, in tones of blue heightened by the various golds of the papier-mâché sculptures. The ceiling is a modern copy of the original painting by Jean-Jacques Lagrenée, kept in store, and represents *Apollo, the Muses and the Graces* (fig. 261).

The stage, vast enough to perform operas, has kept one of its original decors. Artists from the Comédie-Française, the Comédie-Italienne and the Opera took it in turn to play. On one occasion, a performance was given, in the presence of the Emperor Joseph II, of *Iphigenia in Taurida* by Gluck.

261

The Queen had however formed her own company, called the "troupe des seigneurs", consisting of herself, certain members of the royal family and some friends. Marie-Antoinette appeared in *The Village Diviner* by Jean-Jacques Rousseau and in *The King and the Farmer* by Sedaine, among others.

On leaving the Theatre the visitor enters the landscape garden, created by Mique from 1775 in place of Louis XV's botanical garden.

The Belvedere or the Rock Pavilion

This charming pavilion for taking rests, erected on a mound overlooking a small lake, is octagonal in shape: the bas-reliefs above the windows represent *The Seasons*, and the ornamental fronts of the doors are adorned with attributes of *Hunting* and *Gardening* (fig. 262).

Inside there is a circular drawing room, the floor is covered with beautiful marble mosaic, and the walls are embellished with arabesques painted by Le Riche (fig. 263).

Behind the Belvedere is the Orangery and Richard the gardener's old house.

262

262
The Rock Pavilion or Belvedere (exterior)

263
The Rock Pavilion or Belvedere (interior)

263

The visitor returns to the Château du Petit Trianon and walks round it from the left. On the site of Louis XV's greenhouses, a Temple de l'Amour now stands on an islet enclosed in two arms of a tiny river.

264

The Temple de l'Amour

This circular edifice in white marble was built by Mique in 1778 (fig. 264). Twelve Corinthian columns support an entablature ornamented with foliage and a hemispheric cupola, its coffers bearing bas-reliefs due to Deschamps and representing the emblems of Love. In the centre there is an old replica of Bouchardon's *Cupid cutting his Bow from Hercules' Club,* which used to hang here but is now in the Louvre.

A small door provides access to the main courtyard of the Château du Petit Trianon. This is enclosed by railings flanked by two lodgings for guards and a chapel followed by outhouses.

264
The Temple of Love

The Château du Petit Trianon

The staircase[1], the principal ornament of which are the gilded wrought-iron banisters, leads to the reception rooms and the Queen's apartment situated on the main floor.

The Antechamber[2]

In former times this contained two tiled stoves, one on each side of the door leading to the dining room, and heating both rooms at once.

The painting on the overdoor by Philippe Caresme shows *The Nymph Mint metamorphosed into a Plant.*

Busts of *Louis XVI* and the *Emperor Joseph II,* Marie-Antoinette's brother, are the work of Boizot.

The Dining Room[3]

The decoration of this room is a clue to its purpose: the sculptures on the wood panelling and the fireplace are of fruit, and the large pictures evoke various sources of food: *Harvest* by Lagrenée, *Hunting* by Vien, *Grape-Picking* by Hallé and

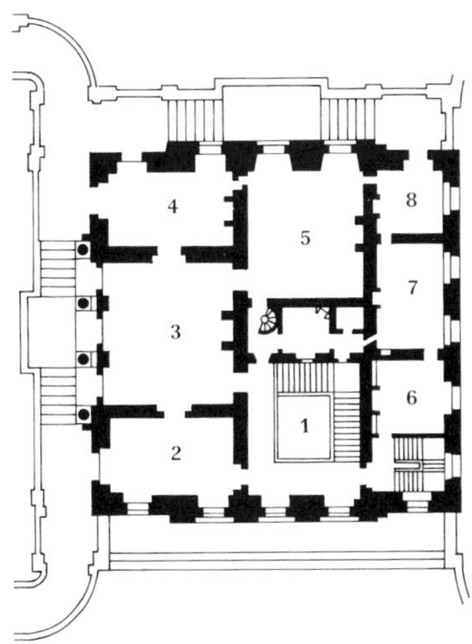

265

Fishing by Doyen. The overdoors depict *Boreas and Orithyia* and *Flora and Zephir* by Monnet, *Venus and Adonis* and *Vertumnus and Pomona* by Belle (fig. 265).

Louis XV ordered the engineer Loriot to make some "flying tables" which were supposed to rise from the ground floor when needed, but they never materialized.

The Small Dining Room[4]

The Lords' Dining Room in Louis XV's time, it was turned into a Billiard Room by Marie-Antoinette.

A chest of drawers and a pier table are worth noticing; they were designed by Riesener for the Petit Trianon. The seats were made for the Queen by Dupain; the light brackets come from Louis XVI's Gamesroom at the Château de Fontainebleau; the oval pedestal table is attributed to Weisweiler.

The Reception Room[5]

The wood panelling, carved by Guibert, is no doubt the finest in the Château. The paintings on the overdoors take their inspiration from Ovid's *Metamorphoses*: *Clytia changed into a Sunflower* and *Apollo and Hyacinth* by Nicolas-René Jollain; *Adonis changed into an Anenome* and *Narcissus changed into a Flower of the same Name* by Nicolas-Bernard Lépicié (fig. 266).

The wonderful bluish steel and gilt bronze lantern was made especially for this room. The light brackets come from the Château de St. Cloud. Only the card-table remains of the furniture of Louis XV's time. The writing table, its marquetry representing Astronomy, is the work of Riesener. The pianoforte by Pascal Taskin and the harp are reminders of Marie-Antoinette's tastes in music. The Savonnerie carpet comes from Marie Leszczynska's apartment at Versailles. On the pedestal table a decorated ostrich egg resembles those offered by the King on Palm Sunday.

The doors on either side of the fireplace lead to the Queen's apartment (visit with a guide).

The Queen's Apartment

This consists of three small rooms on the mezzanine floor, beneath a library and the bedroom of the Queen's chambermaid.

The Washroom[6] used to be Louis XV's botanical library. The washstand was made by Riesener for the Queen's Private Apartment at the Château des Tuileries.

The bedroom[7] is Louis XV's former study; his apartment had been situated on the attic floor. In those days the windows looked on to flowerbeds and greenhouses which are recalled

266

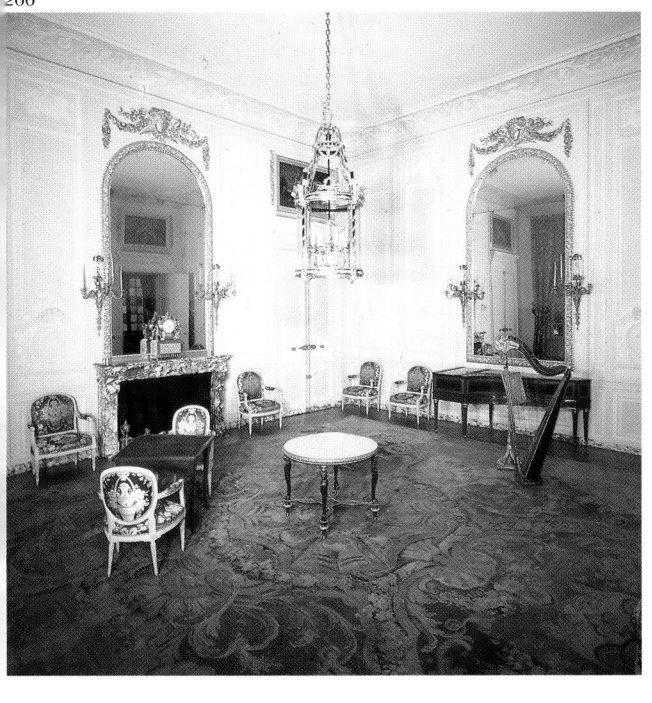

265
The Dining Room

266
The Reception Room

in the flowers carved on the panelling (fig. 267). Marie-Antoinette made this into her bedroom and it was then that the extraordinary furniture was delivered: a chest of drawers (now vanished), a console and a table in mahogany with a gilt bronze motif imitating basketwork made by Schwerdfeger; the bed (disappeared), seats and a screen with a carved wicker-work pattern, ears of corn and jasmine flowers in natural colours, and covered with a bombasine embroidered with wild flowers, all by Georges Jacob; the clock and light brackets are now in the Gulbenkian collection in Lisbon.

The boudoir[8] (fig. 268) was created by Marie-Antoinette in place of a small staircase which enabled Louis XV to go directly to his bedroom in the attic; at the foot of it the King liked to have coffee. The enchanting woodwork, painted in blue and white, was designed by Mique; there are garlands of roses and delicately sculpted arabesques. An ingenious system can shutter the two windows in the evening by means of "moving glass panels" which rise from the groundfloor. The elegant furniture by Georges Jacob was made for the Comte de Provence, the Queen's brother-in-law.

The Attic
Conducted lecture tours

A small staircase leads to the attic floor where the King's apartment and various lodgings are situated. At the time of Louis XV these were occupied by members of his household. Marie-Antoinette put her daughter Madame Royale with her governess here, as well as Madame Élisabeth, the King's sister and some ladies of the court.

The King's apartment consists of three rooms, the main one being the bedroom adorned with elegant woodwork and an alcove hung with a crimson lampas with a Chinese pattern. The Polish-style bed is very like the one Louis XVI had and the chest of drawers was made by Riesener for this apartment.

When the Queen stayed at Trianon, Louis XVI came here three times a day to take his meals with her, but he always spent the night at Versailles.

The suite of lodgings is furnished today with items made for various people who lived in the Petit Trianon in the xixth century: Princesse Pauline Borghese, Napoléon's sister, the Empress Marie-Louise and, in Louis-Philippe's day, the Duc and Duchesse d'Orléans.

The attic floor can only be visited with a guide.

On leaving the Château, the visitor once again goes out of the small door on the left. Following the right bank of the river, he passes in front of the Temple de l'Amour and reaches the Queen's Hamlet.

267

267
The Queen's
Bedroom

268
The Boudoir

The Queen's Hamlet

In 1783 Marie-Antoinette had a dozen rustic thatched-roof houses built at the end of her domain, grouped around a lake and forming a veritable small village. Indeed, contrary to other "hamlets" built at that time, this one, designed by Mique, was not a mere make-believe stage-setting and the Queen did not pretend to be a shepherdhess. This was truly a farm with a farmer in charge, and its produce was sent to the kitchens of the Château.

The Queen's House

This building (fig. 269) is the most important one in the Hamlet. It consists, in fact, of two distinct buildings connected by a wooden gallery, decorated with pots of flowers in blue and white earthenware bearing Marie-Antoinette's mono-

269
The Queen's House
in the Hamlet

269

gram. On the right stands the Queen's House proper, comprising on the ground floor a dining room and a gamesroom, and on the first floor a large drawing room, a small drawing room and a Chinese cabinet room; on the left is the Billiard House consisting of a billiard room on the ground floor and a small apartment upstairs.

From this gallery the mistress of Trianon, simply dressed in plain white muslin with a straw hat on her head, could supervise the work going on in the fields.

The other small houses are: the water mill, the warming house, the boudoir, the dovecote, the steward's house and the barn which could be used as a ballroom but no longer exists. The Preparation Dairy disappeared during the First Empire, the Cleanliness Dairy where pots of milk in Sèvres porcelain were laid out on marble slabs; the Marlborough Tower overlooking the lake, with a fish farm below, and finally the farm itself which today has been partially destroyed.

The Great and the Small Stables

The King's Great and Small Stables are situated below the Parade Ground, between the St. Cloud, Paris and Sceaux Avenues. They were erected by Jules Hardouin-Mansart between 1679 and 1682.

The Great Stable was intended to house the riding horses of the King and the Dauphin in four galleries, with room for keeping the harness, repair shops and granaries for the fodder. It also included several lodgings: for the Master of the Horse, the equerries, pages and their riding masters, the heralds, musicians, grooms and craftsmen.

The Small Stable was reserved for carriage horses and carriages and occupied six galleries. Here were the same annexes as in the Great Stable, as well as lodgings for the First Equerry, the equerries, the pages and their riding masters, the grooms, coachmen, postilions and craftsmen.

At the present day, both Stables are used for various administrative offices: the Small Stable, in particular, houses the Museum Restoration Service as well as workrooms and storerooms for the Musée national du Château de Versailles. The latter occupies four galleries and the Chapel of the Pages of the Great Stable.

There are plans to install a Carriage Museum here, and also a Museum of Sculpture where some statues from the gardens will be exhibited.

270
View of the Indoor
Tennis Court

The Indoor Tennis Court

The Court is outside the precincts of the Château and is situated on the Rue du Jeu de Paume

The game of the "Courte Paume" was the forerunner of tennis. The princes of the royal family enjoyed playing on this indoor court built in 1686.

On 20 June 1789 the deputies of the Third Estate, joined by some representatives of the Clergy and the Nobility, after having found the Session Hall of the National Assembly closed, met here and took an oath not to separate before having given the kingdom a Constitution (fig. 275).

In 1883 the hall was remodelled as a small museum of the Revolution and was decorated as it is today. The statue of *Bailly, President of the National Assembly* is surrounded by busts of the main participants in this historical event. The large picture representing *The Tennis-Court Oath* was done after the drawing by Jacques-Louis David, kept in the History Galleries of the Château.

270

Photographs by the Réunion des Musées nationaux (Arnaudet, Bernard, Blot, Jean, Lewandowski, Marboeuf) with the exception of fig. 42 (Vaulted Ceiling of the Hall of Mirrors) : Varga-Artephot

Premier dépôt légal : 1er trimestre 1991
Dépôt légal : Juin 2000

Printed at the Imprimerie Mame, Tours, in June 2000

Designed by
Bruno Pfäffli

Plans drawn by
Pierre-Alain Paquie

Photocomposotion in "Versailles" by
L'Union Linotypiste

Photoengraving by
N.S.R.G.